The American Expeditionary Forces in the Great War

The St. Mihiel Offensive

Battleground Series

Stamford Bridge & Hastings *by* Peter Marren
***Wars of the Roses* - Wakefield/ Towton** *by* Philip A. Haigh
***Wars of the Roses* - Barnet** *by* David Clark
***Wars of the Roses* - Tewkesbury** *by* Steven Goodchild
***Wars of the Roses* - The Battles of St Albans** *by* Peter Burley, Michael Elliott & Harvey Wilson
***English Civil War* - Naseby** *by* Martin Marix Evans, Peter Burton and Michael Westaway
***English Civil War* - Marston Moor** *by* David Clark
***War of the Spanish Succession* - Blenheim 1704** *by* James Falkner
***War of the Spanish Succession* - Ramillies 1706** *by* James Falkner
***Napoleonic* - Hougoumont** *by* Julian Paget and Derek Saunders
***Napoleonic* - Waterloo** *by* Andrew Uffindell and Michael Corum
***Zulu War* - Isandlwana** *by* Ian Knight and Ian Castle
***Zulu War* - Rorkes Drift** *by* Ian Knight and Ian Castle
***Boer War* - The Relief of Ladysmith** *by* Lewis Childs
***Boer War* - The Siege of Ladysmith** *by* Lewis Childs
***Boer War* - Kimberley** *by* Lewis Childs

Mons *by* Jack Horsfall and Nigel Cave
Néry *by* Patrick Tackle
Retreat of I Corps 1914 *by* Jerry Murland
Aisne 1914 *by* Jerry Murland
Aisne 1918 *by* David Blanchard
Le Cateau *by* Nigel Cave and Jack Shelden
Walking the Salient *by* Paul Reed
***Ypres* - 1914 Messines** *by* Nigel Cave and Jack Sheldon
***Ypres* - 1914 Menin Road** *by* Nigel Cave and Jack Sheldon
***Ypres* - 1914 Langemarck** *by* Jack Sheldonand Nigel Cave
***Ypres* - Sanctuary Wood and Hooge** *by* Nigel Cave
***Ypres* - Hill 60** *by* Nigel Cave
***Ypres* - Messines Ridge** *by* Peter Oldham
***Ypres* - Polygon Wood** *by* Nigel Cave
***Ypres* - Passchendaele** *by* Nigel Cave
***Ypres* - Airfields and Airmen** *by* Mike O'Connor
***Ypres* - St Julien** *by* Graham Keech
***Ypres* - Boesinghe** *by* Stephen McGreal
Walking the Somme *by* Paul Reed
***Somme* - Gommecourt** *by* Nigel Cave
***Somme* - Serre** *by* Jack Horsfall & Nigel Cave
***Somme* - Beaumont Hamel** *by* Nigel Cave
***Somme* - Thiepval** *by* Michael Stedman
***Somme* - La Boisselle** *by* Michael Stedman
***Somme* - Fricourt** *by* Michael Stedman
***Somme* - Carnoy-Montauban** *by* Graham Maddocks
***Somme* - Pozières** *by* Graham Keech
***Somme* - Courcelette** *by* Paul Reed
***Somme* - Boom Ravine** *by* Trevor Pidgeon
***Somme* - Mametz Wood** *by* Michael Renshaw
***Somme* - Delville Wood** *by* Nigel Cave
***Somme* - Advance to Victory (North) 1918** *by* Michael Stedman
Somme - Flers *by* Trevor Pidgeon
***Somme* - Bazentin Ridge** *by* Edward Hancock
***Somme* - Combles** *by* Paul Reed
***Somme* - Beaucourt** *by* Michael Renshaw
***Somme* - Redan Ridge** *by* Michael Renshaw
***Somme* - Hamel** *by* Peter Pedersen
***Somme* - Villers-Bretonneux** *by* Peter Pedersen
***Somme* - Airfields and Airmen** *by* Mike O'Connor
Airfields and Airmen of the Channel Coast *by* Mike O'Connor
In the Footsteps of the Red Baron *by* Mike O'Connor
***Arras* - Airfields and Airmen** *by* Mike O'Connor
***Arras* - The Battle for Vimy Ridge** *by* Jack Sheldon & Nigel Cave
***Arras* - Vimy Ridge** *by* Nigel Cave
***Arras* - Gavrelle** *by* Trevor Tasker and Kyle Tallett
***Arras* - Oppy Wood** *by* David Bilton
***Arras* - Bullecourt** *by* Graham Keech
***Arras* - Monchy le Preux** *by* Colin Fox
Walking Arras *by* Paul Reed
Hindenburg Line *by* Peter Oldham
***Hindenburg Line* - Epehy** *by* Bill Mitchinson
***Hindenburg Line* - Riqueval** *by* Bill Mitchinson
***Hindenburg Line* - Villers-Plouich** *by* Bill Mitchinson
***Hindenburg Line* - Cambrai Right Hook** *by* Jack Horsfall & Nigel Cave
***Hindenburg Line* - Cambrai Flesquières** *by* Jack Horsfall & Nigel Cave
***Hindenburg Line* - Saint Quentin** *by* Helen McPhail and Philip Guest
***Hindenburg Line* - Bourlon Wood** *by* Jack Horsfall & Nigel Cave
***Cambrai* - Airfields and Airmen** *by* Mike O'Connor
Aubers Ridge *by* Edward Hancock
***La Bassée* - Neuve Chapelle** *by* Geoffrey Bridger
***Loos* - Hohenzollern Redoubt** *by* Andrew Rawson
***Loos* - Hill 70** *by* Andrew Rawson
Fromelles *by* Peter Pedersen
The Battle of the Lys 1918 *by* Phil Tomaselli
Accrington Pals Trail *by* William Turner
Poets at War: Wilfred Owen *by* Helen McPhail and Philip Guest
Poets at War: Edmund Blunden *by* Helen McPhail and Philip Guest
Poets at War: Graves & Sassoon *by* Helen McPhail and Philip Guest
Gallipoli *by* Nigel Steel
***Gallipoli* - Gully Ravine** *by* Stephen Chambers
***Gallipoli* - Anzac Landing** *by* Stephen Chambers
***Gallipoli* - Suvla August Offensive** *by* Stephen Chambers
***Gallipoli* - Landings at Helles** *by* Huw & Jill Rodge
***Gallipoli* - Anzac Sari Bair** *by* Stephen Chambers
Walking the Italian Front *by* Francis Mackay
***Italy* - Asiago** *by* Francis Mackay
***Verdun:* Fort Douamont** *by* Christina Holstein
***Verdun:* Fort Vaux** *by* Christina Holstein
Walking Verdun *by* Christina Holstein
***Verdun:* The Left Bank** *by* Christina Holstein
Zeebrugge & Ostend Raids 1918 *by* Stephen McGreal

Germans at Beaumont Hamel *by* Jack Sheldon
Germans at Thiepval *by* Jack Sheldon

SECOND WORLD WAR

Dunkirk *by* Patrick Wilson
Calais *by* Jon Cooksey
Boulogne *by* Jon Cooksey
Saint-Nazaire *by* James Dorrian
Walking D-Day *by* Paul Reed
***Atlantic Wall* - Pas de Calais** *by* Paul Williams
***Atlantic Wall* - Normandy** *by* Paul Williams
***Normandy* - Pegasus Bridge** *by* Carl Shilleto
***Normandy* - Merville Battery** *by* Carl Shilleto
***Normandy* - Utah Beach** *by* Carl Shilleto
***Normandy* - Omaha Beach** *by* Tim Kilvert-Jones
***Normandy* - Gold Beach** *by* Christopher Dunphie & Garry Johnson
***Normandy* - Gold Beach Jig** *by* Tim Saunders
***Normandy* - Juno Beach** *by* Tim Saunders
***Normandy* - Sword Beach** *by* Tim Kilvert-Jones
***Normandy* - Operation Bluecoat** *by* Ian Daglish
***Normandy* - Operation Goodwood** *by* Ian Daglish
***Normandy* - Epsom** *by* Tim Saunders
***Normandy* - Hill 112** *by* Tim Saunders
***Normandy* - Mont Pinçon** *by* Eric Hunt
***Normandy* - Cherbourg** *by* Andrew Rawson
***Normandy* - Commandos & Rangers on D-Day** *by* Tim Saunders
***Das Reich* – Drive to Normandy** *by* Philip Vickers
Oradour *by* Philip Beck
***Market Garden* - Nijmegen** *by* Tim Saunders
***Market Garden* - Hell's Highway** *by* Tim Saunders
***Market Garden* - Arnhem, Oosterbeek** *by* Frank Steer
***Market Garden* - Arnhem, The Bridge** *by* Frank Steer
***Market Garden* - The Island** *by* Tim Saunders
***Rhine Crossing* – US 9th Army & 17th US Airborne** *by* Andrew Rawson
***British Rhine Crossing* – Operation Varsity** *by* Tim Saunders
***British Rhine Crossing* – Operation Plunder** *by* Tim Saunders
***Battle of the Bulge* – St Vith** *by* Michael Tolhurst
***Battle of the Bulge* – Bastogne** *by* Michael Tolhurst
Channel Islands *by* George Forty
Walcheren *by* Andrew Rawson
Remagen Bridge *by* Andrew Rawson
Cassino *by* Ian Blackwell
Anzio *by* Ian Blackwell
Dieppe *by* Tim Saunders
Fort Eben Emael *by* Tim Saunders
***Crete* – The Airborne Invasion** *by* Tim Saunders
Malta *by* Paul Williams
Bruneval Raid *by* Paul Oldfield
Cockleshell Raid *by* Paul Oldfield

The American Expeditionary Forces in the Great War

The St. Mihiel Offensive

12–16 September 1918

Maarten Otte

Series Editor
Nigel Cave

Pen & Sword
MILITARY

First published in Great Britain in 2019 by
Pen & Sword Military
an imprint of
Pen & Sword Books Ltd, 47 Church Street
Barnsley, South Yorkshire, S70 2AS

ISBN 978 152673 495 2

A CIP catalogue record for this book is
available from the British Library.

Typeset in Times New Roman by Chic Graphics

Printed and bound in England by
CPI Group (UK), Croydon, CR0 4YY

Pen & Sword Books Ltd incorporates the imprints of
Pen & Sword Archaeology, Atlas, Aviation, Battleground, Discovery,
Family History, History, Maritime, Military, Naval, Politics,
Railways, Select, Social History, Transport, True Crime,
Claymore Press, Frontline Books, Leo Cooper, Praetorian Press,
Remember When, Seaforth Publishing and Wharncliffe.

For a complete list of Pen & Sword titles please contact
PEN & SWORD BOOKS LIMITED
47 Church Street, Barnsley, South Yorkshire, S70 2AS, England
E-mail: enquiries@pen-and-sword.co.uk
Website: www.pen-and-sword.co.uk

Contents

Dedication

This book is dedicated to Nigel Cave, creator and driving force behind the Battleground Europe Series. His knowledge, vision and energy are very inspiring; its a privilege to work with him. Thanks for everything Nigel!

* * *

American prisoners close to Thiaucourt, 12 September 1918.

Series Editor's Introduction, St. Mihiel

The AEF's St. Mihiel Offensive, 12–16 September 1918, is notable for several reasons. It was the first offensive controlled and fought by the AEF and its newly created US First Army, under General Pershing, albeit with a considerable number of French troops under command. Amongst the major offensives by both sides that took place in 1918 on the Western Front it was the shortest. This was because it had lost its significant strategic objectives shortly before its opening – ie that it was to be limited and any aspiration to press on to vital objectives, such as Metz, railway lines and areas of industrial significance had been vetoed by Foch days earlier. He instructed Pershing to redirect his efforts to the Meuse-Argonne and would have been quite happy if St. Mihiel had been cancelled altogether, although a compromise was reached that enabled the AEF to carry out both offensives (or 'pushes', as the Americans preferred to call them) within an agreed, very tight, timetable. It was also amongst the largest single offensives since the ending of the opening moves of the war in 1914 in terms of manpower and certainly the one that deployed the most aircraft and tanks. As mentioned, it was the shortest, lasting only four days before it was brought to a halt.

It would be hard to argue against the conclusion that it was a considerable success for Allied arms, above all for the Americans. Of course there are always caveats in almost any military operation of such a size. There were command and control problems; the communications systems frequently failed, but never with major consequences; what infrastructure there was over the captured terrain was destroyed and would have provided a major impediment to any major continuation of the offensive; the ground captured was not of itself particularly strategically valuable; the defenders, from formations of dubious military value, were outnumbered by at least 8:1; whilst the Germans certainly intended to abandon it in any case, even if the timing of such a withdrawal remains a source of controversy.

Perhaps the most significant immediate outcome was to give the Americans, not least the higher command, a feeling of superiority. They had managed to achieve in hours what the other Allied armies had failed to do in days, with relatively few casualties whilst imposing substantial losses on the Germans; they felt that their superior morale and enthusiasm would prevail against the hitherto almost impenetrable German defences. Such sentiments would soon be dashed against the realities of the vigorously defended German systems in the woods and ravines and on the ridges that formed the Meuse-Argonne battlefield.

What was achieved by this striking military success? The lines of communication with Verdun were freed from German interference, one of the key reasons why the Germans were so keen to maintain what was a potentially vulnerable salient into the French lines. The closing of the Salient moved the Allies that much closer to strategically important Metz and all-important railway lines that were essential for the maintenance of the German position on the Western Front. However, that is the point – the Allies were closer but in neither case had the major strategic prizes been gained, something of which Pershing was all too well aware but about which he could do little.

In fact the reality is that these vital objectives could not have been achieved after the first phase of the attack – that is the closure of the Salient – without considerable time being spent on preparation for the next phase. This was, of course, not unusual; all the offensives of 1918 were faced with the need to restore roads and railways and generally to provide an infrastructure that could support the next stage. St. Mihiel posed greater difficulties than most, as such work would have to be done over marshy and unpromising terrain, all the time under the view of the guns mounted in untouched positions on the right bank of the Moselle and from the dominating heights along which ran the increasingly formidable Michel Position. The difficulties involved were underlined by the generally rather poor results that were achieved when significant efforts, admittedly rather piecemeal, were made to penetrate this line in the dying days and hours of the war.

For the battlefield visitor, the St. Mihiel Salient provides a rich menu of Great War sites to visit, amongst the best to be found on the Western Front and which serve to illustrate the practicalities of waging the war of 1914–1918. The excellent range of tours that Maarten provides, much assisted by the detailed mapping by Bart Metselaar, makes full use of the potential they offer and, in turn, they act as an excellent commentary on the war in the Salient, which seems to me to be too little known amongst students of that conflict.

Nigel Cave
October 2019, The Vercors

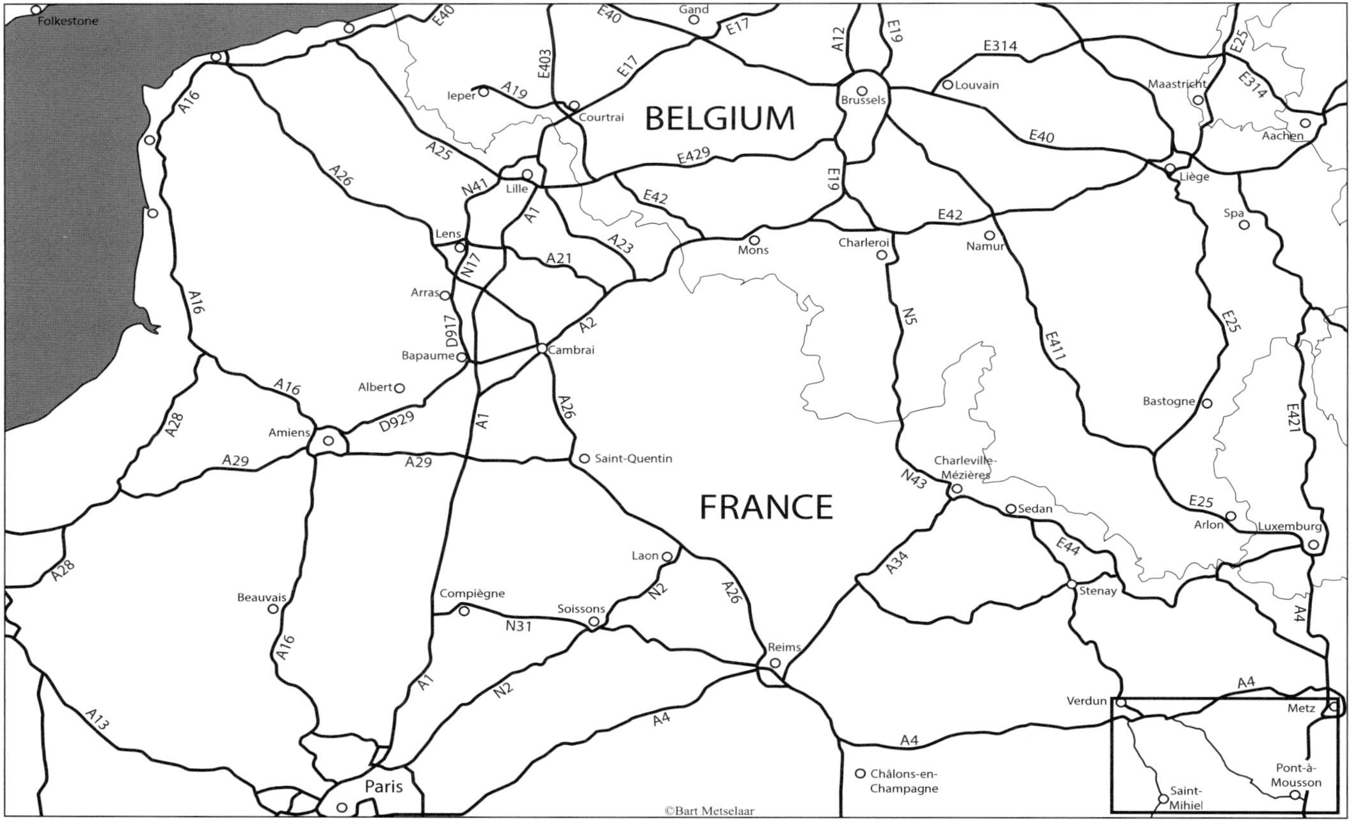

Northern France, Belgium and Luxembourg.

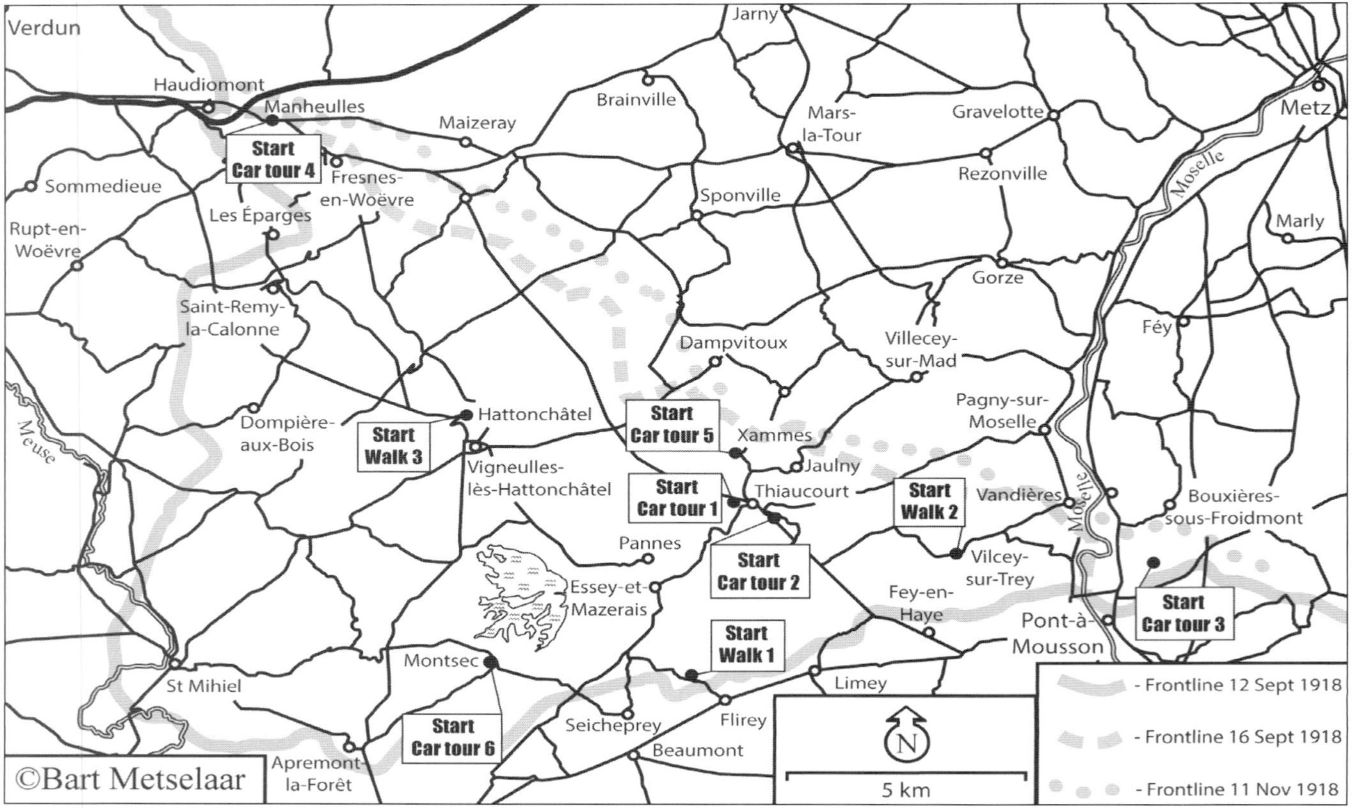

Starting points of the walks and car tours.

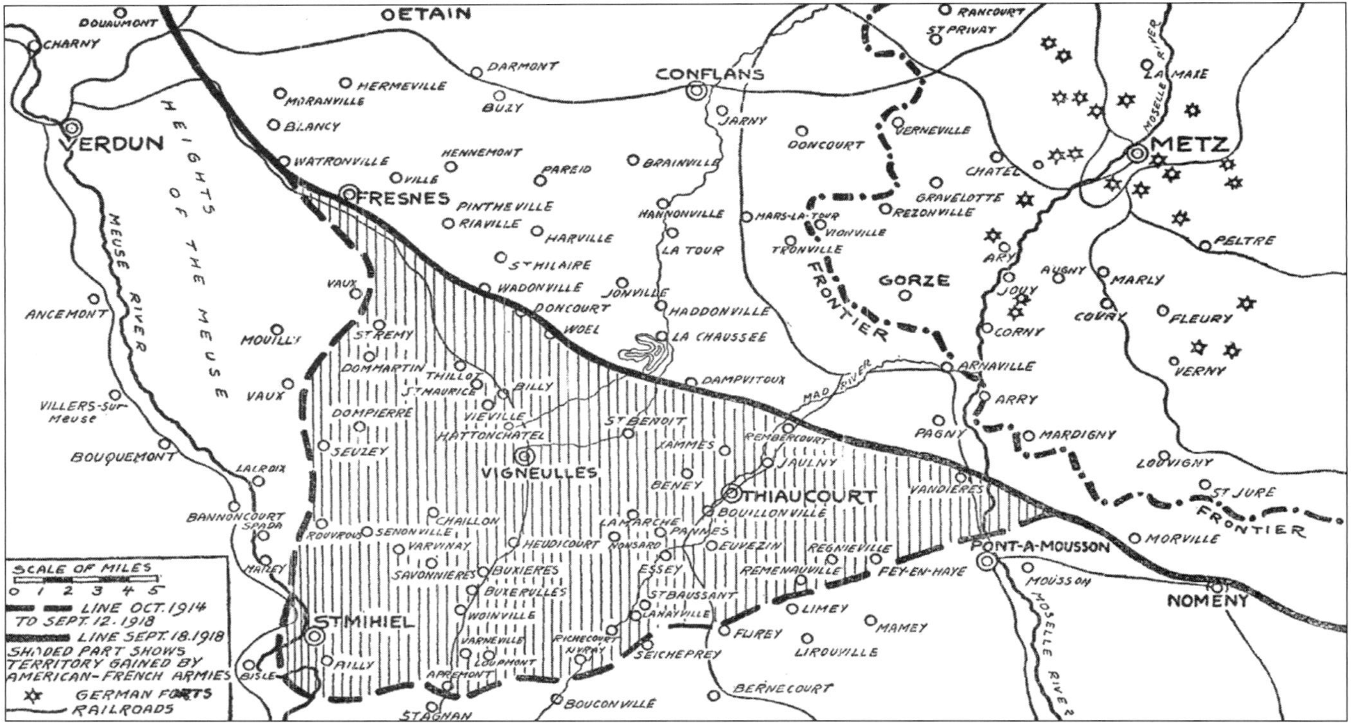

The St. Mihiel Salient, 1914-1918.

Introduction

Note that in this book, 'Salient' is generally used instead of the fuller 'St. Mihiel Salient'.

After the United States declared war on Germany on 6 April 1917, the balance of power, industrially, economically and demographically, finally changed in favour of the Allies. Another psychological turning point of the war came with the halting of the German Spring Offensives of 1918. This series of major attacks came to an end in mid July with the failure of an attack on the Marne. Within a couple of days Foch (1851-1929), the 'Supremo' of the Allied armies on the Western Front, ordered a massive counter-offensive that included a number of American divisions. Between 18 and 20 July the Germans were halted and forced back to their start line; by the early days of August they had been forced back to a line along the Aisne and Vesle rivers.

With significant military success achieved, Foch could now shift the focus of the Allied forces and a major offensive was launched on 8 August south of the Somme. This marked the start of what has become known as the 'Hundred Days Offensive' (or the Advance to Victory), from 8 August to 11 November 1918, a number of successful offensives that were launched along various parts of the Western Front in a series of almost unrelenting hammer blows that forced the Germans to retreat far beyond the Hindenburg Line and which directly led to the Armistice.

For the Allies, 8 August 1918 marked the first of a string of victories, whilst to the German Army this day became known as its 'black day'. Pushed back on a wide front, they lost huge numbers of artillery pieces and machine guns. It was possible to replace the lost *materièl*, but such was not the case with the almost 200,000 casualties that the Allies inflicted on the German army.

The battles fought before the St. Mihiel Offensive opened on 12 September 1918 offered a valuable opportunity for the inexperienced AEF, the American Expeditionary Forces, to gain battlefield experience; the 1st, 2nd, 3rd, 4th, 26th, 28th, 32nd, 42nd, and 77th Divisions were involved in the fighting at Belleau Wood (which lasted almost the whole of June 1918) and Château Thierry (including the counter-offensive there, which opened on 18 July 1918) where they were incorporated into the French front and forced the Germans to retreat from the River Marne. Several other American divisions had been training in quiet sectors with the British;

they experienced enemy shelling for the first time, learnt how to deal with trench life and tried as best they could in the limited time available to become accustomed to the realities of warfare in Europe in mid 1918.

The French and British, threatened with being overwhelmed by the German offensives, originally planned to incorporate Americans divisions piecemeal in their sectors. General John J. Pershing (1860-1948), the Commander-in-Chief of the AEF, however, was resolutely opposed to this idea; he wanted to fight the Germans with an independent American Army, under his command, that would be appointed to a defined sector of the French or British battlefield. This was not his view alone; it was also the clear wish of his political masters in Washington. It was hardly a surprising position – for example, the BEF (British Expeditionary Force) was sent to the continent at the outbreak of the war with clear instructions to its commander, Field Marshal French, that he was to cooperate fully with the French army but that he should maintain his independence and act in the best interests of the BEF. As history shows, Pershing largely got his way, though he did allow, somewhat reluctantly and in light of the emergency situation, American divisions to be deployed under British or French command in what proved to be an important role in halting the German onslaught.

Pershing continued to pursue his primary objective of establishing an independent Army, with its own sector and its own objectives, working in full cooperation with the other allied armies and accepting Foch's rather undefined position as overall Supremo. On 10 August 1918 the First (American) Army was created, with its own sector, although some American divisions continued to serve under direct Allied command elsewhere, and under Pershing's direct command. He combined this new role with that of Commander in Chief of the AEF, a remarkably onerous burden for one man. The first major test in battle of his new, independent, First Army was the successful pinching out of the St. Mihiel Salient.

On the second day of the St. Mihiel Offensive, 13 September, the Salient had already been largely eliminated and the Germans had suffered substantial losses. Officially, the offensive continued until 16 September, grinding to a halt about a kilometre short of the fortified Michel Zone. Although a considerable morale boost for the Americans, it should be noted that the Germans had already made preparations for the evacuation of the Salient to shorten their lines in an operation code-named Loki. In fact it had been the intention of the German High Command since the summer of 1917 to pull back to the Michel Zone – it was from this time that the substantial improvements in it, particularly bunkers constructed at almost ground level, were undertaken, in case of an enemy attack because of the vulnerability of the German positions in the Salient. There is some controversy among historians about when these orders to withdraw were given. After the war the official Loki orders and thousands of other documents were never recovered; however, several available sources confirm that in some places the retreat was already under way before the official order was given at noon on 12 September 1918. In order to draw your own conclusions I have included part of the official captured German orders in Appendix 5.

The remarkably quick success at St. Mihiel gave the Americans, and most notably their commanders, a false sense of superiority, experienced to the fullest a couple of weeks later at the opening of the Meuse-Argonne Offensive (26 September-11 November 1918). It took 400,000 Americans at least three weeks and huge casualties to break through the German Kriemhild Line, well-defended by a mere 65,000 men. As Captain (acting Colonel) George C. Marshall (1880-1959), Operations Section, General Headquarters explained,

> 'A veteran of a single battle like St. Mihiel is prone to draw some erroneous conclusions. Those of the First Division, familiar with the vicissitudes of Cantigny and the terrific fighting at Soissons, felt that they had only participated in a manoeuvre, while the members of a previously inexperienced division considered themselves the victors in a prodigious struggle.'

George C. Marshall.

One important factor to bear in mind is that the topography in the Woëvre Plain has changed in the intervening hundred years. The Lac de Madine is markedly bigger (since 1965) than it was during the war and the area was considerably marshier than it is today. The logistical challenges following the advance on the Hindenburg Line/Michel Zone were very complicated – the old story of utterly inadequate roads dominating. In many ways the St. Mihiel advance increasingly appears to be like a 'traditional' Western Front offensive - early success that would become bogged down in front of a heavily fortified zone after initial gains. In contrast to the Allied offensives in 1917, in the Meuse-Argonne the Germans had no *Eingreif* divisions, or shock troops, to launch counter attacks; whilst in this case they had every intention of pulling out of the Salient when they judged the time to be right. The offensive came to a halt in front of the Michel Zone and therefore it was never really put to the test. What if the

Americans wearing captured German equipment; the two soldiers in the middle wear their German helmets backwards.

Americans had continued the attack immediately after 16 September, would they have been able to break the line? We will never know.

A further factor that should not be forgotten, although it falls outside the scope of this book, is the substantial French contribution to the offensive. Not only did the French army contribute 110,000 soldiers for this joint offensive under American command, they also provided the weaponry; artillery, ammunition, trench mortars, machine guns, airplanes and tanks. None of these were of American manufacture, which was largely due to the munitions resources required for an army expanding from roughly 180,000 men in 1917, to well over 4,000,000 at the end of 1918. Production capacity, logistics and transport are of paramount importance when waging war, let alone when the fighting takes place on another continent. Besides, as a consequence of the dire emergency that the Allies faced on the Western Front in the first half of 1918, the Americans agreed to prioritise the provision of manpower over equipment, the latter of which the British and the French calculated they could provide.

On my first visit to the St. Mihiel Salient, I was struck by the number of memorials, trenches and bunkers and was impressed by the quality of the structures in comparison with other parts of the Western Front; it is clear that the occupants had a lot of time on their hands. Naturally, the German monuments were built during the occupation; a few dozen American monuments were erected after the war, most notably the Montsec American Monument (built in the French sector!), which dominates the area for miles.

This book enables the reader to follow the events that started on 12 September 1918 chronologically and by corps. Short histories are followed by walks and car tours. The composite divisions are treated from left to right; the short histories start on the night of 11–12 September, the night the preliminary bombardment started.

The whole German defence system that was built behind the front line was called the Hindenburg Line, except for the Flandern Line in Belgium and the Michel Zone in the St. Mihiel Salient. However, it is basically the same line, the only difference is in the name given to particular lengths of it. Throughout the book, I use the name Michel Zone instead of the Hindenburg Line.

List of Maps

CHAPTER 1

Setting the Scene: St. Mihiel 1914-1918

1914

On 2 August 1914, the Germans invaded France and Luxembourg and declared war on Russia. Two days later, the German army crossed the Belgian border. The attack on Belgium was immediately followed by the British declaration of war on Germany. The Germans needed to strike at the heart of France to end the problem of fighting a war on two fronts. They were counting on the fact that once Paris was in German hands the French would surrender, after which the German army could turn its attention to Russia. Despite a series of unanticipated setbacks in Belgium, within weeks the Germans had made adequate progress in France and were threatening Paris. Between 25 August and 5 September, the French army had been pushed back on a wide front from the Franco-German border, in the area of this book as far back as the city of Verdun. However, this so-called great retreat ended when the French managed to stem the tide and outflanked the German Armies threatening Paris, which had made important errors in their axis of advance. As a consequence of what proved to be the most significant fighting of the opening stages of the war, during the Battle of the Marne (5 to 12 September) the Germans were forced to fall back to positions between sixty-five and ninety kilometres north of the capital. The opportunity of pushing France out of the war by means of a massive early strike was gone. Soon after what became known as the 'Miracle of the Marne' the war of movement came to an end along the River Aisne and the belligerent armies started to dig in. In the Meuse-Argonne region, the French army had managed to hold on to the northern defences around Verdun.

Creation of the Salient 12-15 September 1914

The St. Mihiel Salient had been developed almost by accident in the opening months of the war; it was the by-product of an attempt to outflank Verdun from the south. The two German wings on the Woëvre Plain were held in check by French troops in Toul in the south and Verdun in the north, but in the centre they encountered virtually no resistance;

Germans leaving for France, August 1914.

French prisoners at St. Mihiel, October 1914.

they managed to push on to St. Mihiel, situated on the right bank of the Meuse River, before the attack lost its momentum and ended in stalemate. Both sides started to dig in and fortified their positions. During the course of the war the front line changed little in this area; for four years, St. Mihiel formed a salient in the French lines.

Located on one of the historic invasion routes into France, the Salient had strategic significance for both parties. The French saw it as a German springboard for future operations, a threat to Verdun and an obstacle to any French drive into Lorraine or east of the River Meuse. It also cut several important French railway lines.

From the German point of view, it created a buffer zone in front of the Briey-Longwy iron basin and coalfields, and the city of Metz. If enemy forces penetrated beyond Metz they could potentially roll up the whole of the German front from the Swiss border to Belgium; whilst it made sure that several French divisions and large quantities of materiél were tied up in the area so that these could not be deployed elsewhere.

Around the same time as the fighting at St. Mihiel ended, the Germans were pushed back along both flanks of the Argonne Forest due to the pressure being exerted by French troops. On 15 September, the retreat in the area came to a standstill on a line running from north of Vienne-le-Château, Varennes, Cote (Hill) 304, Mort Homme, Vacherauville, Les Éparges to St. Mihiel. Heavy fighting in the Argonne Forest and the hills of Les Éparges on the north western lip of the Salient started as both armies attempted to occupy the high ground. The armies quickly adapted to the new static conditions. The war was not only fought in primitive trenches running across the wooded hills and through valleys and ravines, but also underground. Both sides started to dig an extensive maze of tunnels under enemy strongholds in order to place explosive charges; as a result whole sections of trench line and redoubts were blown up. Many mine craters are still visible today, most notably in Vauquois in the Argonne and Les Éparges, about twenty kilometres north of St. Mihiel. Just four months after the outbreak of the war, the war of movement had changed into a stalemate; the idea of a war of movement with a quick and decisive victory had proved a delusion; the misguided hope of many of being home by Christmas was in tatters.

1915

In 1915 the area between Verdun and St. Mihiel was largely dominated by continuous and savage fighting in Prêtre Wood (across the river from Pont à Mousson) on the eastern side of the Salient, and on Éparges Ridge, on its western side. The main goal of the French was to remove the Germans from the heights of Éparges Ridge, which dominated the

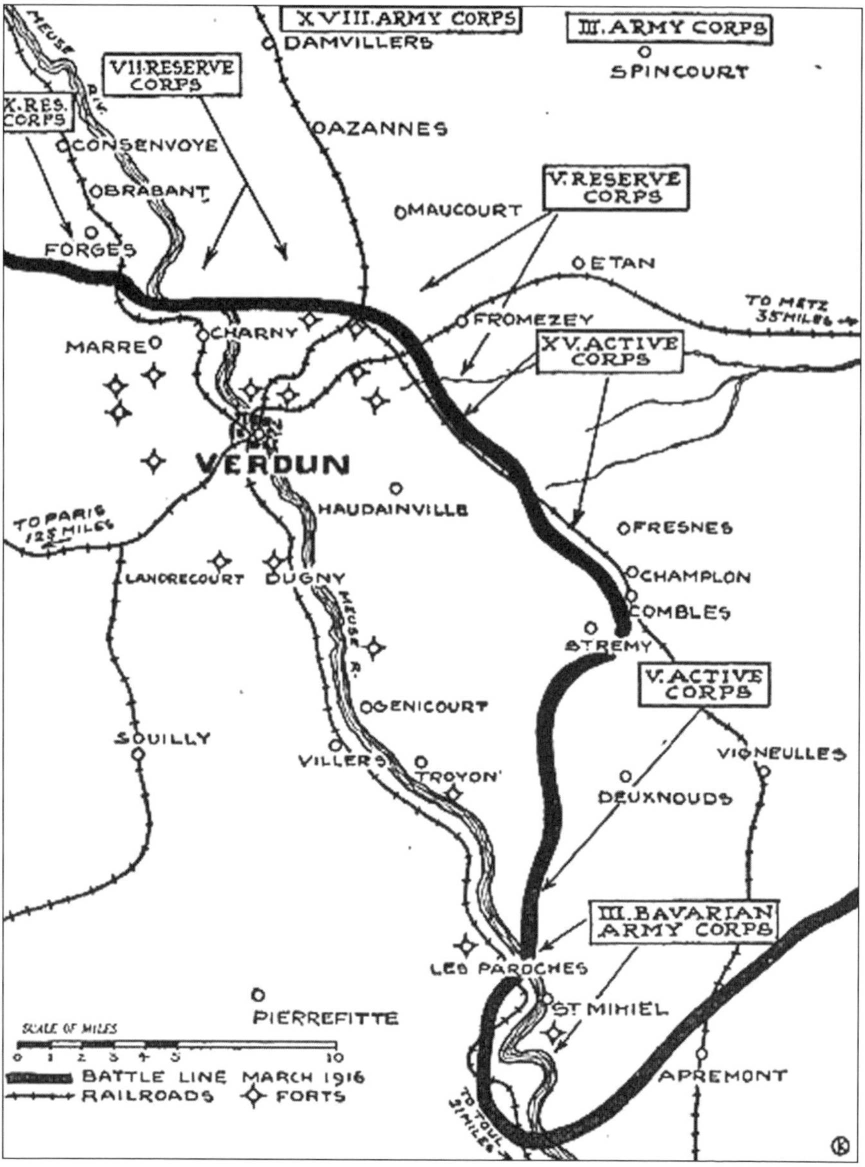

The front line, 1916–1918.

Woëvre Plain below (17 February to 5 April), where both sides had been reinforcing their lines after the fighting had briefly ceased in December 1914. The battle on the rugged and forested hills was fierce and the weather conditions appalling, but both armies quickly adapted to the rain, snow, mud and brutal violence. On both sides a huge amount of energy was spent on tunnelling and mine warfare. For the soldiers protecting their stretch of front line, no other option remained but to go underground. In total, seventy-eight mines were blown, gradually turning the hilltops into huge holes; there are craters that can easily hold a London bus. Without doubt, the most poignant example of underground mine warfare in this area is to be found on Éparges Ridge. An estimated 80,000 soldiers, both French and German, perished on the St. Mihiel front. After April 1915 the sector became a relatively quiet area. Today, the craters are still visible in the landscape and one wonders how anybody could have survived at all in this man-made hell.

Over the course of 1915, armies were expanded, factories were built for the production of the enormous quantities of ammunition, guns, rifles and other weaponry that the armies need on a daily basis. Added to this, there was also the need to create an efficient logistical system for food, clothes, wood, corrugated iron, horses and mail. In spite of the shortages of seemingly everything except manpower, massive offensives were launched during 1915, which cost hundreds of thousands of lives: Neuve Chapelle, Second Ypres, Champagne, Artois, Loos, Gallipoli (Turkey), Isonzo (Italy) and Mesopotamia to name but a few.

1916

This year in the Salient was largely used by both the German and French armies to consolidate their lines; new shelters, improved trenches and developing the infrastructure (ie narrow gauge railways and roads) were the main concern of the soldiers manning the Salient.

Starting on 21 February 1916, the French and the Germans engaged in a massive offensive, now known as the Battle of Verdun, which took place just forty kilometres north of St. Mihiel. By this stage the Salient had become of value as what was in effect a rest area. Whilst the fighting at Verdun continued to rage, at the beginning of July 1916 the British and French in turn launched a massive offensive, on the German line straddling the Somme. However, in the Salient, both the French and Germans largely respected the unofficial ceasefire that only ended with the American-French St. Mihiel Offensive of September 1918.

New doctrine

By the autumn of 1916, in the light of the appalling costs of the fighting on the Somme and at Verdun, the German High Command realized that the country could no longer sustain costly campaigns fighting on two fronts.

The war on the Western Front had gradually changed from the strategy more or less adopted by both sides in August 1914 of a series of battles of annihilation – the destruction of the enemy's ability to fight –

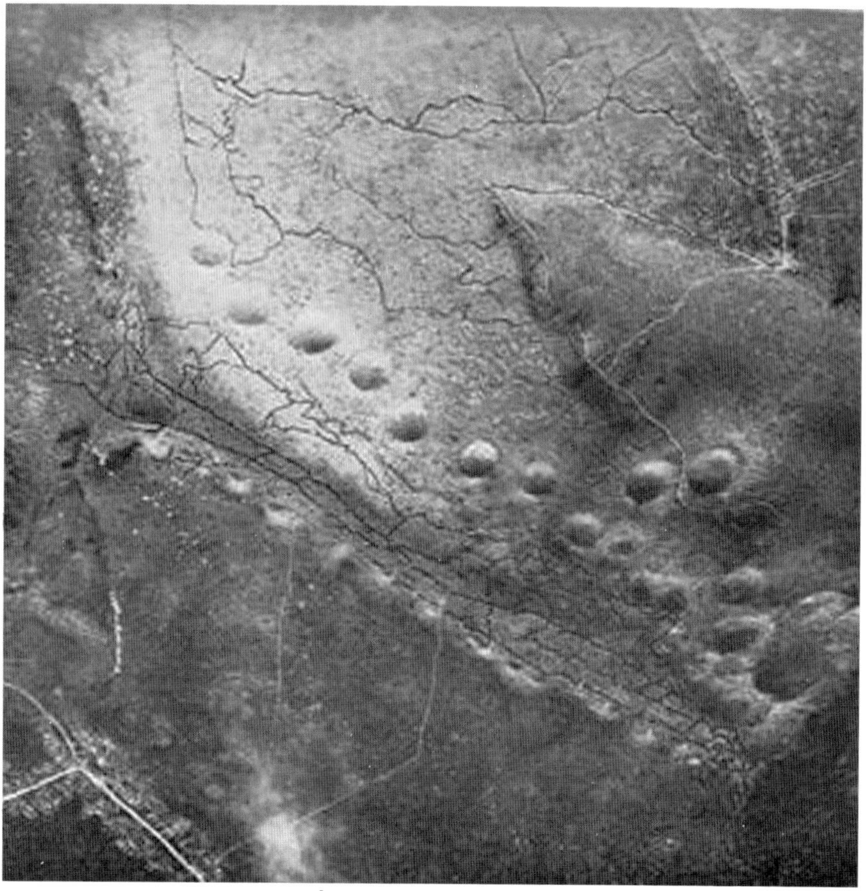

The mine craters at Les Éparges from the air, 1915.

and manoeuvre into a war of stalemate, with much more attention paid to possibilities on the Eastern Front. There was strategic purpose in the German offensive at Verdun (even if it was somewhat obscure), the most significant offensive action taken on the Western Front by them since the early months of the war. Whatever its strategic intent, it rapidly degenerated into an extraordinarily bloody slogging match fought in ghastly, unspeakable conditions. The failure of the Allies to secure a decisive success at the opening of the Somme in July reduced that offensive to an even bloodier battle; fighting on the Western Front had been reduced to a war of attrition. At the same time the mobilisation of industry and technological innovation provided ever more lethal weapon systems made available in staggering numbers. Chief amongst these was the huge increase in artillery pieces, firing shells of greater calibre, with improved fuses and with the capability of firing gas.

French soldiers at their ablutions, one enjoying a shave, 1915.

Erich von Falkenhayn (1861-1922), chief of the German General Staff from September 1914, adopted a doctrine of holding the line at all costs once the fighting had ended that year in the stalemate of entrenched positions. If a position was lost, local commanders were to launch counter attacks to recapture it. By the autumn of 1916 it was clear that this inflexibility was costing unacceptable casualties. Falkenhayn was sacked in late August – the final straw in his downfall being the entry of Romania into the war on the Allied side.

In a war of attrition there was an inescapable fact: the Allies had greater manpower resources than the Germans and there was a real risk that the German army would be bled white first. The duumvirate of Hindenburg (1847-1934) and Ludendorff (185-1937), who succeeded him as professional heads of the German army, sought a new doctrine to enable ground to be held in a way that minimised German casualties whilst at the same time inflicting disproportionate casualties on the Allied forces. The Cambrai Conference of 8 September 1916 was instrumental in working out a new doctrine.

In anticipation of a future Allied offensive, Ludendorff directed military engineers to study the possibility of building two major withdrawal positions behind the front lines of the Western Front. These defence lines became known to the Allies as the Hindenburg Line. Not long afterwards work started on the construction of the new system on the Somme and in Flanders; Once it was completed, in the early spring of 1917, the Germans withdrew in the Somme and Arras sector, shortening the German front line by some fifty kilometres and releasing anything up to a dozen divisions from holding the line and making them available for deployment elsewhere.

1917 and 1918

Still a quiet part of the front line, at the base of the Salient the situation changed rapidly when in July 1917 the Germans started working on the Michel Zone. Thousands of workers were drafted into the area; a building frenzy started at the base of the St. Mihiel Salient. Away from prying enemy eyes and largely out of range of the French guns, the Germans started a building project unprecedented on the Western Front: over a thousand pillboxes were to be constructed on a sixty kilometre wide front, stretching from Étain in the north (twenty kilometres east of Verdun) to Pont-à-Mousson in the south. Ultimately, it shortened the German front line by sixty kilometres and released a little over four divisions, two of

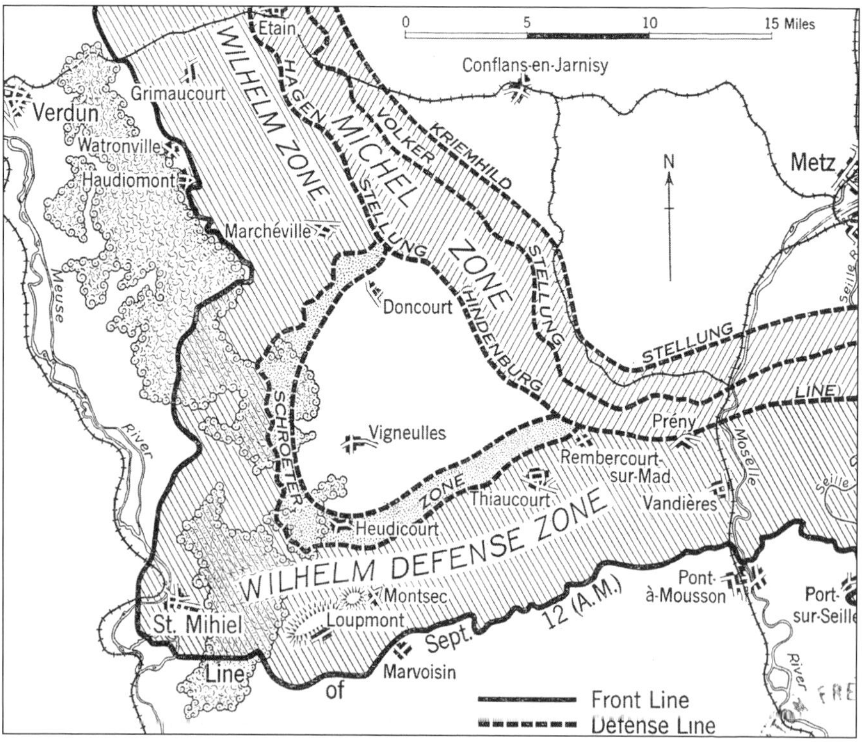

The German defences in the Salient.

the main goals of the building programme. In case of a full-scale enemy attack, the troops were ordered to evacuate the Salient and to retreat to the Michel Zone as fast as possible and only fight rearguard actions to avoid unnecessary casualties and loss of material. Once in the safety of the shelters, the German artillery was to destroy the enemy in front of the defences.

The frantic building activities continued right up to the start of the St. Mihiel Offensive of 12 September 1918. However, when the attack started, the building project was far from complete, save for the Volker Line, the most important. Ultimately, the line was never put to the test, but served as an example for future building programs that both the French and Germans employed in the 1930s to fortify their borders. These lines became known as the Maginot Line and the Siegfried Line, which in turn inspired the building of the Atlantic Wall during the Second World War.

CHAPTER 2

August 1918: the Americans Take Over

The St. Mihiel Offensive started on 12 September 1918, and was the first operation undertaken in the First World War by an independent American Army, under the command of its Commander-in-Chief, General Pershing, and was supported by 110,000 French troops. The plan to develop an Army near St. Mihiel when sufficient troops were available and to reduce the Salient there as a preliminary to more extensive operations in the same vicinity (Metz), was proposed by Pershing and was agreed to by the French High Command at a conference shortly after the arrival of the American Army Headquarters in France. The Americans constantly had this plan in mind and, beginning in January 1918, the front near St. Mihiel was used to give front line experience to American divisions and to acquaint them with the region in which they would later attack.

However, the succession of German attacks in the spring of 1918, the so-called Spring Offensive, made it necessary to postpone the original plan, as all available American troops were urgently needed to bolster the French and British Armies who were at the risk of collapse in other sectors of the front, most notably in the Marne region, not far from Paris. Although by July there were already more than 1,200,000 American soldiers in France, American combat formations were widely distributed along the entire front, either serving in line with the French and British Armies or undergoing training in rear areas.

om The Bystander, London

THE THREE MUSKETEERS

Tommy," "Le Poilu," and "Sammy" Marching Together to the Victory That Certain

When at the start of August (close to the end of the Second Battle of the Marne of 15 July-6 August 1918) it became clear that the reduction of the German-held Aisne-Marne Salient was nearly completed, General Pershing pointed out to Foch that the improved situation made possible the concentration of American formations and insisted that the creation of an American Army be resumed. Although the French, but more specifically the British, urged that American units be left with their forces, Pershing stuck to his position. After much debate, reluctantly an understanding was reached that most of the American formations would soon be concentrated into an independent American Army in the St. Mihiel area. For the time being, only the American 27th and the 30th Divisions stayed with the British.

US collar disc, worn on the left collar.

On 13 August, at the newly established American First Army Headquarters in Neufchâteau, the Army staff began to set up shop and preparations started for the reduction of the Salient. The assembling of formations started soon thereafter and, on 30 August, the American First Army took over command of the front line from Port-sur-Seille, nine kilometres east of the River Moselle, to Watronville, fourteen kilometres south-east of Verdun, a sector that also included the St. Mihiel Salient.

Second Battle of the Marne. The Americans attacked at Château-Thierry and Belleau Wood, see 1 on the map.

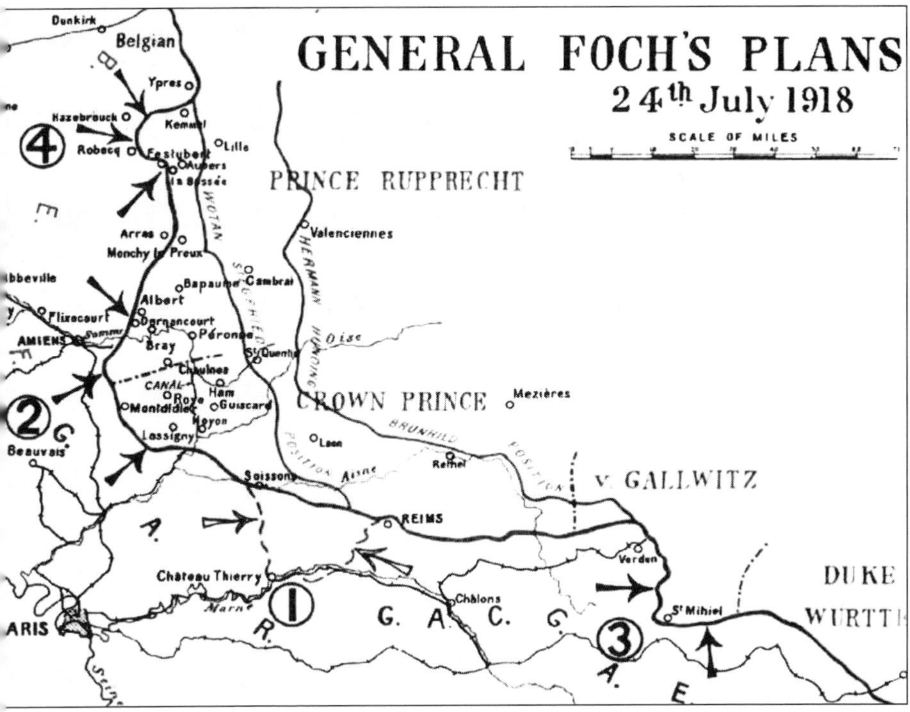

The Salient was shaped roughly like a triangle, with its points near (to the south) Pont-à-Mousson, (west) St. Mihiel and (north) Verdun. At its base, it was forty-five kilometres wide, extended thirty kilometres into the Allied lines and had remained almost unchanged in shape since the end of 1914. Its north-western face ran diagonally across the wooded heights east of the Meuse River, and its south eastern face extended from St. Mihiel to the River Moselle, traversing the Meuse Heights, the Moselle Heights and the intervening Woëvre Plain. This plain is cut by small streams and dotted with woods of varying size. It is comparatively low ground, containing many lakes and swampy areas, thus making cross-country travel difficult, especially in wet weather.

Within the German lines at the southern face of the Salient were the high and isolated hills of Loupmont and Montsec. These afforded the Germans excellent views of a large area of ground behind the French lines. Two German positions, the Wilhelm and the Schroeter Zone, had been prepared in front of the Michel Zone and all had been strengthened by elaborate systems of trenches, barbed-wire entanglements, concrete shelters and machine-gun emplacements. The Michel Zone, however, was the most powerful of the three; since 1917 this zone had been changed into a veritable fortress and close to one thousand pillboxes had been built on a sixty kilometres' wide front. The Michel Zone was to remain intact and in German hands until the Armistice.

The value of the Salient to the Germans

1. It protected the City of Metz, and the German border;
2. It protected the important Briey iron basin and large coal deposits;
3. It interrupted traffic on the main Paris-Nancy railroad;
4. It cut the Verdun-Toul railroad;
5. It threatened the Allied territory in its vicinity, especially west of the Meuse;
6. It forced the French to keep thousands of troops and large quantities of supplies in the area.

It was clear to Foch that the St. Mihiel Salient would first have to be eliminated before any great offensive could be launched against the Briey and Metz region in the east, or to the north, between the Meuse River and Argonne Forest in the general direction of Sedan.

The final American preparations for the attack against the Salient had been underway for just two weeks when, on 30 August, Marshal Foch unexpectedly suggested to General Pershing that the attack on St. Mihiel should be greatly downsized and that most of the American divisions should be used for another attack to be launched around 20 September

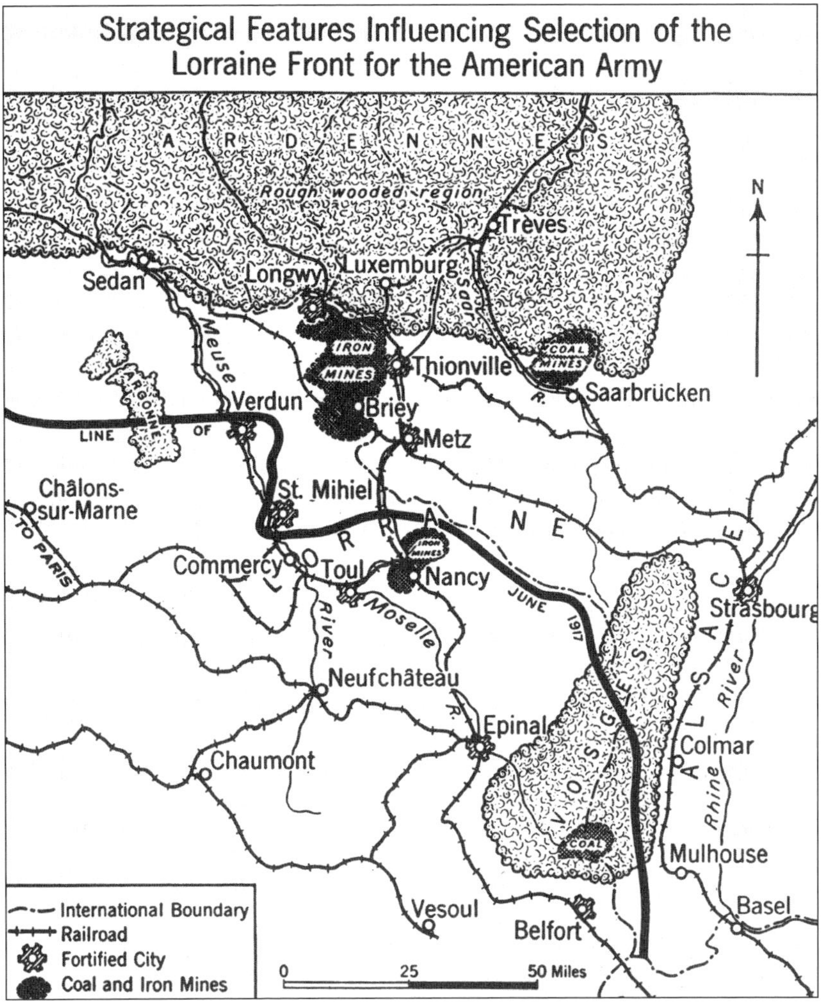

between Verdun and the Argonne Forest. In the new plans, the American divisions would be assigned to operate under French command. Knowing that Pershing was almost fixated on deploying the American Army as a whole, Foch pressed Pershing to undertake not one but two offensives. Additionally, it freed French divisions that could now be deployed elsewhere along the front.

General John J. Pershing.

An extremely annoyed, not to say angry, General Pershing felt that the St. Mihiel Offensive should be carried out as planned and definitely stated that the American divisions would fight *only* as part of an independent American Army. On 2 September, after a series of conferences with Foch, it was agreed that the assault would be carried out, but that its objectives would be strictly limited so that the American (First) Army could undertake another major attack, the Meuse-Argonne Offensive, ten days after the capture of the planned initial objectives for the St. Mihiel 'drive' on 16 September, on the front between the Meuse River and the Argonne Forest. Although quite ambitious, to say the least, but eager to show the French and the British what the Americans were capable of, Pershing agreed.

George C. Marshall, Operations Section, HQ.

Naturally, this agreement weighed heavily upon the largely inexperienced American First Army and staff, as not only was it called upon to bring to an end the offensive at St. Mihiel, it was also responsible for planning the transportation of vast quantities of men and supplies to the Meuse-Argonne front, all within a very limited time frame. From the outset there was a huge shortage of non-commissioned and commissioned officers, which was a problem that continued to haunt the Americans right up to the Armistice. George Marshall wrote in his memoirs that

> '… the inexperience of the hundreds of staff officers involved us in many complications. Instructions directing the concealment of all dumps of supplies and ammunitions which were being established in the area were followed up by inspectors, and one of these enthusiasts required the officer at the largest ammunition dump in the area, La Courtine, north of Toul, to cover it with white [tar]paulins, with the result that a short time after the target was thus accentuated a German airplane dropped a bomb which blew up the entire affair.'

To make matters more complicated, Pershing, not only C-in-C of the American Expeditionary Forces, was also determined to retain command of First Army, an extremely ambitious task for just one man, to say the least.

The Plan of Attack

The final plans for the St. Mihiel operation provided for a main American assault against the southern face of the Salient (IV and I Corps), while at the same time the French (II CAC, ie II Colonial Corps) launched a second attack against the western tip of the Salient. Simultaneously, the American V Corps launched an attack on the northern face in order to join up with the IV Corps and effectively cut off a large chunk of the tip of the Salient.

From left to right, the IV Corps, commanded by Major General Joseph Dickman, attacked from Marvoisin to Limey, with the 89th, 42nd and 1st Divisions in line, and the 3rd in reserve. I Corps, under the command of Major General Hunter Liggett, continued the line from Limey to Pont-à-Mousson, with the 2nd, 5th, 90th and 82nd Divisions in line and the 78th in reserve.

V Corps, commanded by Major General Cameron, composed of the 26th Division, the French 15th (Colonial) Division, part of the 4th Division and the remainder of the 4th in reserve, was to make a secondary attack from the Meuse Heights to the south from the direction of Hattonville.

It was Foch himself who added the French troops to the American assault force; in this way he hoped to keep pressure on the tip of the Salient in order to enable the Americans to execute the pincer movement

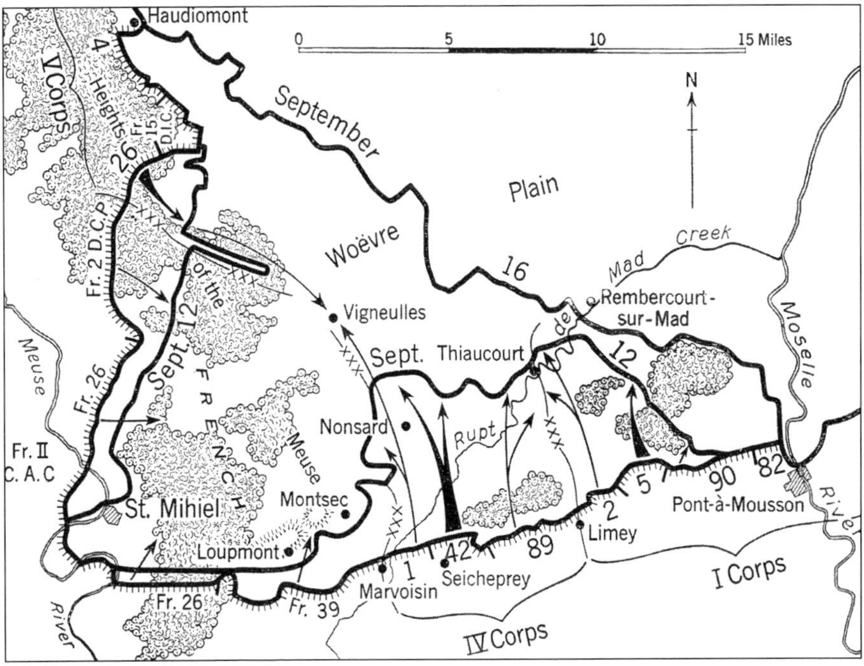

The American plan of attack.

more easily. The French II Colonial Corps, comprising three French divisions, the 39th Division, 2nd Cavalry Division (dismounted) and the aforementioned 15th (Colonial) Division, each occupying large sectors of the front line around the tip of the Salient, was to support the left flank of the main American attack. When the fighting ceased on 16 September, the French Corps had successfully liberated over one third of the Salient.

The man largely responsible for the plan of attack was the brilliant Captain George C. Marshall, attached to the Operations Section at General Headquarters. Starting with a small-scale plan involving six divisions, this ultimately evolved to a large-scale attack deploying no less than fourteen American divisions. The ever-changing conditions on the Western Front and Allied politics of 1918, made it necessary for Marshall constantly to adapt his plans; the final version was only finished a few weeks before the start of the offensive. Marshall played an important role in the organization of troop movements, among many other things. For most of 1918, Marshall was busy studying the questions of ocean tonnage and ports of debarkation, methods of training new divisions, securing French and British artillery pieces and ammunition. The constant change of plans took a heavy toll on planners like Marshall. He later wrote that

> '… an interview between General Pershing and Marshal Foch might result in some seemingly insignificant amendment to the general plan, but it usually resulted in a wide disturbance in the lower echelons. An inch at the top became a mile at the bottom.'

We cannot imagine the huge problems facing the Operations Section when, on the afternoon of 8 September, they received orders to begin planning the troop movements for the Meuse-Argonne Offensive; they were still deeply engaged in work preparing for the St. Mihiel Offensive that was due to start just four days later. Marshall, in his own words 'rather disturbed', took a long walk to think things over. He returned to his office a few hours later.

> 'Fully recognizing the gravity of my dilemma', *he wrote later*, 'I called a stenographer and started the dictation of the preliminary order for the Meuse-Argonne concentration, realizing that it must reach the various army corps immediately if the corps commanders were to be given time to make the necessary rearrangements prior to the jump-off at St. Mihiel. In less than an hour I had evolved a method for the procedure and had completed the order, which not only covered the preliminary movement of troops but also involved the regrouping of the organizations

remaining on the St. Mihiel front at the close of the battle, and outlined instructions for the defensive organization of the positions which they were expected to capture.'

The next day, General Pershing 'thought it was a fine piece of work'. Thanks to extraordinarily talented men like Marshall, who were capable of planning the whole affair on the back of a beer mat, so to speak, Pershing got away with the seemingly impossible task that Foch had imposed on him.

George 'organizer of victory' Marshall was one of the most influential men in the American army during the first half of the twentieth century. After the Second World War, Marshall, by now US Secretary of State, was one of the main instigators of the plan that eventually came to carry his name, the Marshall Plan, the plan to help Europe recover from the war. He served as Chairman of the American Battle Monuments Commission from 1949 to 1959; in 1953 Marshall was awarded the Nobel Peace Prize in recognition of his post-war work. Marshall died at Walter Reed Hospital in Washington D.C. on 16 October 1959 at the age of 78.

Of the three American corps and the fourteen American divisions that took part in the attack, two of the corps and four of the divisions had never before been engaged in offensive combat. Therefore, First Army had the 35th, 80th and 91st Divisions in reserve for use in case of necessity. The US Army's need for additional planes, artillery, machine guns and tanks was largely met by the French and British.

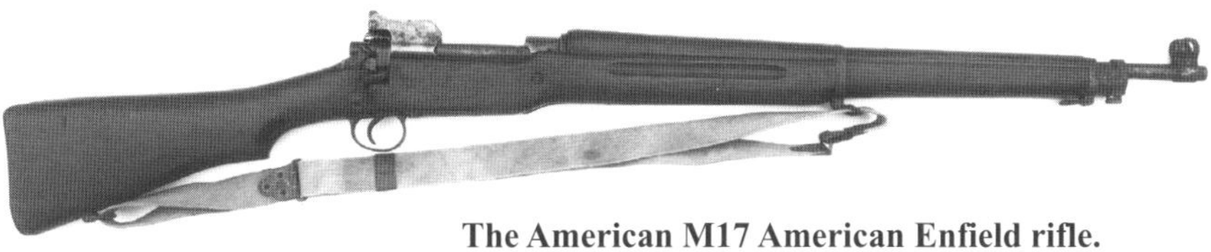

The American M17 American Enfield rifle.

More than 500,000 Americans (216,000 in line) and about 110,000 French were involved in the offensive – from muleteers, clerks, engineers, to the soldiers in the front line. Apart from the Springfield and M14 American Enfield rifles and small arms like the Colt 1911, most of the equipment of the AEF was supplied by the French. For example, the American Air Service, commanded by Colonel William 'Billy' Mitchell, was supplied with 1,481 airplanes of French and British manufacture. In addition to this, the commander of the Independent Air Force – effectively a branch of the RAF, Major General Trenchard, supplied the Americans with eight night bombing squadrons for the forthcoming offensive. As well as supplying fuel for the aircraft, the Americans also contributed a handful of British designed, American built De Havilland DH-4 planes, nicknamed flying coffins because they were notorious for catching fire.

Chief of Air Service Brigadier General William L. 'Billy' Mitchell.

The Americans were also provided with about 400 French tanks, 350 of which were the light Renault FT17s, mainly operated by French drivers; 144 were operated by Americans. About 2,700 French artillery pieces of all calibres were used and approximately 3,300,000 rounds of artillery ammunition were brought into the area in preparation for the offensive. The secret movement of such a large number of troops to the battle front and the many details involved in planning the operation and in providing the necessary special troops put a tremendous strain on the Army's staff. However, they faced up to the task given to them with great enthusiasm. George Marshall later wrote that,

American-built De Havilland DH4 bi-plane.

'It was growing increasingly difficult to conceal Pershing's intentions. Everyone was enthusiastic and each felt that his individual part was of momentous importance and, therefore, an exception to the rules or regulations, with the result that, despite drastic orders to the contrary, the traffic on the roads in the daytime had grown to such proportions as to ensure its observation by the enemy. Every officer desired to make a personal reconnaissance of the ground over which he was to operate, and there were frequent violations of the orders against promiscuous reconnaissances in the daytime.'

On the night of 11-12 September, First Army was in position, ready for battle.

The Germans

The German Army holding the Salient comprised eight divisions in line; four divisions were held in reserve, well behind the Michel Zone. It should be noted that a German division was in no way comparable in size to an American division: by this stage of the war they were, at best, a little over a third the size.

Max von Gallwitz.

The German High Command suspected that the enemy was preparing an attack but they believed that it would not take place until late in September. However, as early as 1 September, Ludendorff sent a message to Army Group Gallwitz that '*... there are increasing reports to the effect that the Americans intend to attack Metz on both sides of the* [River] *Moselle.*' From that moment on, the Germans were in the highest state of readiness. Three days later, Ludendorff wrote to Gallwitz that:

'The forces for repulsing a broad attack against the greater portion of the south front of Composite Army C are not at present available. The attack is therefore not to be met in the present forward combat zone, but in this case avoiding it by withdrawal into the Michel Zone is contemplated although only in the event of an enveloping attack.'

Although no official orders had been issued, from the start of September supplies and weaponry were gradually moved from the front line to the Schroeter Zone, the system of defences in the centre of the Salient, and further back. On 10 September, Ludendorff wrote to Army Group Galwitz HQ:

> 'I request that you abandon the proposed attack [*in case of a small-scale American operation the Germans had been contemplating a counter attack*] and begin to execute the measures for the occupation of the Michel Positions according to plan. The withdrawal of the troops from their present positions and the resultant abandonment of the position itself is, if possible, to be postponed as long as the tactical situation will permit, even after the evacuation of the St. Mihiel foreground, in order that time may be gained to improve the general situation.'

The German plan allowed eight days to destroy anything of value and transfer war materiel to the rear. The actual withdrawal of the troops, code named Loki, was to take place during four successive nights, each division covering the other. However, the American attack started earlier than anticipated and the Germans were caught by surprise whilst preparing for the Loki orders.

On 12 September, at 1.00 am, the American bombardment of the German positions began and was so intense and overpowering that the

Destroyed German truck. (Collection Tom Gudmestad)

Hardware supply depot in Vigneulles that was burned by the retreating Germans.

German guns left in the Salient could not make an effective reply. The fact that several of the forward artillery batteries had already been withdrawn to the intermediate zone, the Schroeter Zone, did not help matters.

The Americans attack

Thursday 12 September

At 5.00 am, the rain-sodden infantry climbed out of their trenches into No Man's Land. Despite the lack of tanks – only a few had come up in time to assist the troops through the wire entanglements – the attack advanced on schedule. According to the plan, the greatest advance was to be made by IV Corps and the left of I Corps; to gain the objectives of 12 September required an advance of ten kilometres. In its execution the 1st Division, on the left flank of the main attack, captured Nonsard and entered the woods to the north; the 42nd Division pushed on beyond the villages of Essey and Pannes, while the 89th seized Bouillonville. In I Corps' sector, the 2nd Division captured Thiaucourt, and the 5th drove through Vieville-en-Haye, with its eastern flank bent back to connect with the 90th Division, which was at the pivot of the main attack on the first day.

On the western face of the Salient the intensive fire of the French artillery continued until 8.00 am, when the infantry of V Corps launched its assault from the north. The Germans, not knowing what day the attack was going to take place, were surprised by the severity of the assault and were forced to give up ground on all fronts. As a result the official

German order to retreat to the Michel Zone, the so-called Loki Movement, was given around midday. However, the speed of the American and French attacks was such that thousands of German soldiers and large quantities of equipment fell into American hands. At nightfall V Corps had advanced about four kilometres.

While the attacks on the two faces were progressing, reports indicated that the Germans were retiring from the tip of the Salient in front of the French troops, although French raids into the German lines near St. Mihiel itself met with considerable opposition, mainly from machine-gun units.

Early in the evening of 12 September General Pershing, with the idea of cutting off the retreat of as many Germans as possible, directed that troops of IV and V Corps be rushed with all speed to link up in the vicinity of Vigneulles. Part of the 26th Division marched along a narrow forest road directly to the heart of the Salient; soon after 2.00 am Vigneulles was in American hands but the two divisions had not yet joined up.

First Division Memorial, marking the closing of the Salient.

Friday 13 September

At dawn, the 26th Division met patrols of the 1st Division just north-east of Vigneulles. This marked the closing of the Salient and the German soldiers who had not retired beyond that point were cut off and captured. Practically all objectives had been gained by the evening of 13 September, and the organization of the new position, roughly along the line between Vandières and Haudiomont, was begun. Because the attack had gone so well, the transfer of American units to the Meuse-Argonne region was started on the night of 13 September, three days before the scheduled completion of the St. Mihiel Offensive.

Saturday 14 to Tuesday 17 September

While the remaining German troops were fighting rearguard actions, it was of great importance to keep pressure upon the fleeing German soldiers. Deep raids and local attacks were continued, especially on the eastern part of the front, where things had run less smoothly; on 16 September, after several fierce German counterattacks, the 90th Division finally captured Rappes Wood and much adjoining territory.

Incredibly, by 17 September, the worn-out German Army had been increased to ten divisions with a further ten divisions in reserve, an actual increase of seven divisions during the period of the offensive. They scraped the bottom of the barrel for reinforcements in anticipation of the big American push towards Metz and into Germany. For the Allies, the attack on the Salient had the added advantage that it more or less kept twenty German divisions engaged; troops that for the time being could not be deployed elsewhere.

On 20 September, only the American 26th, 42nd, 78th, 89th, 90th and four French divisions were left to consolidate the front. These divisions, and those which entered the line from time to time as relieving units, continued to strengthen their positions and to conduct local attacks to secure vantage points in order to occupy the best possible positions in the event of an advance on Metz.

The Americans had suffered 8,600 casualties, yet more than 15,000 prisoners and about 400 guns had been captured, and over 500 square kilometres (approximately 200 square miles) of territory, with its remaining French population, had been liberated. The railroads in the vicinity of St. Mihiel, although heavily damaged, had been freed for future Allied use and the immediate threat of the Salient against the surrounding country had been removed and cleared the path for the Meuse-Argonne Offensive. Perhaps most significantly, the most important obstacle to a possible advance toward Metz or Sedan had been overcome.

The creation of the American Second Army

The divisions that had occupied the St. Mihiel sector and the divisions that were going to engage in the Meuse-Argonne all fought under the flag of the First Army. To command such a large number of divisions, dispersed over a wide area, was an extremely difficult job for General Pershing. He was wearing too many hats; besides Commander-in-Chief of the AEF, he was also commanding First Army, an impossible job for just one man. With very slow progress being made on the Meuse-Argonne front, it was decided that the divisions stationed at St. Mihiel (and those further south) were to become the new American Second Army, and those at the Meuse-Argonne would be known as the First Army. On 12 October, Major General Robert L. Bullard became the commander of the newly organized Army. He took command of the front between Fresnes-en-Woëvre and Port-sur-Seille, then held by the 7th, 37th, 79th, 92nd and two French divisions; the US 28th Division was in reserve. On 16 October, General Pershing relinquished his command of the First Army to Major General Hunter Liggett.

Sectors Held by American Divisions in the St. Mihiel Region

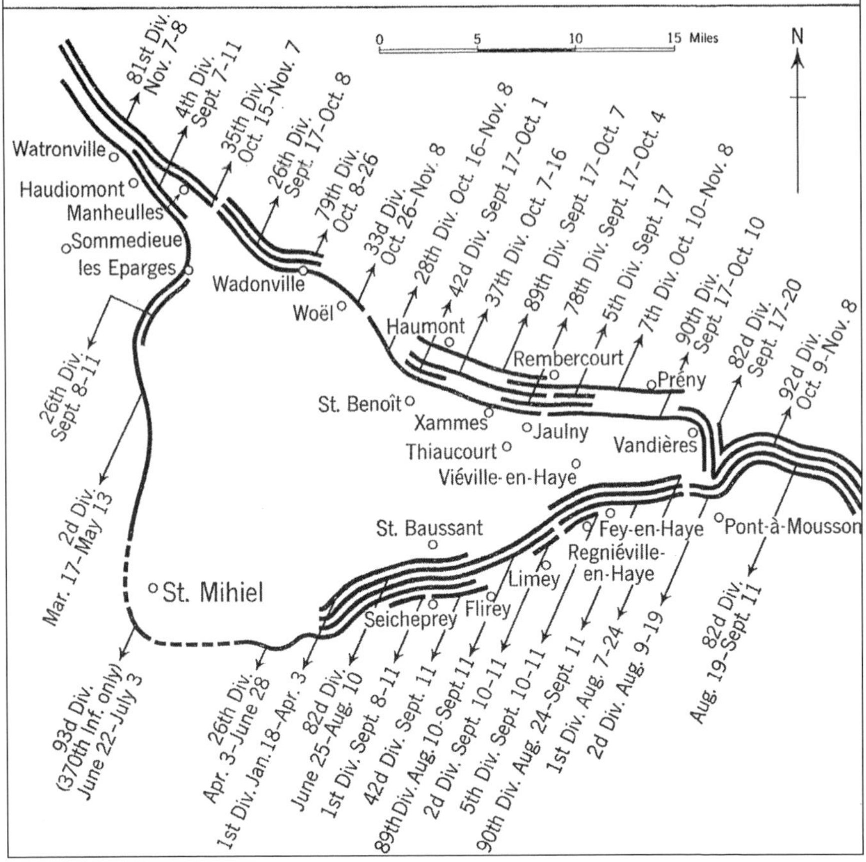

The lack of decisive results in the Meuse-Argonne, especially when contrasted with successful offensives by the French and British to the north, was a crucial factor in this decision to split the AEF into two armies – something that Foch had proposed in August. Although this might seem an obvious move, given the huge numbers of American troops in France, Pershing had his doubts about finding the right men to command these armies. However, circumstances on the ground made the change almost inevitable. On 29 September, after four days of battle and in spite of overwhelming numbers, the Meuse-Argonne offensive had bogged down in front of the Hindenburg Line; it took over two more weeks to breach it. The situation was so serious that it required all the American divisions to expend the utmost energy in the fight. The Second Army, therefore, had the role of holding the St. Mihiel front for the time being, principally with tired divisions, which could be rested there and prepared for another tour of duty in the Meuse-Argonne. However, active patrolling and raiding continued as much as possible to keep the pressure on the Germans and the artillery carefully aimed at targets in anticipation of a possible major offensive to be undertaken later.

Early in November it became clear that the Allied attacks, stretching from the Meuse to the North Sea, along with other important factors like the explosive social and political situation in the Fatherland, were causing such huge losses in terrain, manpower and materiel that there remained no other option for the German Government than to start negotiations for an armistice.

November 1918: Renewed American attacks in the St. Mihiel sector
On 5 November, General Pershing ordered the Second Army to begin advancing its lines in preparation for an offensive in the direction of Briey. The Second Army planned to launch these attacks on 11 November, but on the evening of 9 November a message was sent by Foch that directed that vigorous pressure be applied immediately along the whole front. The 7th, 28th, 33rd and 92nd Divisions began the planned attacks at once. According to an official American source (the ABMC's American Armies and Battlefields in Europe: A History, Guide and Reference Book), *the scarcity of troops prohibited strong concentrations but in spite of this and of stubborn resistance encountered, the Americans made a considerable advance.* In truth, they only moved about a hundred

American First and Second Army plan for the never executed attack on Germany, 14 November 1918.

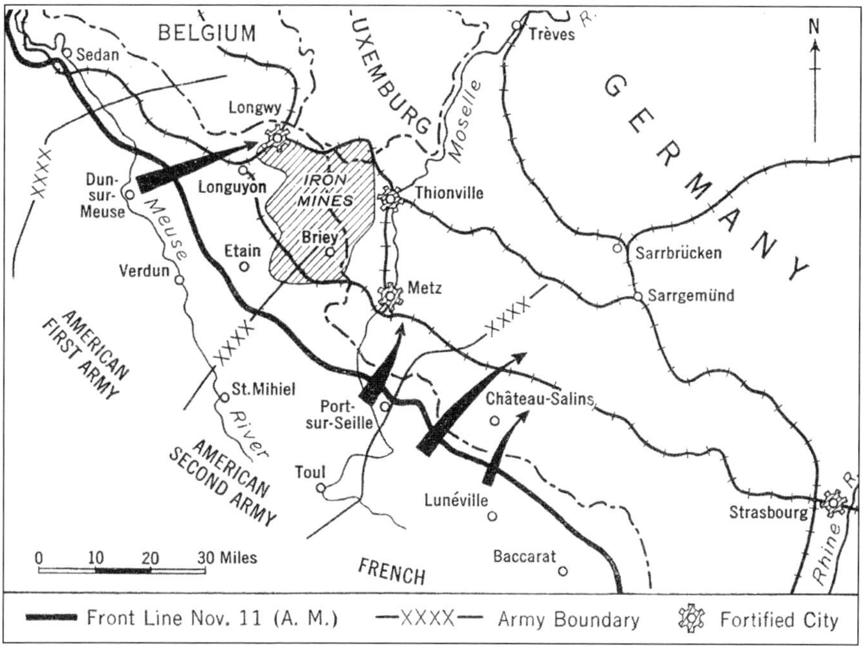

metres closer to the outer defence lines of the Michel Zone, although they now occupied a more favourable position should the green light for a new offensive be given.

In case the negotiations with the Germans failed, Foch had decided upon an offensive east of the River Moselle, to the right of Pont-à-Mousson, and asked that six American divisions be designated to take part in it. General Pershing had long favoured an attack in that direction and had been planning to launch one there following the St. Mihiel Offensive. He therefore selected the 3rd, 4th, 28th, 29th, 35th and 36th Divisions for the task, with the stipulation that these formations should operate under the command of the American Second Army. The plans prepared by the Second Army for its part in this offensive provided for a powerful drive in a north-easterly direction, from the area around Port-sur-Seille, east of the River Moselle. On the right flank, a French army group was to attack at the same time and the American First Army, from its location in the general vicinity of the Meuse River, was to push eastward in the direction of Longwy.

The date of the start of this combined offensive was fixed by the French for 14 November. The American divisions directed to take part on that section of the front east of the River Moselle were already moving toward their new positions when the Armistice came into effect on the morning of 11 November.

It is highly likely that the Americans would only have been able to break through the formidable Michel Zone by paying a very high toll in human life. Even today, to anyone visiting the Michel Zone, it is clear that an attack in this area would have been extremely costly. [For more details about the Michel Zone, see **Car Tour 5.** The Michel Zone.]

In September 1919, one year after events described in this book had taken place, Field Marshal von Hindenburg tried to explain the German tactics in his memoirs *Aus Meinem Leben*, In My Life. There, he states that the retreat was already well underway at the start of the American attack. Indeed, most of the German heavy artillery had already been moved to the Schroeter Zone.

> 'On 12 September 1918, the battle started on the until then quiet front between Verdun and Pont-à-Mousson. Since the start of our attack in autumn 1914, we had been improving our lines, assuming that we were ready to inflict a killer blow to our enemy. We have never really understood why the French left us in this great big salient for so many years. Had the enemy made a powerful attack on both sides of the basis of this triangle, then we would have been in big trouble. It is possible that people think that we were stupid

not to give up this vulnerable position when the Battle of Verdun started. However, because of our possession of the St. Mihiel Salient we were able to put serious pressure on the French and seriously restrict their freedom of movement; we were able to cut the vitally important Valley of the Meuse in the south, leaving them only a one track railway line to supply the garrison [of Verdun].

'Only when at the start of September 1918 the front line between the River Meuse and the River Moselle became a little bit too alive to our taste, we decided to evacuate the Salient and to retreat to the long since prepared Michel Line. Before this movement had ended, the French and the Americans launched their attack and inflicted serious losses on us. However, for the rest of the war we managed to keep the Michel Line.

'The attack launched in the Champagne on 26 September, and the attack of the Americans in the Meuse-Argonne were different insofar that the American Army operated as an independent army for the first time, and in spite of the fact they had been able to take large parts of our territory, our lines were never broken; we faltered, but never fell.'

CHAPTER 3

IV Corps

A short narrative

The 1st (the 'Big Red One') Division

Maj. Gen. Summeral.

The left flank of IV Corps was protected by the 1st Division, commanded by Major General Charles P. Summerall. This regular army division was constituted on 24 May 1917 and was the first American division to leave for France (14 June 1917), as the First Expeditionary Division. Marshal Joffre (1852-1931), visiting the US in April 1917, urged that a large military force should be sent to France without delay; the French army was at the end of its tether and badly in need of replacements. The regiments that made up the First Division, the 16th, 18th, 26th and the 28th, were all relatively experienced; they had all seen much field service during the Mexican Punitive Expedition, though its immediate relevance to the nature of the fighting on the Western Front was at best tangential. However, lots of organizing still needed to be done before the division could act like a division; the last units arrived in France on 22 December. Acting as Pershing's personal 'trophy division', the division took part in parades to show the French and British people that the Americans were actually on the continent and ready to fight; big crowds went out to see the 'Sammies' (after 'Uncle Sam'), as the French nicknamed the American soldiers. From 18 January to 18 April 1918, the 1st Division replaced a French division in the St. Mihiel sector.

However, things became more urgent when on 21 March 1918 the Germans started their Spring Offensive. German shock troops smashed through the French and British lines and pushed the defenders back to within sixty kilometres of Paris. The Allies were in considerable trouble and every man available (or at least every man available to the BEF in France – there were thousands of troops in Britain) was thrown into the fray. Consequently, the American 1st Division was deployed at Cantigny,

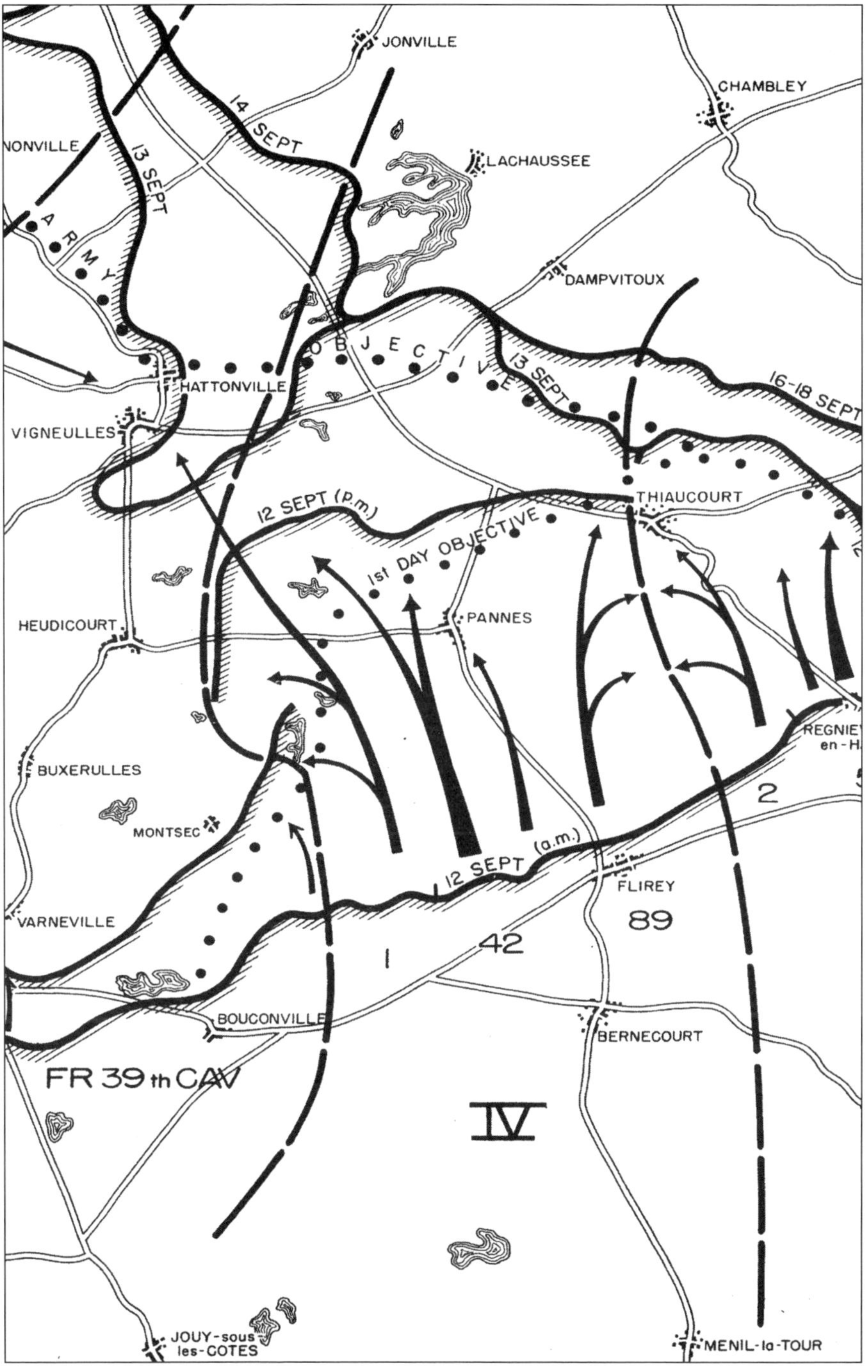

IV Corps Sector.

a town that they promptly captured from the Germans. In spite of several counterattacks, the Americans held on to the town, but suffered 1,603 casualties, including 199 killed in action. The American success at Cantigny assured the French that American divisions could be depended upon in the line against the German attack on Paris. The victory at Cantigny was followed by attacks at Soissons, Château-Thierry and Belleau Wood. At the start of August 1918 the 1st Division found itself in the Lorraine sector. According to plan, it had taken over a quiet stretch of front line at Saizerais, a small village about eight kilometres to the south of Pont-à-Mousson. To intimidate the Americans and to extract information, the Germans of the 255th Division were very active and several trench raids were undertaken. Two Americans were killed and forty-nine wounded during this period. On 10 September, after a period of training at several places close to the River Meuse, the engineers were the first to occupy the line at Marvoisin, from where the 1st Division would launch the attack; their task was to cut lanes in the German barbed wire.

Thursday 12 September
Strong winds and driving rain.
The front assigned to the 1st Division extended from Xivray to Seicheprey, a distance of about two and a half kilometres. The left flank was covered by the French 39th Division, the right by the American 42nd. The general axis of attack was the town of Nonsard, some eight kilometres to the north, behind the double row of barbed wire of the Schroeter Line and beyond the reach of the American guns. Because the attack was supposed to be a surprise, the preliminary bombardment started at 1.00 am and lasted for only four hours. It was anticipated that this would not be enough time to cut the enemy wire, so details from the 1st Engineers were to accompany the platoons in the first wave with wire cutters and Bangalore torpedoes, a tube-like, lengthy device that was filled with explosives and which was manoeuvred underneath enemy wire to blow gaps in the entanglement.

In the pitch-black night of 11 to 12 September, the Americans crept silently, platoon after platoon, into the front line trenches; at 1.00 am the sky lit up with the muzzle flash of the 2,700 guns that were providing the preliminary bombardment to soften up the German defences. Soldiers standing on high ground remembered seeing an arc of fire, clearly marking out the Salient's perimeter. Every known German battery and machine-gun emplacement was deluged by gas and high explosive shells. Cold and wet, the men sat in their trenches, waiting for first light and the signal to go over the top.

At 5.00 am, the 75mm field guns started a rolling barrage that moved one hundred metres every four minutes. The infantry clambered out of their slippery trenches under the protection of a wall of shrapnel shells. Montsec, a prominent hill and the eyes of the German artillery, was a special target; it was under constant fire from a battery of 75s firing nothing but smoke shells to blind the observers. In spite of this, German shells started falling all along the front line, inflicting the first American and French casualties. The first objective was the village of Richecourt, on a line north of the Rupt de Mad Creek. Supported by a few tanks that had already crossed the stream in the Allied sector, this target was met within thirty minutes of the start. Here the barrage halted for about twenty minutes, to allow the engineers to lay wooden footbridges across the stream. Part of the 18th Regiment occupied Tombois Wood to form a buffer against a possible German counterattack from Montsec, while the rest of the division moved north to Quart en Reserve and Raté Woods (the latter quickly corrupted into Rat Wood), in the direction of Nonsard. Here, German resistance stiffened notably as the Americans reached the barbed wire defences of the Schroeter Line. However, one battalion outflanked the German positions on the left and with the help of French Reneault FT17 tanks the wire obstacles were destroyed. Anyone who resisted was killed and the remainder taken prisoner. During the action several Americans were wounded and killed. Reserve troops were brought forward and between 9.30 and 10.00 am the advance on Nonsard continued. By now several villages within the Schroeter Line were in flames; according to Major General Fuchs' orders the retreating German troops destroyed everything of military value in their wake.

German barbed wire in the 1st Division sector. Note Montsec on the left.

American Chauchat light machine gunners at work in St. Baussant, 12 September 1918.

While the engineers started to rebuild the roads in the liberated area, the 1st Division regrouped and prepared for the third and last objective of the day. Four kilometres from their jump-off positions, the Doughboys just needed to advance one kilometre to reach Nonsard and Lamarche-en-Woëvre; this line was reached at about 12.30 pm. The losses had been far less than anticipated and most of the wounded had already been moved to the rear by the medical evacuation chain.

Upon learning the news that the advance had gone so well, IV Corps Commander Major General Joseph Dickman decided to exploit the situation and ordered the 1st Division to advance to the first phase of the second day's objective. Because of the successful advance of the 26th Division in the north, this could be the break the Americans needed. If the two divisions could join up, the Germans would effectively lose the tip of the Salient and this would certainly speed up the capture of the entire Salient.

As far as conditions allowed, artillery was transported by truck closer to the front line and thus extending their range; however, the wheels of the lorries often became bogged down in mud, a result of poor roads made worse by the fighting and poor weather. Finally, at around 5.30 pm, the 1st Division resumed the attack and without much opposition they advanced along the Nonsard-Heudicourt Road (this road no longer exists; the extraction of sand and gravel has created a large lake in its place) and the Nonsard-Vigneulles Road, the present D179. Patrols were sent out and managed to reach the Vigneulles-St.Benoît Road, the present D901. To reach this road, the Americans advanced through Vigneulles and Nonsard Woods; this area was far from clear of Germans. Every now and then the Americans stumbled upon isolated pockets of resistance and sometimes this was so fierce that the Americans were forced to retreat. The fighting continued into the night and in fact no one knew the division's exact location until the next morning. Many prisoners were taken, but also large numbers of Germans managed to escape under the cover of darkness.

Friday 13 September
Cloudy and rainy, poor visibility.
During the night, the 6th Brigade (30th and 38th Regiments) of the 3rd Division was called up as a reserve and contact was made with the left flank of the 42nd Division. At first light, the tired troops of the 1st Division were on the move again. At 6.20 am, the 28th Regiment entered Hattonville and captured some prisoners; forty-five minutes later, they entered Hattonchâtel and met up with elements of the 26th Division; the tip of the Salient was now cut off. It was now a matter of clearing the area of Germans as there were still many isolated groups of soldiers who were trying to reach the Michel Zone and were hiding in barns and houses.

By noon, the artillery had advanced as far as Nonsard Wood; in spite of the terrible conditions of the ground they had made pretty good progress. The engineers had been working around the clock on the roads, clearing obstacles left by the Germans and erecting temporary bridges,

A Renault FT17 tank at Seicheprey, 12 September 1918.

First Division supply train at St. Baussant, 13 September 1918. Note the absence of a road surface and the barren waste land all around.

making this progress possible. Ammunition trucks, as well as kitchen wagons, field kitchens and field ambulances made it to the new front line.

During the morning of the 13th, the Second French Colonial Corps, which operated on the 1st Division's left, moved up to Vigneulles; this was a clear sign that the area had been cleared of Germans. On the previous day the French had launched a series of trench raids all along the front line in order to keep the Germans manning the tip of the Salient engaged. In spite of this, the Germans were not yet beaten; their heavy artillery pounded many of the woods and villages that were now the new front line; many Americans fell victim to the occasionally intense shelling.

Saturday 14 September
Fair weather, good visibility.
For the 1st Division, by this stage the fighting in the Salient had effectively stopped altogether. Now it was all about getting as many supplies as possible to the front in case of a counter-attack. By noon a new bridge had been built across the Rupt de Mad Creek to speed up the movement of the endless stream of traffic. The first Supply Train, which had reached Nonsard Wood the previous day, was forced to leave it due to intensive German shelling. While the villages of Heudicourt, Vigneulles, Hattonville and Hattonchâtel were burning, the Americans discovered alternative accommodation in the elaborate rest camps that the Germans

had constructed behind the front line. According to the *History of the First Division*,

> 'There were billets and recreation rooms and the most artistic cottages and bungalows elaborately furnished from the homes of the defenceless villages. Club houses for officers and men, with pianos and moving pictures, gave evidence of the pleasure that was afforded. There were extensive and well-fitted stables, and forage in abundance for the officers' chargers, some of which were left in the hasty flight. Other evidences that the comfortably housed garrison did not expect the Americans to advance so rapidly were the uniforms and personal effects of officers, including their arms, and freshly cooked food.'

The 1st Division, according to its history, had lost ninety-three killed and 451 wounded in the attack.

On Thursday 19 September the division moved out of the sector in preparation for the Meuse-Argonne Offensive.

The ruins of St. Baussant: a machine gun battalion of the 18th Regiment, 1st Division, moving up to the front line, 13 September 1918.

Troops of the 1st Division moving to the front line, St Baussant, 12 September 1918.

The 42nd 'Rainbow' Division

Maj. Gen. Charles T. Menoher.

The 42nd Division, commanded by Major General Charles T. Menoher, was placed in the centre of IV Corps. The 42nd, a National Guard division, was activated in August 1917, four months after America's entry into the war, drawing men from all over the United States. They sailed for France in November 1917, and were among the first divisions of the AEF to arrive there. Upon arrival the 42nd Division was subjected to an intensive training programme with the British and French to learn the basics of trench warfare that for the past three years had dominated strategy on the Western Front, with neither side advancing much further than they had in 1914. In the summer of 1918 the 42nd took part in two major operations: the Champagne-Marne and the Aisne-Marne, before the division was transferred to the St. Mihiel sector. Like the 1st Division, they were a relatively experienced formation in comparison to many of the other American divisions.

Thursday 12 September
Strong winds and driving rain.

In the days prior to the attack on the Salient, the artillery units had, as far as possible under the circumstances, dug and camouflaged new battery

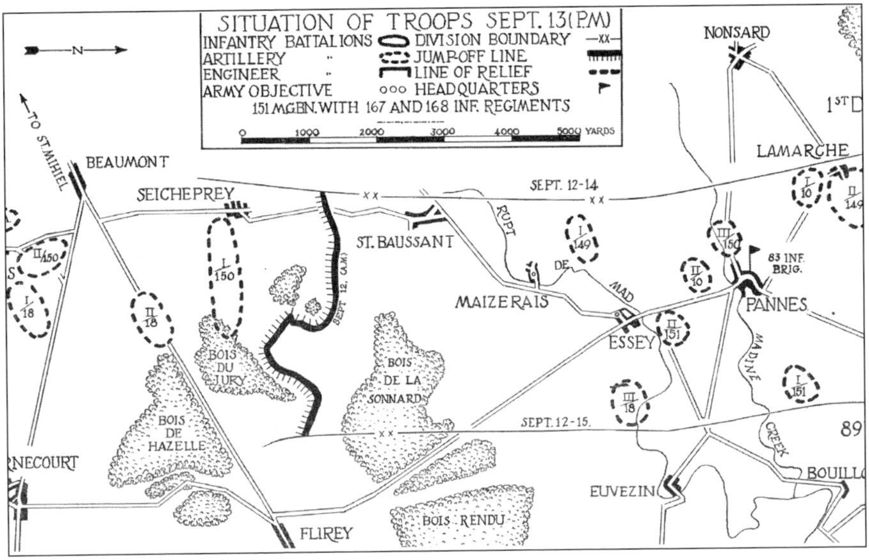

Area of attack of the 42nd Division.

positions and established their firing data after moving the guns unobserved into these positions at night. The troops were all hiding in de la Reine Wood, four kilometres to the south of the jump-off lines. Private Martin J. Hogan, 165th Regiment, 42nd Division, noted:

> 'The woods were cold, damp and dreary, and as we slept a chilly wind rippled icy puddles against our necks and down our shirt collars. However, we slept well; we were tired. About seven o'clock in the morning word came that we must hurry our advance, that we had no time to lose. There had been but mighty little sleep, but we were glad to speed out of this wet nightmare. About eight o'clock [in the evening] we began our slow advance. After some time of cautious movement we quickened our pace. There was considerable ground to be covered so that we should be in our positions before the great barrage started, and we were soon off to our part of the line double-quick. About twenty minutes to one we reached an open field, fringed with hills, and the men wondered where the trenches ran. It was unusually quiet along the line – the deadly quiet before the storm.'

The 42nd Division was assigned to a two and a half kilometre wide sector between Seicheprey and Flirey; their first objective was the village of Pannes, where they also had to cross the Madine Creek, about four kilometres into enemy territory.

At 5.00 am the troops went over the top and quickly took Sonnard Wood and St. Baussant. The barrage had been so intense that they had already ran over the first opposition before the Germans had had the opportunity to catch their breath. At 7.00 am it was Private Martin Hogan's turn to advance on the German lines. After the war, he proudly noted that:

> 'We wondered what had seized upon the Germans' guns, for we waited and waited in vain for their answer. There probably was no answer to that levelling hail that the Americans put over on the morning of the first big all-American [sic] offensive. It was the deadliest gunfire that I heard during my stay in France, and German prisoners told us that never before had they been called upon to face such a withering storm.'

Indeed, German retaliation had been weak and the troops in the front line were caught on the hop by the American attack; it had been anticipated that the assault would not take place for another week or two. The troops of the German 10th Division tried to evacuate the front line as quickly as possible but the Americans were too fast; many Germans were taken prisoner. Unexpectedly, the 42nd Division quickly captured Pannes, its first objective, around noon. It was decided not to waste too much time there and so amidst the burning barns and houses, the attack continued onto the second objective.

In spite of the American success, many organizational problems surfaced. Along the whole line of advance the regiments, battalions, companies and platoons experienced considerable problems in maintaining contact with each other; whatever there was, if any, was often lost and on many occasions divisional and regimental boundaries were crossed, which added to the confusion. The advance had to be stopped repeatedly in order to extricate troops. Quite often, support troops moved too quickly and became mixed up with the assault companies. This chaos also led to a high number of stragglers and shirkers; thousands of soldiers simply lost their way; for some reason they became separated from their units or just called it a day and 'disappeared'! Although the Military Police quickly set up checkpoints in the newly occupied area, they had little success, as there were simply too many soldiers in the former Salient for their efforts to be effective.

The second objective, the Army objective for the first day, stretched from St-Benoît-en-Woëvre to halfway to Dampvitoux Woods, roughly along the present-day D901. Again, except for some scattered German shells landing here and there, almost no opposition was met. Private Martin Hogan noted:

> 'We started slowly at the beginning, keeping under cover and going forward in open battle formation, but quickened our pace when the battalions ahead began cleaning up what remained of a dazed enemy at such breakneck gait. The attack generated into a double quick rollick forward in a go-as-you-please and get-there-as-fast-as-possible line of battle. We ourselves saw no signs of the Germans, we found no resistance.'

At nightfall all the goals that had been set out for the first day had been reached; thousands of German prisoners had been sent to the rear. In the abandoned villages that had not been destroyed by shellfire or burnt down by the Germans, rich booty was found. Many soldiers set out to find German souvenirs. Iron Crosses, officers' boots, postcards, Luger pistols, sausages, wine and beer; some took as much as they could carry.

A wounded American officer being given first aid. Note the German prisoner on the left that is, according to the original caption, 'awaiting to assist in carrying him back to the dressing station.' The medic on the left wears his overseas cap under his helmet and also carries a French canteen. Pannes, 12 September 1918.

167th Regt, 42nd Division front line near St. Benoit, 15 September 1918.

Friday 13 September
Overcast and rainy weather.

During the night the neighbouring divisions, the 1st (left) and the 89th (right), had tried to make contact with each other but for some reason they failed. Before daylight the 42nd Division was ordered to pack up and push on again. The 83rd Brigade (165th and 166th Regiments) was to continue north in order to meet up with the French 39th Division, while the 84th Brigade (167th and 168th Regiments) turned right in the general direction of Dampvitoux a fortified village inside the Michel Zone. This was never reached; the main reason for going in that direction was to keep the pressure on the Germans. Indeed, everywhere along the front line it was noticed that German resistance had grown stronger; they had already partially recovered from the first blow.

As the advance continued, Private Hogan recalled:

> 'The country was ruined. The battalion had reached some places that morning just as Germans were frantically digging their way with bleeding knuckles out of their smashed-in dugouts. Some men wore the flesh away to the bone in such struggles against death by burial alive. And they were taken to the rear jabbering and yelping with pain. The advance was again ordered. This time the way lay through a swamp [now part of Lac de Madine], and [the] going was hard. Still, beyond the swamp on a road ahead, [the present-day D133] we saw [rolling] kitchens, which fact made the go through the swamp the most spirited go of the day. We were famished.'

Château St. Benoit. American soldiers posing with German prisoners, 13 September 1918.

An American platoon guarding an outpost, 12 September 1918.

Around noon reports came in that a large columns of German troops was passing along the St-Benoît-Dampvitoux Road, the modern-day D901. Promptly, two companies of the 168th Regiment proceeded along the railway track that ran parallel to the road. Suddenly, a group of about forty German soldiers appeared out of the woods. The Americans immediately attacked, resulting in one German soldier being killed straight away, whereupon eighteen others surrendered; the remaining Germans escaped. This kind of action is typical of the fighting during the second day on the 42nd Division's front. By nightfall, the goals for the day had been reached; according to Foch's orders, the advance was halted a few hundred metres in front of the Michel Zone.

Brigadier General Douglas MacArthur, commander of the 84th Brigade, spent the night in St-Benoît Château and recalled:

> 'The morning of the second day's attack we not only reached but passed the Army objective. I am sorry to say that we missed capturing the headquarters of the 19th German Army Corps in St-Benoît Château. Amongst much other evidence of their hasty departure, we found a fully set dining room table and a prepared meal.'

MacArthur, a strong advocate of pushing home the attack to Metz, sent a message to HQ to ask for permission to continue the advance. Naturally, this permission was denied, but it shows MacArthur's strong character. For Pershing it had been a blessing that the offensive had gone so well; this left him more time to prepare for the Meuse-Argonne battle.

After the war MacArthur (1880-1964) became a well-known five-star general and a field marshal of the Philippines Army. He was the Chief of Staff of the United States Army during the 1930s and played a prominent role in the Pacific theatre during the Second World War. He received the Medal of Honor for his service in the Philippines Campaign, which made him and his father, Arthur MacArthur Jr., the first father and son to be awarded the medal. His star was extinguished during the Korean War at the beginning of the 1950s, when he was sacked by Truman.

Another famous 'star' of the 42nd Division was Major William 'Wild Bill' Donovan. (1883-1959) of the 165th Regiment. He became one of Pershing's favourites and was awarded the Medal of Honor on 14 October 1918 during the Meuse-Argonne Campaign. After the war Donovan was involved in US foreign intelligence organizations and later became the leader of the OSS, Office of Strategic Services, the forerunner of the CIA.

Saturday 14 September
Fair weather, clear sky.
This day was mainly used to reinforce the front line; wire fences were put up, foxholes were dug and during the day a constant stream of material was brought in, as far as the roads allowed. It also marked the day that General Pershing visited the front at Essey, a village three kilometres from the jump-off line of 12 September. During this visit

Pershing spoke with Colonel Hughes, Chief of Staff of the 42nd Division. Hughes had not been at all pleased about the lack of supplies. In front of a group of soldiers and officers, Pershing claimed that 'soldiers never get tired but can always go on; that it is only the high-ranking officers who sometimes get tired.' If this was his way of making a compliment to the tired troops, we will never know. Anyway, without a second's hesitation, Colonel Hughes said, 'General, that is only true provided they are adequately fed and their clothing and shoes kept in good condition. This division has not been receiving the supplies of all kinds which are necessary!' In low level cold tones, 'like air from an arctic region', Pershing said: 'Hughes, I repeat that the soldiers never get tired, it is only the high ranking officers who sometimes get tired!' and left. However, before he left, he told his aide, Major Quackmeyer, to make a note for him to check who was responsible for this and to take the necessary steps to improve the situation.

The next few days were spent in consolidating the positions, repairing roads and bringing in supplies. On 19 September part of the 42nd Division was transferred to the Argonne, although the majority remained in the Salient, only to leave on 30 September, when the sector was taken over by the 89th Division. The 42nd lost 1,215 men during the operation.

The 89th 'Middle West' Division

The 89th Division, a National Army Division, commanded by Major General William M. Wright, was placed on the right flank of IV Corps and was also tasked with protecting I Corps' left flank. The division was activated in September 1917 and trained in Camp Funston, located at Fort Riley, Kansas. The draftees were primarily drawn from the Mid West, ie Kansas, Missouri, South Dakota, Nebraska, Arizona, Colorado and New Mexico. The division sailed for France in June 1918.

Maj. Gen. William M. Wright.

Thursday 12 September

Strong winds and driving rain.

The 89th Division's front line ran a little north of Flirey and Limey, two small villages on the main road from St. Mihiel to Pont-à-Mousson, today's D958. The general direction of attack was from this road to Dampvitoux, about ten kilometres north. The function of their attack was to support the 42nd Division on their left flank, which was to deliver the main blow. In the role of a support division, it was also tasked with assisting the 2nd Division on their right; if the 2nd Division was delayed, for whatever reason, the 89th was to capture Thiaucourt, one of the larger

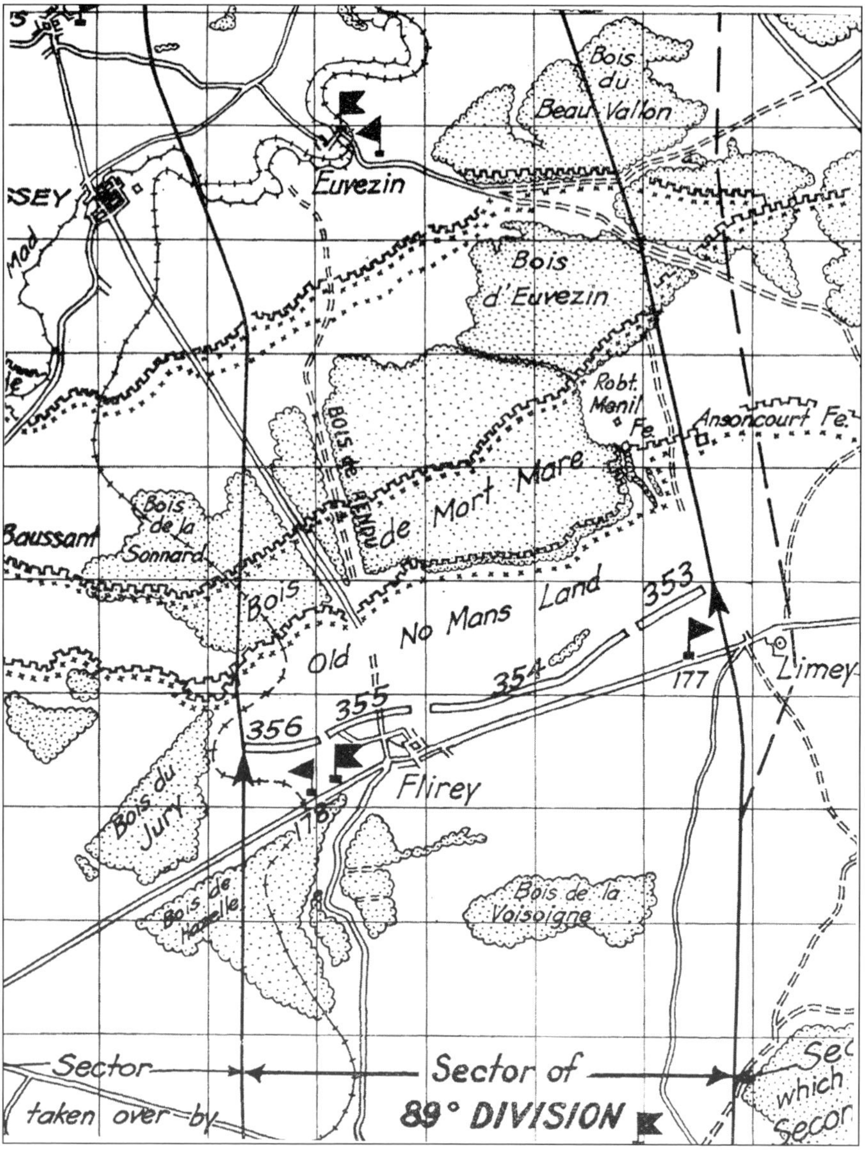

Map of the 89th Division sector.

settlements in the area, and later turn it over to the 2nd Division.

Directly in front of the American front line lay Mont Mare Wood, situated along a heavily fortified ridge that the Germans regarded as a key position in their defences as it was situated roughly between St. Mihiel and Pont-à-Mousson. The ridge and slopes were all covered with trenches, wire and strongholds; two farms, Robert Mesnil Farm and

Ansoncourt Farm, had been transformed into fortresses. The 89th was to crack three well-prepared German defence lines defended by the 77th Reserve Infantry Division. (There are some books and maps that incorrectly name it the 77th Division; this formation did not exist.) In order to avoid the unnecessary casualties that would be caused by a frontal attack, it was decided to try to outflank the woods by attacking its left and right flanks; the 356th and the 355th Regiments (178th Brigade) on the left, the 354th (in reserve) and the 353rd (177th Brigade) on the right.

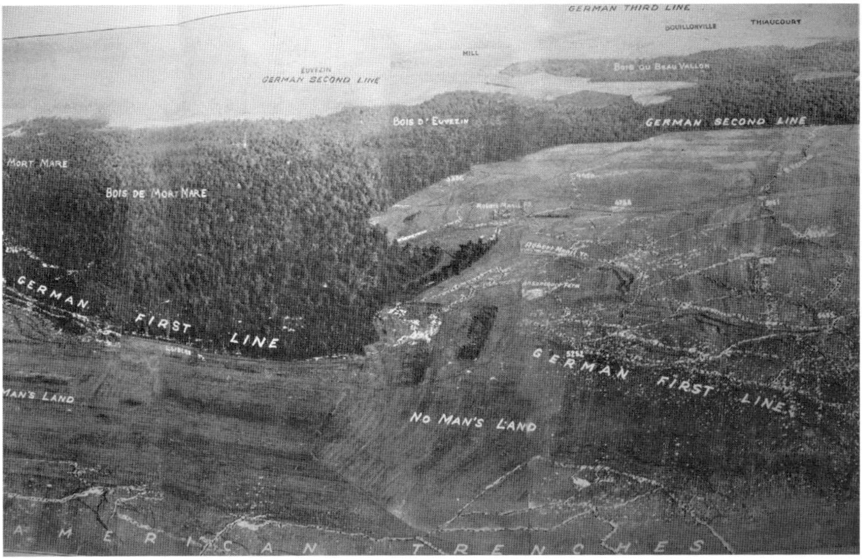

Recconaisance photo of the German front line in the 89th Division sector opposite Flirey.

Modern-day view from the German trenches at Ansoncourt Farm in the direction of Limey. Note the complete lack of cover.

A destroyed German shelter in Mont Mare Wood, 2019.

At first light the assault companies left the safety of their trenches and, under cover of the rolling barrage, advanced to the edge of the woods. When the barrage lifted, they were met by a hail of machine-gun fire; once more it became clear that this weapon was the cornerstone of the German defences. Nevertheless, forward platoons were busy cutting the wire, while other platoons attacked the machine-gun positions. German defences included three trench lines, concreted machine-gun positions and deep dugouts. Fortunately, the lines were scarcely held but still the Americans suffered approximately 200 casualties before the lines were broken. Once the first machine guns had been overrun the first Germans surrendered. In some sectors Alsatians, of French origin and forced to serve in the German Army, surrendered in droves. In other sectors German resistance was heavy and machine guns, especially, inflicted heavy casualties on the 89th. When both brigades passed along the flanks, hundreds of Germans surrendered; many were wounded; most injuries had been inflicted by the preliminary barrage that had caught them by surprise.

A major disappointment on the first day was that the weather had been too bad to deploy aircraft. As most of the divisions reached their objectives on time, due to poor visibility, there was not much glory to reap for the newly established American Air Service. Colonel 'Billy' Mitchell's pilots were grounded for most of the day. However, Second Lieutenant Bleckley of the 50th Aero Squadron took a chance; he flew off at 6.15 am, but was forced to return to the airfield before too long. He wrote that the '*clouds were so low* [I] *could not see very much,* [besides] *quite a bit of allied artillery activity'*. Only a few weeks after the reduction of the Salient, Bleckley was awarded the Medal of Honor; he and his pilot, First Lieutenant Harold Goettler, were the ones who pinpointed the exact location of the Lost Battalion. Bleckley and Goettler were shot down by the Germans, but somehow they managed to reach their own lines and crash-landed the plane. Both were killed in the crash, but the information needed was found in Bleckley's hands.

Like Bleckley, and in spite of the weather, dozens of other American pilots took off, eager for action. However, many lost their way due to bad visibility.

Medal of Honor
John Hunter Wickersham (3 February 1890-12 September 1918).

J.H. Wickersham (1890-1918), Medal of Honor.

He was born in Brooklyn, New York. He moved to Denver when he was a small boy, where he also received his education. After high school, he went to the First Officers Training Camp at Fort Riley, Kansas in May 1917. He was commissioned a Second Lieutenant and assigned to Company H, 353rd Infantry, 89th Division.

Advancing with his platoon from Limey, Wickersham and his men operated on the far right flank of the 89th Division. Their first objective was Ansoncourt Farm, in order to try to outflank the heavily fortified Mont Mare Woods from the right. However, Ansoncourt Farm was part of the German first line defences and was changed into a stronghold. Between Limey and the farm lay a wide open valley without any form of shelter. Early in the morning of 12 September, at 5.00 am, E and F Companies were leading the attack and soon encircled the stronghold that comprised three machine guns. The gunners killed, G and H Companies rushed in to support E and F Companies and to continue the attack. On approaching Ansoncourt Farm, Wickersham was severely wounded in four places by the exploding of a high-explosive shell. Before receiving any aid himself he dressed the wounds of his orderly, who had been wounded by the same shell. Although weakened by the loss of blood, he ordered his platoon to advance and accompanied them on their march as they moved forward. Due to the fact that his right hand had been disabled by wounds, he continued firing his revolver with his left hand until, exhausted by loss of blood, he fell and died from his wounds before first aid could be administered. He was posthumously awarded the Medal of Honor and is buried in St. Mihiel American Cemetery, Plot B/19/12.

Deserted German trenches in Mont Mare Wood.

The 89th now continued on to Euvezin and Beau Vallon Wood. On the right flank enemy resistance had slackened and contact was made with the 9th Regiment of the 2nd Division, while other troops mopped up isolated German pockets of resistance and rounded up prisoners in Mont Mare Wood. This, however, was no easy task; at the far end of the woods a large body of German defenders had been looking to attack from the front and not from the rear. Hand-to-hand fighting followed and a large number of prisoners and machine guns were taken. However, there were still some persistent snipers firing pot shots from the trees. At 10.30 am, the last of the snipers were eliminated and the woods were firmly in American hands.

The left and right flanks of the division were now reunited, and, having passed the main line of resistance, Euvezin and Beau Vallon Wood were taken. The attack now focussed on Bouillonville, two kilometres north of Euvezin, while part of the 177th Brigade advanced on Thiaucourt. The Doughboys halted on the heights south of Bouillonville; patrols were sent out to check on the strength of the German garrison. Lieutenant Colonel Boschen and a few men of the 353rd Regiment entered the village, shortly to return with several hundred German medical troops who had been cut off by American artillery fire.

At 10.50 am, a somewhat panicked German General Fuchs reported to higher command that:

'... the enemy is south-east of Thiaucourt and Tautecourt Farm. The 77th Reserve Division appears to be annihilated. No information yet concerning the counterattack of the 31st and 123rd Divisions. At the time of this report, the enemy has, therefore, already advanced to within one kilometre of the main line of resistance of the Michel Position. Furthermore, the left wing of the 10th Division has undoubtedly been outflanked and driven back by the six-kilometres penetration near Thiaucourt. There is not only the danger of a breakthrough at the vital point of the Michel position, but also a serious threat to the line of retreat of the Mihiel Group [192nd Division and the 5th Landwehr Division] which are still in the Salient.'

Captured German dugout in Bouillonville. Fitted for comfort with a piano, carpets and electric lighting, 20 September 1918.

At 11.00 am, the order was issued to start the withdrawal at once.

Bouillonville, known by the soldiers as Souppy Town [bouillon is French for a broth type soup], was also the scene of the extraordinary feat of Sergeant Harry Adams, Company K, 353rd Regiment. He saw a German soldier run into a house; he followed just in time to see the man disappear into an opening in the hillside behind the house that led into a large dugout. Adams had only two rounds left in his Colt revolver. In spite of this, he fired both of them into the door and called on the occupants to surrender. Soon the first German appeared at the exit of the dugout; more and more poured out until the surprised sergeant found himself the sole custodian of approximately 300 prisoners, seven officers included. When he marched the column of prisoners out of the village, at first his platoon commander, Lieutenant Chase, was under the impression that the Germans were launching a counterattack. Back in the American lines, Adams realized that he had taken 300 prisoners with an empty pistol.

Sgt Harry Adams.

The attack had gone so well that orders were received to push on to the second day's objective, the Beney-Xammes line, north of Bouillonville. By 6.00 pm, these objectives had been reached; the German 77th Reserve Division had been virtually destroyed.

Sergeant First Class Jay E. Shetler (1887-1960)

On 12 September, 2018 a sound but corroded US Army condiment can was found on an overgrown hillside in Hazelle Wood, just south of Flirey. Exactly one hundred years before, Mess Sergeant First Class Jay E. Shetler of Company A, 301st Engineers, had set up his unit kitchen on that very spot. The 301st had arrived in Flirey a few short hours after the men of the 89th Division had left the village to go over the top.

Mess Sgt 1st Class J.E. Shetler. (Shetler Family Archive)

At noon that Thursday, the Engineers had arrived in the village to a scene of total devastation. Having been a target of German guns for more than three years, the village had been totally destroyed. The original village, east of the main north-south road, had been abandoned. The villagers who had not fled had moved to the west side of that road. Hauling stones and other useful parts of the destroyed buildings from the east side of the road, they built as much of a new village as they could on the west side.

On that September afternoon in 1918, the battle would have been only a few kilometres to the north; the thunderous sounds and ground concussions of artillery fire would have been clearly heard and felt in the camp. In this cacophony of war, Sergeant Shetler and his five cooks set up the company kitchen and began putting together a meal for the men of the companies who were already out in the area repairing roads. They would be coming back at nightfall for a meal and Sergeant Shetler would be expected to have something ready for them, a feed to give them renewed energy to return to their work, as it was expected they would work well into the night.

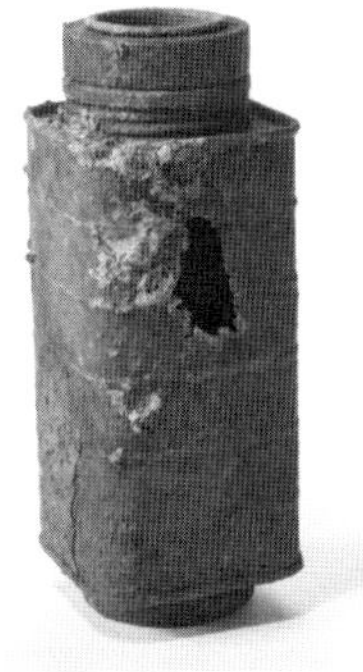

Condiment can found in 2018 at the spot of Shetler's kitchen. (Shetler Family Archive)

During the five days they were in Flirey, each of the companies (A-E) were sent out on short (sometimes long) details repairing roads, cutting through barbed wire and stringing communication lines amongst other tasks. Sergeant Shetler's kitchen, based in the camp near Flirey, was busy from before dawn until after dark preparing and serving meals made from whatever food was available to them at that time.

Friday 13 September
Overcast and rainy weather.
During the night the weather temporarily cleared. In Bouillonville and Xammes, fires were still burning in the stoves of the German military kitchens and huge kettles of food were found, still hot. Thus it was lucky for the men of the 89th that the enemy provided their dinner; the American field kitchens were nowhere to be found. The sky had a reddish glow, as fires blazed all around the area; the Germans had set numerous military supply stores, barracks and villages on fire to prevent them from falling into the hands of the Americans.

The second day's objective had already been reached on the first day and the engineers moved into the sector to consolidate the area. This mainly involved rebuilding roads and reinforcing the front line. As well as the 314th Engineers, many other troops were also involved in this work. It was vitally important to move the artillery closer to the new front line. In spite of serious shortages of road-making material, the construction of the road from Flirey to Euvezin and Bouillonville made good progress. Rubble from the burnt-out and destroyed villages was used and by noon a light motor transport of the 340th Machine Gun Battalion was picking its way along the improvised road. It is important to bear in mind that, although the Germans had retreated to the Michel Zone, most of the Salient was still subjected to German shellfire. The Zone was largely constructed on high, dominating ground; the Americans were under constant German observation and as a result many of the newly established ammunition and engineer dumps were blown up by German shelling. Fortunately, the weather became overcast and rainy weather obscured most of the troop movements during the day.

Brigade headquarters were also moved closer to the front: General Winn, 177th Brigade, (353rd and 354th Regiments) established his HQ in Bouillonville; Genaral Hanson, 178th Brigade (355th and 356th Regiments) in Euvezin. The 354th Regiment, which up to that time had been largely held in reserve, moved to Bouillonville.

Saturday 14 September
Fair weather, good visibility.
The final line was established between the villages of Haumont-Lès-Lachaussée, Dampvitoux Wood and Xammes. By now the Americans feared that the Germans were preparing a counter attack but this proved to be a false alarm. Finally, on the third day the telephone communications were sorted out. During the first couple of days Division HQ had been in communication with Brigade HQs, but contact with the troops had been a shambles. The main reason for this was that the telephone wire carts could not advance as quickly as the infantry because of traffic jams and the lack of good roads. Communication by plane had been a disaster; the divisional observation plane flew into the American artillery barrage and fell to the ground in flames.

Observing the German lines: Xammes being shelled in the background, 15 September 1918. Note the observer's canned lunch in the foreground.

The 89th Division stayed in the sector until 9 October. By that time it had taken over the sectors of the 42nd and the 78th Divisions; the 78th Division had previously taken over the sector of the 2nd Division. By the time they had finished fighting at St. Mihiel, the 89th had suffered an estimated 833 casualties, dead and wounded.

Second phase: Monday 16 September to Saturday 9 November

Between 16 September and 9 November the Americans holding the St. Mihiel front undertook numerous trench raids and small-scale attacks to straighten out the front lines in order to occupy more favourable positions in case the order was given for a full scale attack on Metz. This second phase, as I like to call it, led to the strange situation that the divisions that remained in the sector sometimes lost more casualties during this period of occupation than they had during the St. Mihiel Offensive. For example, the 89th Division lost 833 men in the battle, but lost 1,351 men during the occupation of the sector from 17 September to 7 October. These casualties were mainly caused by German shellfire and the Spanish Flu; this was the period, from September to November, that the often fatal second wave of the 1918 pandemic influenza spread globally.

Third phase: Sunday 10 November to Monday 11 November

The last two days of the war saw a lot of activity in the Salient as several divisions prepared for a major attack. All along the American front line attacks were launched against the outposts of the Michel Zone. During this period armistice negotiations were in full swing; in order to keep pressure on the Germans it was thought best to keep them as pressured as possible.

The 28th 'Keystone' Division

The 28th Division was a Pennsylvania National Guard Division, commanded by Major General Charles H. Muir. The original units were officially established in 1879, which makes it the oldest division-sized unit in the armed forces of the US. The division had been organized at Camp Hancock, Georgia, from May to 11 October 1917, when it received thousands of new recruits and was reorganized into the two-brigade four regiment scheme, and thus became the 28th Division. Camp Hancock only existed from 1917-1919, and was one of sixteen US Army National Guard Mobilization and Training Camps built

Maj. Gen. Charles H. Muir.

from scratch in the second half of 1917, when the American Army was rapidly expanding.

Understandably, the rapid expansion of the AEF had major drawbacks. The living conditions of the 28th Division at Camp Hancock were dismal; when the men first arrived at the camp they were given summer uniforms; however, these were not replaced by warmer clothes until the winter was over. Blankets were scarce too; it was January 1918 before there were enough blankets to go around. Training equipment was pathetic; there was only one bayonet for every three men, machine guns were made of wood, just like the rifles, and there was just one 37mm gun for the whole division, nearly 30,000 men. It must be noted that the problem of shortages in the training camps, on every level, lasted well into 1918. After two months of 'let's make the best of the situation' training, the division went overseas in April 1918; by the beginning of May all units had arrived safely in France and begun training with the British.

In July 1918, like several other American divisions, the 28th Division was moved into the front line to help the Allies to stop the German advance south of the Marne River and east of Château-Thierry. The 28th fought hand-to-hand battles and suffered heavy losses but stood their ground. Other campaigns the division was involved in were the Champagne-Marne, Aisne-Marne, Oise-Aisne and Meuse-Argonne battles, before they were finally moved into the St. Mihiel sector. On 10 October they took up positions around Thiaucourt. On 25 October, Major General Muir was replaced by Major General William H. Hay, who commanded the 28th Division until the Armistice. In the line from 16 October, they occupied a two kilometre wide front just north of Haumont-lès-Lachaussée.

Maj. Gen. William H. Hay.

Monday 11 November

Overcast with some rain.

A minor front line correction was carried out on the last morning of World War One. Unopposed, safe from the ever-present shellfire, the 28th Division moved the American line a few hundred metres closer to the Michel Zone. Strangely, the divisional history of the 28th Division does not mention the last two weeks in line.

From 16 October to 11 November, the 28th Division suffered a total of 1,059 casualties. This was the period when the war was coming to an end, so, this number can possibly be explained by the presence of the so-called Spanish Influenza, which by that time had become a pandemic.

Car Tour 1

IV Corps Area

Duration: A full day's tour
Distance: 60 kilometres
Maps: IGN 3213 SB, Vigneulles-lès-Hattonchâtel, 3214 SB, St-Mihiel and 3314 SB, Pont-à-Mousson.

This circular tour starts and ends in Thiaucourt at the St. Mihiel American Cemetery and Memorial (N48°57.417′ E005°15.133′) and is designed to cover the general area of the attack as fought by IV Corps. From left to right, the 1st, 42nd and 89th Divisions were involved.

Thiaucourt is a small town with a petrol station, supermarket, restaurants and lunch facilities. There are also a few shops in Vigneulles-les-Hattonchâtel. With the exception of the American Cemetery, there are no public rest rooms along this route. All points of interest are easily accessible by car; walking boots are not needed but a pair of binoculars would come in handy. However, make sure you bring some provisions for a picnic along the way.

GPS coordinates Car Tour 1

(1) St. Mihiel American Cemetery and Memorial	(N48°57.417′ E005°15.133′)
(2) Bouillonville German Cemetery	(N48°56.556′ E005°50.299′)
(3) Bouillonville railway bridge	(N48°56.617′ E005°50.160′)
(4) Virolet and Sismangolu Monument	(N48°55.063′ E005°48.482′)
(5) German gun battery	(N48°54.409′ E005°48.081′)
(6) German observation post	(N48°53.678′ E005°47.562′)
(7) Plaque on French War Memorial	(N48°52.194′ E005°47.441′)
(8) Memorial plaque on church	(N48°52.179′ E005°47.439′)
(9) State of Connecticut Fountain	(N48°52.169′ E005°47.456′)
(10) Lorraine-USA Monument	(N48°52.508′ E005°50.841′)
(11) Flirey railway bridge	(N48°52.377′ E005°50.724′)
(12) Flirey French Cemetery	(N48°51.959′ E005°50.449′)

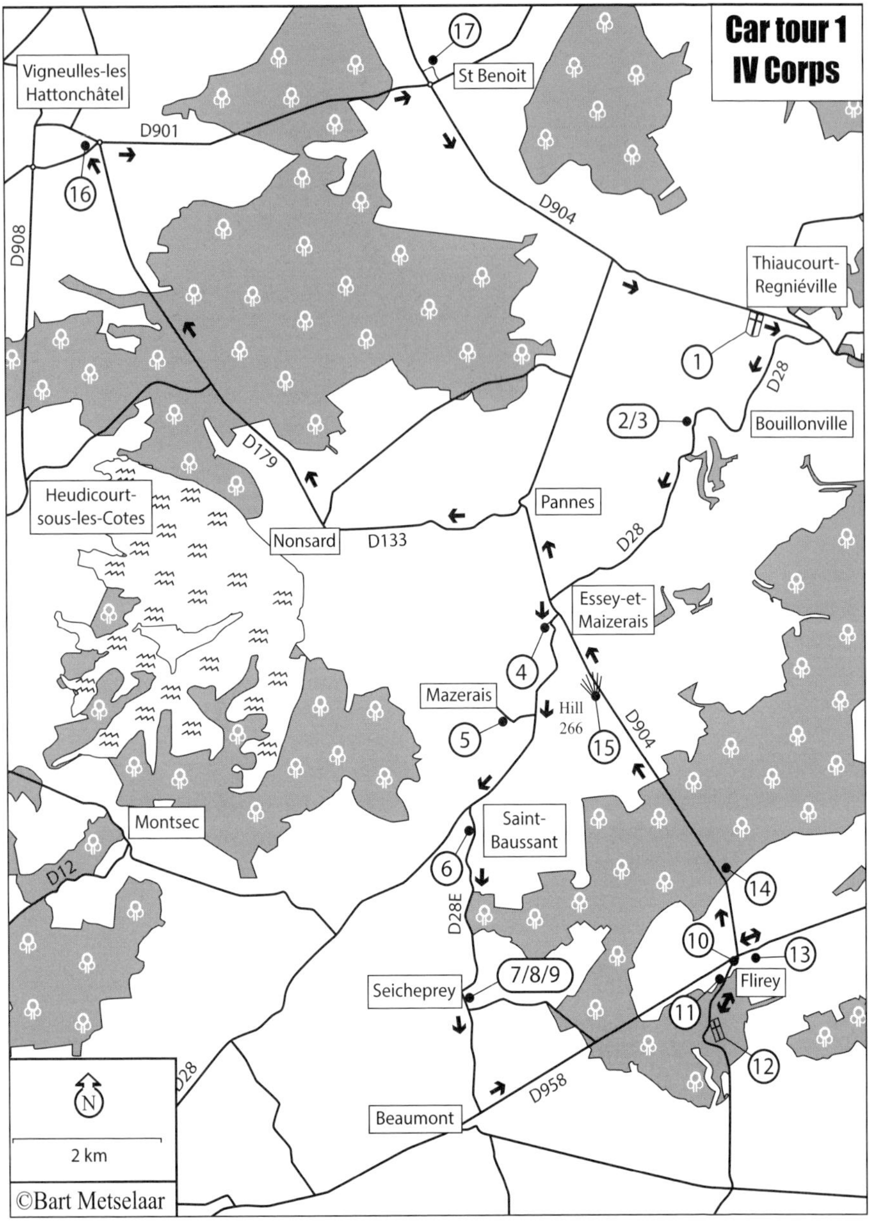

(13) Flirey church and village ruins	(N48°52.551′ E005°51.076′)
(14) Flirey mine craters	(N48°53.215′ E005°50.735′)
(15) Hill 266, Patton and MacArthur	(N48°54.484′ E005°48.160′)
(16) First Division Monument	(N48°58.703′ E005°42.910′)
(17) St. Benoit Château Ruins/MacArthur	(N48°59.261′ E005°47.069′)

The cemetery in 1921.

The tour starts at the **St. Mihiel American Cemetery and Memorial (1)** (N48°57.417′ E005°15.133′) situated along the D3, not far from Thiaucourt. This cemetery was started in September 1918; immediately after the liberation of Thiaucourt a place was needed to bury the dead. This happened in nearly every village in the Salient, but after the war it was decided that the temporary American cemetery at Thiaucourt was going to become the concentration cemetery for all American dead. This meant that every temporary graveyard or isolated field grave in the Salient was cleared and the bodies reburied in Thiaucourt.

MYTH: You are not on American soil when you enter the cemetery. However, the French government has granted free use of the land as a permanent burial ground without charge or taxation; it remains under the administration of the United States until – or rather if – the decision were made to cease to maintain the cemetery, a very unlikely eventuality. The same details of land tenure apply to the Commonwealth War Graves Commission's sites and memorials, including burials in communal cemeteries.

The entrance gate of the cemetery.

Construction of the chapel.

On entering the cemetery, toilets and a small interpretation centre are on the left. On the right side you will find the office of the superintendent and his staff. These people speak both French and English and are there to help you and to answer your questions. It always helps if you come prepared and have done your homework; if you are looking for a particular grave site this can easily be found on the ABMC website under ABMC burials.

This well maintained cemetery was dedicated on 30 May 1937, and holds 4,153 burials including forty-six Jewish and 117 unknown casualties. Beyond the burial area to the south is the white stone memorial, consisting of a small chapel, a peristyle with a large rose-granite funeral urn at its center, and a map building. The chapel contains a beautiful mosaic portraying an angel sheathing a sword. On two walls of the museum are recorded the names of 284 of the missing. Small bronze rosettes mark the names of the six soldiers (so far) subsequently found and identified. On the wall facing the door is a large map of inlaid marble depicting the St. Mihiel Offensive. Second Lieutenant Wickersham of the 89th Division is the only Medal of Honor recipient (of three awarded during the battle) buried in this cemetery, in Plot B row 19 grave 12. For more information see also Car Tour 6, stop 9.

The cemetery is divided into four plots by paths and trimmed Linden trees. At the centre is an American eagle surmounting a sundial inscribed with 'Time will not dim the glory of their deeds'. Another interesting monument can be found on the right side of the cemetery, between plot B and D. The statue of an officer in front of a cross, made by sculptor Paul Manship, was initially paid for by the Beale family to honour Walker Blaine Beale. However, as personal memorials are against ABMC policy, the statue was dedicated to all the soldiers buried in the cemetery and is now owned by the United States Government.

The statue that was donated to the cemetery by the Beale family.

A temporary American cemetery somewhere in the Salient.

First Lieutenant Walker Blaine Beale, 310th Regiment, 78th Division, was born on 22 March 1896, in Augusta, Maine, at the home of his maternal grandparents, James G. and Harriet Blaine. He was the only child of Thuxtun Beale and Harriet Blaine Beale but his parents divorced when he was very young. Walker graduated from St. Paul's School in New Hampshire in 1914 and enrolled in Harvard that fall.

In July of 1916, he went to Officers' Training Camp in Plattsburg. He trained with the Harvard Unit in 1917, which was followed by a three month course in First Officer Training at Fort Myers and was finally assigned to the 78th Division, a National Army Division, at Fort Dix. In the last week of May 1918 the Division sailed for Europe. Because of the shortage of officers, 1st Lieutenant Beale became acting captain of Company I, a position he held until his death. Sadly, his captain's commission came through after he was killed. On 8 June his formation arrived in England but was later transported to France, where it received several months of additional training.

Walker Blaine Beale.

At the beginning of September 1918, the 78th Division was ordered to the Meuse. During the St. Mihiel Offensive it served as a reserve unit for I Corps and was not involved in the fighting. When on 16 September the offensive ended, most of the American divisions that had been participating in the elimination of the Salient were hastily moved to the Meuse-Argonne. The 78th Division took over a large chunk of front line in I Corps' Sector. They were to strengthen the American positions and from time to time to conduct local attacks. On 18 September, close to Xammes, Beale and his company were moving out to the front when a shell exploded that hit Beale and two other lieutenants. Seriously wounded, the men were taken to a field hospital. Walker's uncle was a famed conductor Walter Damrosch. Damrosch published a book in 1923, *My Musical Life*, in which he recounts the day that Walker was fatally wounded.

Beale's headstone, plot D/2/2.

> 'My nephew was killed on the 18th of the following September 1918 at Saint-Mihiel. Reconnoitering to assure the safety of his men, he leaped a fence to join three fellow officers. A shell tore them to pieces. This was in the early afternoon. Walker was taken to a field hospital and died at eleven that night.'

Walker was born into two powerful American families. His paternal grandfather was General Edward Beale. Walker's grandfather and father served as United States Ambassadors to several countries; his father served as ambassador to three different countries at the same time, a not unusual situation in the pre-1914 diplomatic world. Beale is buried in plot D, row 2, grave 2.

Visiting Hours

The cemetery is open daily to the public from 9 am to 5 pm, except 25 December and 1 January. It is also open on French holidays. During opening hours a staff member is on duty in the visitors' building to answer questions and escort relatives to grave and memorial sites. Tel +33 (0)3 83 80 01 01.

Take the D3 to Thiaucourt. Pass the church and turn right onto the D28 to Bouillonville. The Americans quickly changed the name of the village into Souppyville or Soup Town. Upon leaving Bouillonville, you see the **Bouillonville German Cemetery (2)** (N48°56.556′ E005°50.299′) on the right side of the road. Park in front of the gate. The terraced cemetery was started in September 1914. In the early months of the war the French and German armies were trying to secure control of the Meuse Heights and suffered severe losses. When it became clear to the German high command that the French were not going anywhere they started to dig in, a strategy that was quickly followed by their adversaries What followed was a battle of attrition that lasted until April 1915. In total, 12,000 men were killed, wounded or missing. From April 1915 to April 1917, seventy-eight large underground mines were exploded on the 800 metres wide front line at Les Éparges (at the northern edge of the Salient), adding to the death toll. Not surprisingly, several hospitals were built in and around Bouillonville, as the ravine offered much-needed protection against shelling.

The part of the cemetery that was started in 1914 is situated on the valley floor. At the back of the cemetery are several contemporary headstones and the original cemetery monument that is inscribed with

Bouillonville German Cemetery during the war; note the abutment of the railway bridge top right.

the Prussian motto *Für Gott, König und Vaterland*, For God, King and Country. Soldiers from many different German states that composed the Empire lie buried here; but for the most part they are from Bavaria. During the war, the cemetery was expanded twice, each time using a higher terrace of the hill. These terraces can be reached by stairs but also by car. At the top terrace there are many crosses bearing the 12 to 16 September date.

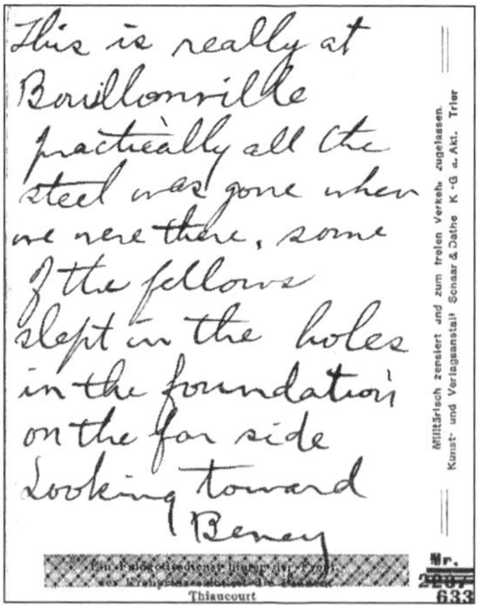

This is really at Bouillonville practically all the steel was gone when we were there, some of the fellows slept in the holes in the foundation on the far side looking toward Beney

Militärisch zensiert und zum freien Verkehr zugelassen.
Kunst- und Verlagsanstalt Schaar & Dathe K.-G. a. Akt. Trier
Thiaucourt
Nr. 633

The back of a postcard written by an American soldier. (Collection Tom Gudmestad)

Across the fence at the back of the lowest terrace of the cemetery you can also see the concrete remains of a pier of the **Bouillonville railway bridge (3)** (N48°56.617′ E005°50.160′). The bridge was dynamited by the French in September 1914 and finally demolished after the war. If you look over the fence, you can clearly see the concrete remains of the abutments and parts of the cast iron superstructure. When you walk back to your car, look across the valley; on the left the concrete remains of the abutment can be seen on top of the ridge.

Return to your car and continue along the D27 to Essey. At the T-junction, turn left onto the D904. Cross the bridge and

A good view of the demolished bridge. (Collection Tom Gudmestad)

The concrete remains of the abutments.

immediately turn right; this is the Chemin de Ville. At the end of this street, cross the Rue du Moulin and drive into the Rue de Vadepré, a quiet little street with a few bungalows. The **Virolet and Sismangolu Monument (4)** (N48°55.063′ E005°48.482′) is immediately on your right. The MF 44 Squadron was created on 4 April 1915, MF standing for *Maurice Farman*, the make of the six planes that formed the squadron. Less than two weeks later, the unit, consisting of five pilots, four observers, sixteen mechanics and fifty-one soldiers, was moved to the Meuse to assist the French attacks on the Meuse Heights. Their job was mainly aerial photography and to relay targets for the artillery.

The Virolet and Sismangolu Monument.

On 15 June 1915, the MF699, flown by Adjutant Jean Sismanoglu and observer Eugène Virolet, was on a reconnaissance mission in the Flirey sector. Not long after take off, they came under attack by a German fighter plane, flown by Lieutenant Schlemmer and First Lieutenant Baer. As the dog fight turned in favour of the French, the Germans broke off the fight and retreated to their own lines. However, possibly thinking about the honour of being the first of the MF44 squadron to down an enemy plane, the French started to pursuit the Germans. Unfortunately for the French pilots, the German plane led them straight to an anti-aircraft battery that immediately shot the MF44 to shreds; from an altitude of 1,200 metres, the engine block fell on a house, thereby partly destroying the building. The rest of the plane, including the bodies of the French airmen, came down in pieces and were scattered across the street where you are now standing. The next day, the remains of Virolet and Sismangolu were buried with full military honours by the Germans in the German cemetery opposite the communal cemetery.

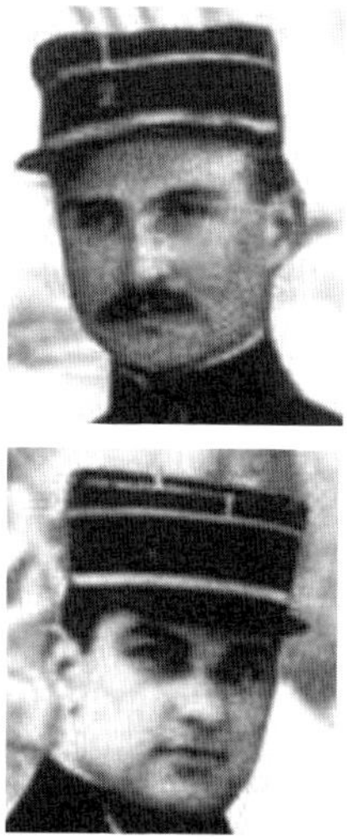

Eugène Virolet and Jean Sismangolu.

Go back to the Rue du Moulin and turn right. At the T-junction take a right turn and continue along the D28. After about one kilometre, turn right at the signpost *'Chapelle St. Gibrien'*. Cross the bridge over the

The original graves made by the Germans for the French airmen.

Rupt de Mad Creek and continue to the hamlet of Maizerais, which comprises two farms. At the end of the farm track, on the right, you see the concrete structures of two **German gun batteries (5)** (N48°54.409′ E005°48.081′). A real gem, eight gun concrete emplacements, ammunition stores, shelters and the command post in various conditions of decay are still present. The guns were trained on the area between Seicheprey and Flirey and hidden behind a railway bank and a series of low hills. Assuming the Germans used the 77mm field gun in this battery, this means that two batteries, ie eight guns, could fire a total of eighty rounds per minute with an effective range between five and eight kilometres, a formidable weapon. Built in the sector that was liberated by the 42nd Division, the battery was one of the prime targets of the American artillery. Unfortunately, at the time of writing no information could be found about the events that happened during the liberation nor about the German crews. Looking at the damaged pillboxes, it is possible that the guns were (partly) destroyed by the preliminary American bombardment but the guns could just as well have been evacuated by the Germans. It is known that at least one of the bunkers was destroyed by the current (2019) farmer's father.

NOTE: The gun battery and shelters are built on private property; if you

One of the gun emplacements.

kindly ask the landowner, who is often to be found walking around nearby, he will probably show you around. When last encountered the dogs were remarkably friendly – but of course this cannot be guaranteed! A few words in French can work miracles as does a bottle of beer or other suitable offering. This is a very worthwhile visit and a rare chance to visit a battery site, in such a complete state, like this.

Return to the main road and turn right onto the D28. After about one kilometre you enter the sleepy village of St. Baussant. At the T-junction, take the D28a to Seicheprey. Behind the third farm on the left (Rue de la Renommière 15), the Germans built a large **observation post (6)** (N48°53.678′ E005°47.562′). You can park your car at the side of the field next to the farmhouse. The bunker stands on private property but you can take a look from the farm track that runs alongside it. Originally, the bunker, dating from the end of 1915, was built inside a house. The walls of the existing structure were used to camouflage the building of the bunker, but also offered extra protection against shelling. The observation post is equipped with two observation slits that are aimed at

The Maizerais gun battery.

German observation tower hidden between the buildings of a French farm.

the front line at Seicheprey and Flirey. It was also fitted with a map room, a telephone exchange, living quarters, electric lights and wood stoves. Apart from the fighting in 1914 and in April 1918 (when the Germans pushed the French and Americans of the 26th Division out of their front line trenches and almost took Seicheprey and Flirey), this was a relatively quiet sector. St. Baussant was taken at first daylight of 12 September 1918 by the 42nd Division. Patton and his 327th Tank Battalion also passed through the village.

Carry on along the D28a to Seicheprey. Park at the church. In Seicheprey there are three monuments dedicated to the Americans. Surprisingly, they have no direct connection with the St. Mihiel Offensive, but with a large-scale German attack on 20 April 1918 (see also stop 9). The first monument is a **plaque on the French War Memorial (7)** (N48°52.194′ E005°47.441′) that stands on the left of the church building. The monument is dedicated to the people of Seicheprey, but also to the French and American *poilus* who fell during the liberation of Seicheprey. *Poilu* is a French nickname meaning the furry, shaggy one, after the appearance of the French soldiers that were allowed to grow a beard.

Walk to the entrance of the church; to the left of the entrance, you can see a bronze **memorial plaque (8)** (N48°52.179′ E005°47.439′) that is dedicated *to the god of the armies in recognition and remembrance of the American troops, January-November 1918.*

In a field to the right of the church stands the **State of Connecticut Fountain (9)** (N48°52.169′ E005°47.456′). This fountain, dating from 1923, is dedicated to the 26th Division, 102nd Regiment, for their part in the Battle of Seicheprey on 20 April 1918. This is one of the earliest American monuments in the region.

After a failed attack on Apremont-le-Forêt on 10 April 1918, the Germans launched a large-scale attack on Seicheprey to test the American strength and to capture prisoners for interrogation. In the early morning of 10 April around 3,000 German shock troops started the attack on

State of Connecticut Memorial Fountain.

Seicheprey. Under the cover of thick mist and a heavy bombardment, the first 400 Germans attacked the front line trenches occupied by American and French soldiers. Fierce fighting broke out but the surprise had been complete; quickly, the Germans pushed on to the centre of Seicheprey. However, the American-French army managed to hold the line. The next day, after thirty-six hours of brutal hand-to-hand fighting and heavy shelling, the Germans were pushed out of the village and back to their own lines in Hauts de Mad Woods. The German casualties amounted to an estimated 1,200 men. The Americans buried 164 of their own men. Furthermore, they lost 800 wounded (many were gassed) and 150

Americans were taken prisoner. Because the Americans and French repulsed the Germans from Seicheprey, they declared themselves victors. However, the Germans from the 10th Division also looked upon themselves as victors; they were ordered to test the strength of the freshly arrived American Army and also to return with prisoners: mission accomplished. In fact, both sides lost a roughly equal number of men.

Miss Skinner, (see Walk 3) was the initiator and leader of the effort to rally American cities to adopt French villages during the postwar reconstruction. In March 1919 she established the American Committee of Villages Libérés in New York City. Through this committee the people of Connecticut raised the money for the memorial fountain, the monument designed to provide drinking water to the people of Seicheprey. It also emphasizes the friendship between France and the US.

Drive past the church and take the D28a in the direction of Flirey. Once you have entered Flirey, go to the church and park here. On the other side of the road you can see the large **Lorraine-USA Monument (10)** (N48°52.508′ E005°50.841′). This monument was erected in the 1930s as a gift from the Department of Lorraine to thank General Pershing and the American divisions that 'sacrificed their lives for France' during the St. Mihiel Offensive. Forty-eight bronze stars (symbolizing the then forty-eight states of the Union) surround a bronze bas relief showing American soldiers in a heroic pose.

Return to your car and drive to the crossroads; take a right turn onto

The Lorraine-USA Monument at Flirey.

A huge tail back of traffic in Flirey in September 1918, with the destroyed railway bridge above centre.

the D904 in the direction of Bernécourt. After about one hundred metres you see a valley on your right hand. Park on the side of the road – there is space by the access for agricultural vehicles – and look at the then and now photo in the book. This is the site of **Flirey Railway Bridge (11)** (N48°52.377′ E005°50.724′). Blown up by the French in September 1914, the bridge was scrapped after the war.

A photograph taken from a similar viewpoint. Remnants of the left buttress (in particular) may be seen in what is now a wooded area on the left.

Flirey in 1918.

Carry on along the D904 until after one kilometre you arrive at **Flirey French Cemetery (12)** (N48°51.959′ E005°50.449′), on the left side of the road. Park here. The cemetery was started in 1919 and served as a concentration cemetery for bodies found in the area around Flirey, including Mont Mare Woods and the temporary French cemeteries of Fey and Seicheprey. In total, 4,407 soldiers are buried in this cemetery, including twenty-two Russian, three Belgian and three Romanian soldiers. It has been recently renovated.

Return to Flirey; at the crossroads turn right onto the D958, direction Limey. Just after you leave Flirey you come to the area where the town was originally built. The village was almost entirely destroyed during the war. The only thing left standing are the **ruins of the church (13)** (N48°52.551′ E005°51.076′). The ruins can be visited via a small road

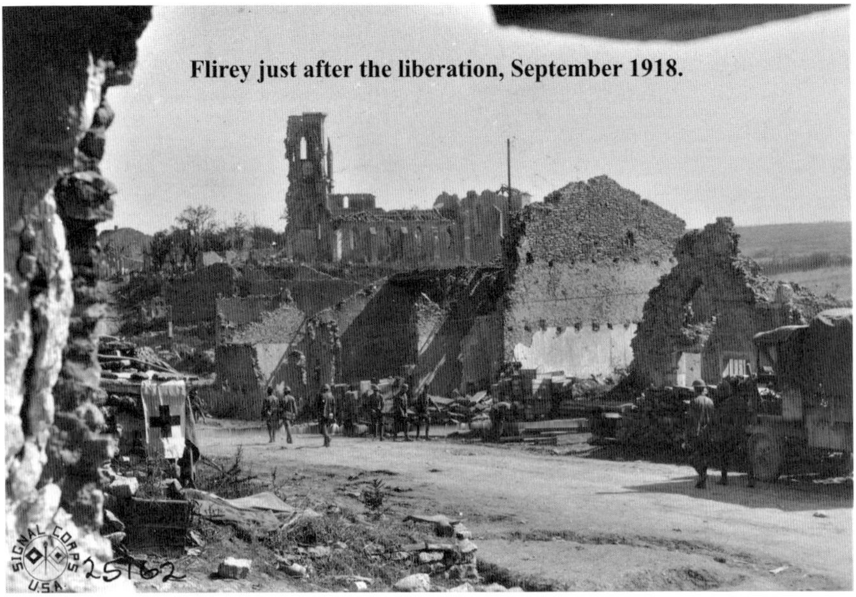

Flirey just after the liberation, September 1918.

The ruins of Flirey church; all that remains today of the original village.

on the right. You can park next to the cemetery. Information panels on the walls of the cemetery and the church show the history of the church before and during the war. All in all it is an impressive testimony of the brutal fighting that took place in this village that has roots to the third century when it was a thriving community, situated as it was along the Roman road from Pont-à-Mousson to St. Mihiel.

Return to Flirey; at the crossroads, turn right onto the D904. When you reach the forest, take the track on the right to visit the **Flirey mine craters (14)** (N48°53.215′ E005°50.735′). The craters are the remains of the intensive mine warfare fighting during the winter of 1914/1915.

One of the Flirey mine craters.

Memorial to the French troops that fought in the area for four years.

Turn your car around and drive back to the main road; turn right onto the D904. After you have left the forest you once more pass a patch of trees on the left. A few hundred metres further on, as the road starts to descend, a track starts on the left. Park at the side of the road and walk along the track for about one hundred metres. Although the exact spot seems to be lost in the mist of time, by combining all possible information, Hill 266 is the most likely location where **Patton and MacArthur (15)** (N48°54.484′ E005°48.160′) met for the first time.

At first light on 12 September, immediately following the bombardment, the doughboys of the 84th Brigade, commanded by MacArthur, supported by Patton's 327th Tank Battalion, started toward their objectives of Essay, Pannes and St. Benoit. By 6.30 am, MacArthur was in Sonnard Woods, 500 metres into enemy territory, where he was pushing forward elements of the 84th Brigade, the 167th and 168th Regiments. At about that same time, Patton was advancing his command post to the town of Seicheprey, about two kilometres west of MacArthur's position.

With reports coming in that some of Patton's tanks had become bogged down on the battlefield, Patton began heading north-west to

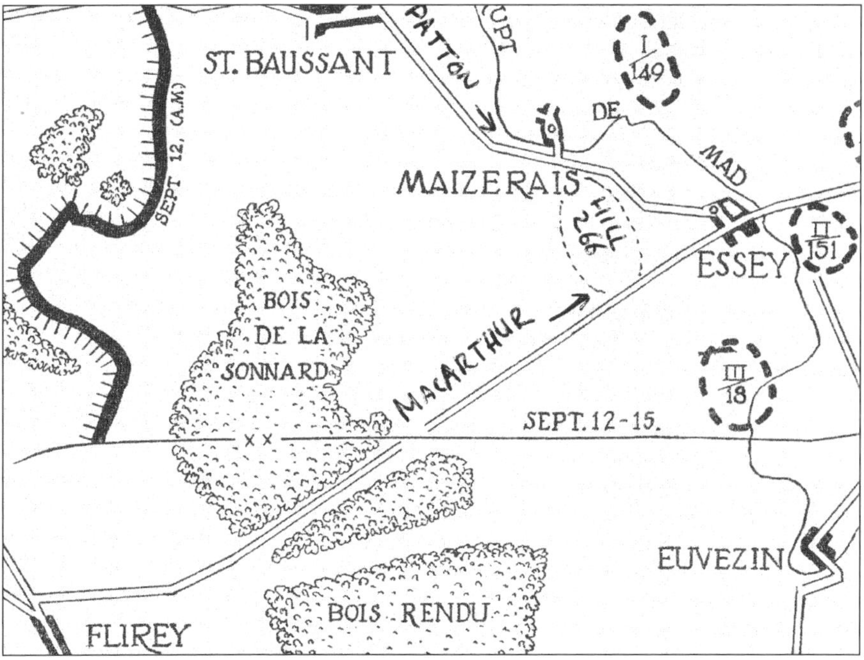

Meeting of Patton and MacArthur.

Trenches in the St. Buissant area, 12 September 1918.

View from Hill 266 over Essey.

assess the situation. When he reached his men, Patton found out that one major problem was that, as a result of the thick mud, the tanks (these were lightweight, two-man tanks, Renault FT-17s) burned three times as much fuel as had been expected. According to a letter to his wife, his reaction to being shelled when he was walking around on the battlefield was: 'I admit that I wanted to duck and probably did at first, but soon saw the futility of dodging fate.' As Patton headed north-west to the town of Essey, MacArthur was making his way north through Sonnard Woods to the same place. Before the ridge where Patton was walking gradually drops down to Essey, Patton spotted MacArthur on a small hill on that same ridge and walked over to him. It was then that a barrage started towards their position and, according to legend, 'it was there that they stood, looking towards Essey, while everyone else ran for cover'. According to Patton's account, which he wrote a few days later:

> 'I met General MacArthur commanding a brigade, he was walking about too. I joined him and the creeping barrage came along towards us, but it was very thin and not dangerous. I think each one wanted to leave but each hated to say so, so we let it come over us. We stood and talked but neither was much interested in what the other said as we could not get our minds off the shells.'

Continue to Essey-et-Maizerais, pass through the village and drive to Pannes. Here, several of Patton's tanks came to a grinding halt because they ran out of petrol. During the St. Mihiel Offensive Patton learnt several important lessons that would prove valuable for the American tank in battles and wars to come. It may sound simple, but one of the lessons learnt in Pannes was to strap extra tanks of petrol to the tanks (though of course it did provide the possibility of an attached firebomb to the vehicle). Remember, tanks were a fairly recent (1916, British)

invention and much was discovered by trial and error by the inexperienced American tank commanders. However, Patton was a quick learner and made sure this lesson was immediately put to use during the Meuse-Argonne Offensive a few weeks later. It was during the latter offensive that he discovered that strapping a hundred litres of fuel to the outside of a tank did not add to the average live expectancy of a tank crew.

Colonel George S. Patton.
George S. Patton (1885-1945) graduated from West Point in early 1909 and started his career as a cavalry officer. In 1916 and 1917 he served in Mexico prior to embarking for Europe as an aide-de-camp to General John J. Pershing. The tank, this new British invention that was to play such a big part in Patton's life, was first used on 15 September 1916 during the Battle of Flers-Courcelette, part of the Battles of the Somme 1916. Upon learning of this new British weapon, Patton sought opportunities to observe British and French tank training and began petitioning for authorization to establish an American tank school. In mid-December 1917 permission was granted and he opened a tank school in France at Bourg.

Patton's tank of choice was the French-built Renault FT-17 because of its mobility. His vision was that his tanks would move quickly over the battlefield, just like cavalry. Patton applied lessons from the cavalry to tanks and their mobility; feeling that tanks were meant to move as an independent force to cause breakthroughs and disrupt the enemy's ability to fight. Unfortunately the American High Command did not share his vision; they were convinced that tanks were best used as infantry support, moving ahead with the infantry and acting as their protection from German strong points. Nevertheless, on 20 August 1918 Patton's efforts were rewarded when he was placed in command of the newly created 304 Tank Brigade.

On 12 September 1918, Patton's orders were to send his tanks forward, while he stayed behind in his headquarters; however, he disobeyed this particular order and advanced with his tanks towards their objectives. American tanks were ordered forward early in the morning. The infantry were sent up shortly after the relatively slow tanks had made their initial progress. Once in contact with the Germans, tanks were ordered to clear trenches and machine gun nests using their machine guns and guns. As the tanks removed the more difficult pockets of resistance, the infantry moved forward and eliminated the remaining defences. In this way tanks and infantry supported each other. After the German front line near St. Baussant had been breached, the villages of Maizerais and Essey were taken. The tanks then quickly moved forward to the village of Pannes where, to Patton's great frustration, one after another they came to a standstill due to lack of fuel. With only four operational tanks left, Patton carried on, took Pannes and just made it to its northern outskirts when the remaining FT-17s ran out of petrol. In spite of the successful attack, the majority of the tanks never made it into the battle because of mechanical failures or a lack of fuel.

One of the lessons Patton took from the Offensive was that infantry was unable to support a tank advance. This reinforced Patton's belief that tanks were destined to be an independent force within the army and not simply infantry support. For Patton, the most valuable lesson he took from St. Mihiel was that tanks required their own logistical support. Three weeks later, at the start of the Meuse-Argonne Offensive, tanks were seen with extra jerry cans of petrol strapped to their side.

Go back to your car and continue to Essey and Pannes. Once in Pannes, leave the D904 and turn left onto the D48; pass through Nonsard. Here the road changes into the D179; continue to Vigneulles-les-Hattonchâtel. When you reach the roundabout, take the third exit. Immediately after leaving the exit make a stop at the parking space alongside the road. The **1st Division Monument (16)** (N48°58.703′ E005°42.910′) that is placed here commemorates a historic event that took place on 13 September 1918, when the 1st and 26th Divisions met and cut off the tip of the Salient. The day before, on 12 September, at 5.00 am, the 1st Division had left Seicheprey. In the early hours of 13 September, after a day and a night of fighting, the division arrived

First Division Memori in Vigneulles.

in Vigneulles. By closing the gap that morning, thousands of German soldiers got trapped in the pocket and hundreds of guns and tons of supplies were captured. This spot unofficially marks the end of the offensive; officially it continued until 16 September. However, by the night of 13 September most of the fighting was over.

If you look at the wooded ridge behind the monument, Hattonchâtel can be seen. This village and Vigneulles, among others, were captured by the 26th Division. During this time, the 1st Division lost ninety-eight men killed and 489 men wounded or missing.

Return to the roundabout and continue straight along the D901 to St. Benoît. This little hamlet is more or less built around the roundabout. Take the third exit onto the D904. After fifty metres, turn right into the *Rue du Château*. Right in front of you you see the ruins of **St. Benoît Château** (in fact more or less the main part of an abbey) **(17)** (N48°59.261′ E005°47.069′). Although on private property, the owners do not mind if you make a brief stop to take a look at the ruins.

In 1132, the first Cistercian abbey was built on this spot. Besides dwellings for the monks, eventually six stone barns were built. At the start of the 18th century, due to the lack of maintenance, the buildings were in such poor condition that it was decided to demolish the complex altogether. In 1740 the first stone was laid for a new abbey. By using the capital from two other abbeys in the area, there was no lack of money. The result was a sumptuous building that looked more like an 18th century château than an abbey. In 1784, as a consequence of debts incurred by the commendatory abbot (a layman) a large part of the property was sold; only the two wings that once stood behind the facade you see today

Facade of St. Benoit Château.

Château St. Benoit whilst in use by the Americans.

remained in the monks' hands. During the French Revolution of 1789 the wings were destroyed by revolutionaries and only the privately owned Château Benoît remained.

Occupied in September 1914 by the Germans, the château first served as a hospital before it became into use as a general headquarters building. Typically, many Frenchmen blame the Germans for the destruction of the château; they claimed the Germans set the place on fire before retreating to the Michel Zone. On the contrary, German officers, knowing the war was all but lost, had prevented the burning of the Château. On numerous occasions they had refused to carry out scorched earth orders. However, it is the victors that write history. True, eventually the German army *was* responsible for the destruction of the château, but only after the Americans used the building as an observation post to direct artillery and machine guns that were placed near the château.

In the afternoon of 12 September 1918, the German XIX Corps HQ that occupied the château was evacuated to Metz. On 13 September the château was taken by the American 167th Regiment and became the HQ of 84 Brigade. General Douglas MacArthur, commander of 84 Brigade, who spent a few nights in the Château, boasted:

> 'The morning of the second day's attack we not only reached but passed the Army objective. I am sorry to say we just missed capturing the HQ of the 19th German Army Corps in the St. Benoit Château.'

General MacArthur in one of the rooms of Château St. Benoit.

On 24 September 1918, the Germans, after American provocation, fired a few salvoes of incendiary shells at the château. MacArthur noted:

> 'From the cupola of the château which, until the Germans destroyed the château with shellfire, was a favorite observation post for the higher ranking officers of the division, to say nothing of visitors to Corps headquarters, I could see the dust of the German trains retreating down the roads towards Metz. Prisoners captured insisted that there was only a small garrison in Metz. I could only come to one conclusion: it was no time to stop! What a wonderful thing it would have been for the division to go ahead, even though the outer defences of Metz might have held it up!'

Return to your car and drive back to the roundabout. The second exit, the D 904, takes you back to Thiaucourt.

Walk 1

The Trenches of Hauts de Mad Woods

Duration: Half a day's tour
Distance: Two and a half kilometres
Maps: IGN 3314 O, Thiaucourt-Regniéville

The circular walk starts and ends in Hauts de Mad Woods, not far from Flirey. This rural village has no shops, cafés or petrol station, so be sure you bring everything you need for a picnic. The walk takes about two hours and follows tracks through the woods; these can be muddy at certain times of the year. Sturdy walking boots and a flash light (torch) are recommended. In summer, a good brand of insect repellent is indispensable.

To reach the start of the tour, drive to the church in Flirey. At the crossroads, take a left turn onto the D904, direction Maizerais. Just before you leave the village take a left turn onto a narrow road, signposted 'Tranchée Allemands'. After about two kilometres and soon after you enter a wooded area, you will see an information panel and a parking space on the right; park here. **(N48°53.050′ E005°49.461′)** Don't leave anything of value in your car.

Commencing in 2004, the trenches have been cleared by different groups of local youth in a project that encourages cooperation between local communities. Supported by the ALHIMIC, the *Association Lorraine d'Histoire Militaire Contemporaine*, every year a group of fifteen or more local youth spend the first two weeks of July restoring the trenches. All credit for this tour must go to ALHIMIC; without their effort this unique trench system would not be accessible to the public. The route is well signposted and information panels (only in French, of course) with photos and drawings explain the purpose and history along the way. Therefore, only a short explanation will be given at each stop.

On 12 September 1918, this trench system, built and improved since 1914, was the first objective for the men of the 168th Regiment, 42nd Division. They left their trenches in Flirey at 5.00 am behind the rolling barrage. In spite of a sea of mud, the Americans quickly managed to reach the thinly held German lines. After the German machine guns were

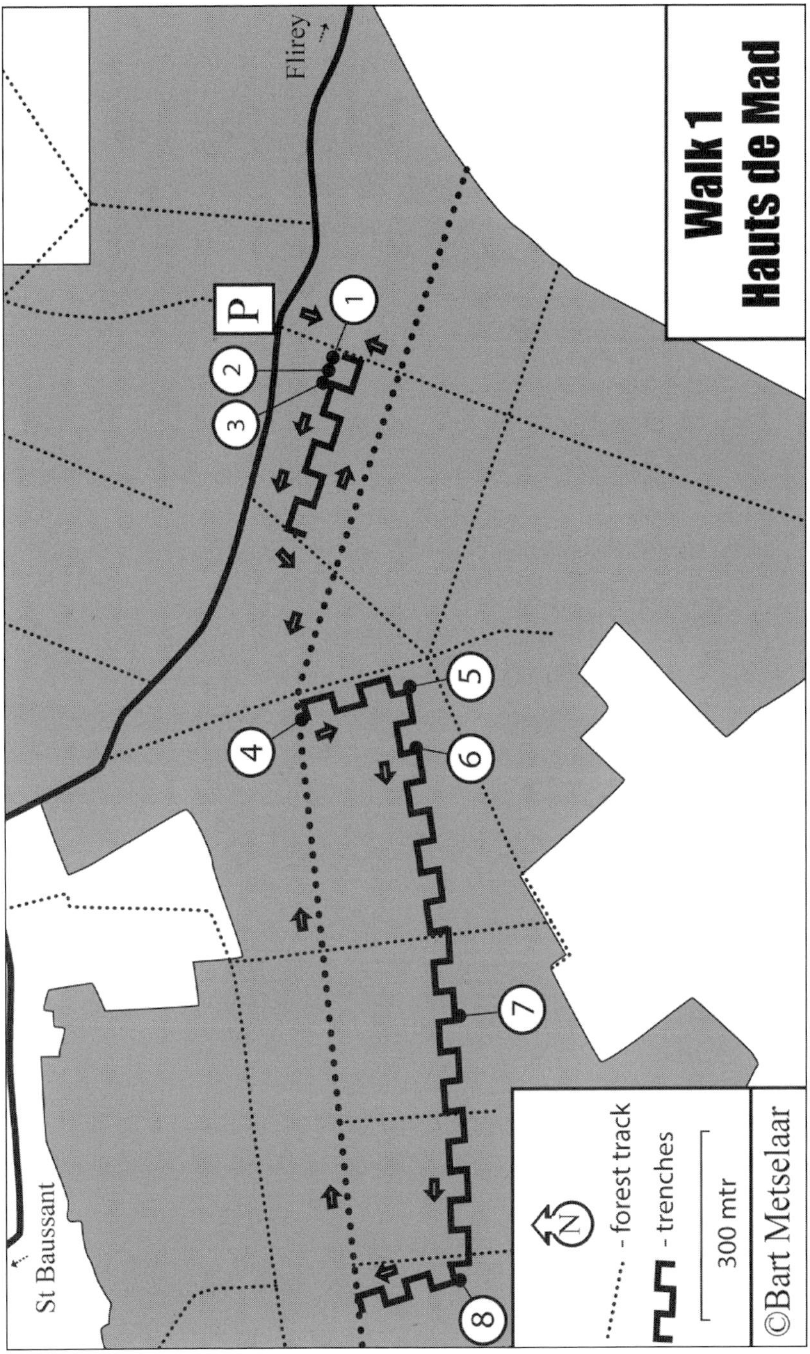
Walk 1
Hauts de Mad
Flirey
St Baussant
P
1
2
3
4
5
6
7
8
- forest track
- trenches
300 mtr
N
©Bart Metselaar

silenced, the Hauts de Mads Wood (or Sonnard Wood) was quickly occupied by the doughboys. The third rate German 77th Reserve Division was completely numbed by the American bombardment and the war-weary and unmotivated troops surrendered in droves.

GPS coordinates Walk 1

(1) Masonry trench (N48°52.995′ E005°49.362′)
(2) Underground shelters (N48°53.004′ E005°49.299′)
(3) Observation post (N48°53.020′ E005°49.229′)
(4) Reconstructed trench (N48°52.995′ E005°49.112′)
(5) Machine-gun position (N48°52.915′ E005°49.001′)
(6) Trench fortified with concrete (N48°52.007′ E005°49.090′)
(7) Concrete dugout (N48°52.913′ E005°48.944′)
(8) Observation post and concrete trenches (N48°52.910′ E005°48.852′)

The walk starts across the road opposite the car park. Follow the trail for about 200 metres until you see the **Masonry trench (1)** (N48°52.995′E005°49.362’) on your right. The first hundred metres of trench are made from local stone instead of the usual wooden and wire mesh construction. In front of the trenches you can see an example of a barbed wire obstacle. Originally, these would be broad belts, sometimes

Trenches built from local stone.

as much as fifty metres deep. The barbed wire is attached to so-called pig tail or cork screw pickets. These pickets were used by all belligerent countries and are therefore a common sight along the old front-line.

A few metres from where the trenches start are the remains of two **Underground shelters (2)** (N48°53.004′ E005°49.299′). At the entrance, you can clearly see the so-called Siegfried sheets of corrugated iron, often used by the Germans to reinforce tunnel or *Stollen* entrances.

Shelters.

A little bit further along the trail stands one of many **Observation posts (3)** (N48°53.020′ E005°49.229′) that were built whenever they were needed. Also clearly visible are the fire steps built into the parapet. These made sure that the soldiers were able to fire over the parapet, the side of the trench facing the enemy.

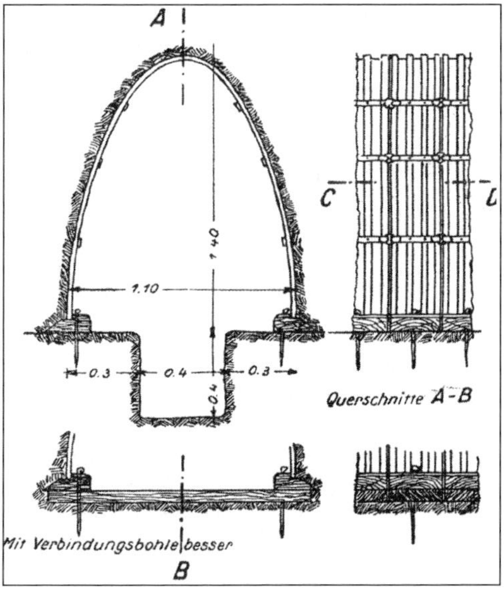

Technical drawing of Siegfried sheets. (Seeßelberg)

One of the many observation posts.

When you have finished the first part of the walk turn left onto the trail that leads you to the main track; turn right here. Continue for about one hundred metres and then turn left (indicated) where we return to the trenches.

The **reconstructed trench (4)** (N48°52.995′ E005°49.112′) was originally part of the German first line trench from 1914 to March 1918. It was in March 1918 that the Germans launched strong patrols against the French in order to break through to Flirey. This failed; however, they managed to push the French out of the woods (by then reduced to mere stumps and shell holes) and immediately started to reinforce their new positions with four concrete pillboxes. These were constructed during the night. The advantage of this new position was an enhanced ability to observe French (and later American) troop movements.

The reconstructed trench clearly shows how trenches were reinforced and what kind of material was used. Generally speaking, the trenches along the Western Front were constructed this way, using a mixture of timber, branches, chicken wire, on occasion corrugated iron and sandbags. It is important to realize that not a great many trenches were built of stone or concrete. Built into the parapet are two *Infanterieschild Model 1916,* more popularly known as sniper's shields – although they were not exclusively used by snipers. Snipers tended to use more concealed positions to take pot-shots at the enemy. Made of heavy gauge

Reconstructed trench.

iron, these were generally used as protected and camouflaged firing positions for the regular infantry. Inside the trench you can see wooden boxes to store hand grenades and ammunition. These were mostly built from empty ammunition boxes; if you take a closer look at the walls of the concrete trenches you can still see their imprint.

Walk along the trenches until you come to the concrete remains of a **Machine-gun position (5)** (N48°52.915′ E005°49.001′). This rectangular structure was built by using wooden form work; the concrete arrived in

Concrete machine-gun position with the roof blown off.

The infamous Maxim MG08 machine gun.

wooden barrels and was mixed on the spot. Inside, the form work was usually left in place as an extra layer of protection and to absorb shrapnel or bullets. The French and later American first line trenches were situated some 500 metres away.

One of the corner stones of the German defences was the Maxim machine gun, the MG 08. This water-cooled gun was capable of firing 500 rounds per minute, but in practice and to avoid the gun from over heating and to save ammunition, short bursts were fired. Three to five men were needed to operate the gun; an officer, two loaders and two operators.

The machine-gun post and surrounding trenches were badly mauled during the American preliminary bombardment that started at 1.00 am in the morning of 12 September 1918; the partly deserted and severely under-manned positions were quickly taken by troops from the 42nd Division.

A little further along the track you see a **trench fortified with concrete (6)** (N48°52.007′ E005°49.090′) Wooden stairs of recent date allow you to walk through the trenches. The imprint of corrugated iron sheets used for form work is clearly visible in the concrete at the lower part of the parapet.

About a hundred metres from Stop 6 lies a deep **concrete dugout (7)** ((N48°52.913′ E005°48.944′). The trenches and the dugout itself are

Trenches reinforced with concrete.

flooded. This was a common problem along the front line. Lots of time and resources were spent in keeping water out of the trenches and shelters. Even in summer this spot remains flooded, so it does not take too much imagination to think how difficult the situation might be in the winter. Pumps were needed to get rid of the water.

At the point where the trenches make a sharp turn to the right, you see a flooded **observation post and concrete trenches (8)** (N48°52.910′ E005°48.852′). Also visible in the woods behind the front line trenches are communication trenches. These were used to get troops, ammunitions and other supplies to the front.

Flooded trench.

Flooded concrete trench.

Continue along the trenches until you come at a sign that points at the main track running through the woods. When on the main track, follow this for about one kilometre; be sure to take the second track on the left. This leads you back to your vehicle.

Close-up of a fire step.

CHAPTER 4

I Corps

A Short Narrative

The 2nd ('Indianhead') Division

Maj. Gen. John H. Lejeune.

The 2nd Division, a National Army Division, commanded by Brigadier General John A. Lejeune, US Marine Corps, was placed on the left flank of I Corps. The composition of this division was somewhat unusual; in order to send a full division to France quickly, it was decided that it would contain the 3rd Infantry Brigade (9th and 23rd Regiments) and the 4th Marine Brigade (5th and 6th Marines). All of these formations were, as far as the American army as a whole was concerned, highly experienced, with battle honours dating from 1860. Some of the Marine regiments had been established as early as 1798.

The 2nd Division was constituted on 20 September 1917 and sailed for France over a period of six months from June 1917 to January 1918. Together with the 1st Division, the 2nd Division served as the vanguard of the Americans in France; it was to show the Allies that the Americans meant business and served as a major morale boost for the French and British. Upon their arrival in France, there were almost hysterical crowds, singing and cheering, waiting at the docks to greet the 'Sammies'.

In June 1917, the first troops to arrive in France went into training under the guidance of the French. According to the 2nd Division History, *'this experiment was found unsatisfactory; the difference in language, temperament and methods caused little progression to be made'.* Therefore, in August 1917, the division was training following an American training programme. This was followed by a month's service by battalions in a French division in a quiet sector. In March 1918, the 2nd Division moved to the Lorraine front and were stationed between St. Mihiel and Verdun, along the River Meuse.

As explained in the short history of the 1st Division (see chapter 3),

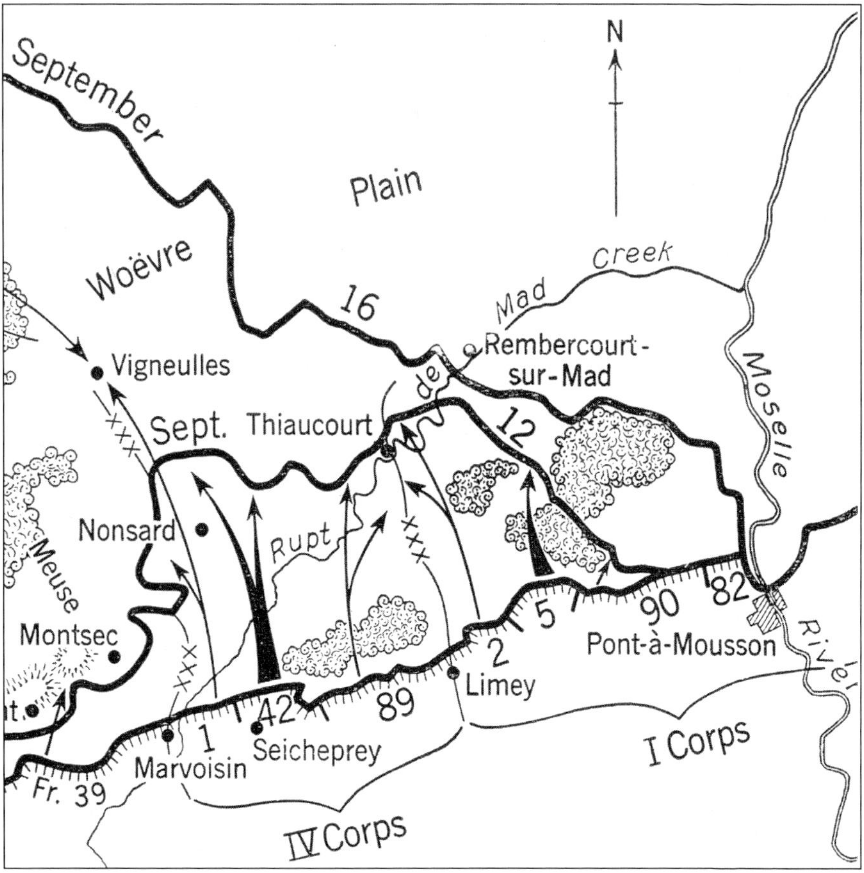

I Corps sector.

because of the German breakthrough on the Marne, the French were in desperate need of reinforcements; the 2nd Division was first moved to the Marne front, more specifically to Château-Thierry. The Division distinguished themselves in 1918 in the hard fighting at Belleau Wood (June), Soissons (July) 1918 and (in due course) at Blanc Mont (October). When they marched into the St. Mihiel Salient, between 1 and 3 September, the 2nd Division was already regarded as one of the best fighting formations of the AEF.

Thursday 12 September
Strong winds and driving rain.
On 8 September, the 2nd Division, after absorbing replacements for the quite severe losses sustained in fighting over the last couple of months, started to move into the line and took over a two kilometres' wide front line from the 89th and the 90th Divisions. The outposts were left unaltered

as long as possible; this line was fully taken over on the night of 11-12 September. The line, sandwiched between the positions of the 89th and 5th Divisions, ran roughly between Limey and Remeneauville. The area had no distinctive features; it was a rolling wooded landscape, but the ravine at the Rupt de Mad Creek at Thiaucourt, one of the bigger villages – almost a town – could create serious problems. The main line of resistance ran along the Promenade des Moines Ridge, some 500 metres from the jumping-off lines of both the 89th and 5th Divisions. A second defence line had been built along the southern edge of Eiche Wood.

The first phase of the American assault was to take Eiche Wood. The second objective, to be achieved after crossing the Rupt de Mad Creek, was the taking of a line between Thiaucourt and Jaulny, a village two kilometres to the north-east of Thiaucourt.

The rain was falling very heavily when, at 1.00 am, the artillery preparation started; in the pitch black the muzzle flash of the guns lit up the night. When dawn broke, the first companies went over the top, each in four consecutive waves, about fifty metres apart. The first waves were closely followed by machine-gun, mortar and one-pounder gun teams for extra firepower once the leading units had moved beyond the rolling barrage. Enemy machine guns opened up; the first walking casualties started to pour back through the advancing troops. Medics were called in, the first soldiers were killed. Great quantities of wire and shell holes had to be dealt with but generally the Doughboys encountered surprisingly little resistance. The freshly torn-up ground may have caused problems for the infantry but it was an even bigger headache for tanks; they all got bogged down in the mud if they had not already broken down. However, at best, the German lines were weakly held, in defiance of Major Neuman's order that the outpost zone should be continually occupied by machine-gun crews.

W. Jackson. (Coll. Frances Kerber and Paula Gilbert)

Warren R. Jackson, an infantryman with the 95th Company, 6th Marines, attached to the 2nd Division, remembers when he left Limey for No Man's Land on that rain-drenched morning.

> 'Going down the zigzag trench to follow up the advance of the attacking troops, we soon found ourselves on a rise with destruction and desolation ahead of us. It must have been half a mile or more to the main front line trenches and that chaotic mass of wire. The advancing waves were just reaching the crest of the

ascent beyond. As we advanced, I came to where an officer had been wounded and left a bright new helmet. It seemed that my mind might have been on other things just then but, discarding my old helmet, I adorned myself with a new one. How many there were killed of wounded among those ahead of us I do not recall, but I do not remember seeing many who had fallen.'

The American artillery barrage had taken a serious toll on the defenders and many had fled during the night. About 300 Germans of the 419th Regiment, 77th Reserve Division, were rounded up that morning. The combined pressure of the 2nd and the 89th divisions proved too much for the German Division; the line was breached. At 10.00 am, after a five hour struggle through the mud and driving rain, the first objective was taken.

14 September 1918: 6th Marines fighting another battle: hunting for cooties (lice).

Although there were hundreds of wounded and dozens of soldiers who were killed, in comparison with Soissons the number of casualties was relatively low. Not all the American casualties had been inflicted by

Traffic jam in Limey, 13 September 1918.

the enemy; while waiting for the barrage to lift, one of the men of the 6th Marines was pulling a fork out of his overcoat when one of the prongs caught in the pin of a hand grenade in the same pocket, setting off the detonator. There was normally a five second delay after pulling the pin. Panic-stricken, he tried to get the grenade out of his pocket just as it went off. He was killed instantly.

As planned, the American artillery started a standing barrage which had a two-fold objective - to prevent German soldiers from leaving the battle zone and to block any attempt to push reinforcements into the liberated sector. This time was used to round up prisoners and to reorganize the division before the barrage ended at 11.00 am.

When the barrage lifted the Americans continued to their second objective, a line between Thiaucourt and Jaulny. Here, the remnants of the 77th Reserve Division attempted to make a stand on the ridge that runs south of Thiaucourt, but it was all to no avail; the remnants of the 419th Regiment, some 250 men, fled to Xammes. At 1.00 pm Thiaucourt was liberated and it was decided to exploit the situation to push on to the Xammes-Jaulny line, the Army's objective that day. Without encountering any opposition worth mentioning, the Thiaucourt line was reached at about 2.00 pm; it was immediately organized for defence as a German counterattack from the Michel Zone was feared. Almost incredibly, throughout the day the 2nd Division had been able to keep in touch with the neighbouring 89th and 5th Divisions.

William McFee

William McFee was commissioned as a first lieutenant on 8 June 1918 and assigned to the 2nd Division. Early in September, he was assigned to the First Battalion, 9th Regiment, 2nd Division, as a battalion surgeon. In the days just before the St. Mihiel Offensive he put his thoughts and worries about the forthcoming offensive into words in his 1918 pocket notebook:

> 'This period spent in woods in leaf tent. Rain every day. Hail came through tent and wet everything. Thinking a good deal about the coming battle and possibilities. Decide what to do in case of hopeless wounds.'

1st Lt. William McFee. (Coll. Peter Wever)

On 12 September, he wrote:

> 'Barrage opens at 1 AM. Am shaking [with] cold & excitement. Attack success. Sleep in Th[iaucourt].'

His notes for 13 September reveal the dangers he encountered:

> 'Start to find battalion. Am stopped on road by own barrage. Was about to get in No Man's Land. In P.M. am shelled by own erratic battery – close call. Germans shelling other end of forest road. Very tired. Sleep in Dutch [German] abri.'

Back in the United States, he pursued a career in surgery and eventually became a professor of clinical surgery. During the Second World War he was commissioned a colonel and became the commanding officer of the 2nd Evacuation Hospital and a consulting surgeon to the Fifteenth Army. He was responsible for the treatment of casualties evacuated from Omaha Beach during D-Day. On 16

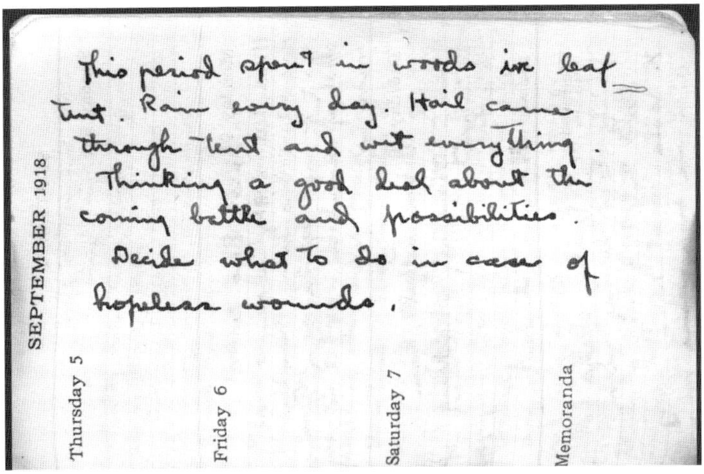
This period spent in woods in leaf tent. Rain every day. Hail came through tent and wet everything. Thinking a good deal about the coming battle and possibilities. Decide what to do in case of hopeless wounds.

Entry of McFee's diary. *'This period spent in woods in leaf tent. Rain every day. Hail came through tent and wet everything. Thinking a good deal about the coming battle and possibilities. Decide what to do in case of hopeless wounds.'* (Coll. Peter Wever)

February 1974, at the age of 83, William McFee died in New York City. He is buried in Virtue Cemetery in Concord, Tennessee. His legacy is honoured at St. Luke's – Roosevelt Hospital Center in New York City, by the William MacFee [after the war, he changed his name to MacFee] Professorship in Surgery.

The Gorz Group, which comprised the 10th Division and 77th Reserve Division of I Bavarian Corps, was pushed out of the Wilhelm and Schroeter defence zones; in the north, the Combres Group was being pushed back all along its front. By now the Mihiel Group, consisting of the 5th Landwehr Division and 31st Division of I Bavarian Corps, which had been occupying the tip of the Salient, was in immediate danger. Therefore General Fuchs started issuing orders to start the Loki Movement, the evacuation of the Salient and the withdrawal to the Michel Zone.

Friday 13 September
Overcast and rainy weather
The next morning part of the American artillery was moved to Four Wood, about two kilometres north of Limey. All day and all night the Germans had been harassing the Americans with machine-gun fire, coming from north of Jaulny, so it was decided to launch a small-scale attack in that direction. The area between Jaulny and Rembercourt-sur-

Railroad station in Jaulny after the American bombardment, 18 September 1918.

Mad was by now, effectively, a sort of No Man's Land; the German outposts were easily pushed back.

As the Regniéville-Thiaucourt Road, the present-day D3, was in reasonably good condition, it was used by both the 2nd and its neighbouring 5th Divisions to bring ammunition and other supplies forward. Now another well-known Great War problem presented itself: traffic congestion. In spite of Herculean efforts, only limited amounts of supplies reached the front line.

Saturday 14 and Sunday 15 September
Fair weather, good visibility.
As a German counter attack was still feared, the front line troops were relieved by the reserve troops. The occasional German shell exploded, but it was a relatively calm night. Most of the weekend was used to straighten out the line. There was a whole zone between the American front and the Michel Zone that was occupied by neither the Germans nor the American Army. Not counting improvised German outposts that remained here and there, the area had been largely abandoned by the German army; the Germans were now entirely focussed on reinforcing

the Michel Zone in anticipation of a possible American attack in the direction of Metz. The Divisional HQ of the 2nd Division had been moved to a group of old German dugouts in Haie l'Evéque Woods, some four kilometres north of Limey.

David Ephraim Hayden, Medal of Honor

David Ephraim Hayden (2 October 1897 – 18 March 1974) was a United States Navy Hospital Corpsman and earned the Medal of Honor for his valiant actions in Thiaucourt. Hayden was born in Florence, Texas and enlisted in the Navy in October 1917. He received his training at San Diego Naval Base, California, and in Quantico, Virginia. During the war he was attached to the 2nd Battalion of the 6th Marines as a hospital apprentice, first class. On 15 September, in Thiaucourt, Hayden ran through heavy enemy fire to administer first aid to a wounded marine, Corporal Creed. For this action he was awarded the Medal of Honor. Hayden stayed in the services until the summer of 1920. He then served as a US Marshal in California until the age of seventy. He died on 18 March 1974 and is buried in section 35, lot 1864, in Arlington National Cemetery.

David E. Hayden, Medal of Honor.

For gallantry and intrepidity at the risk of his life above and beyond the call of duty. During the advance, when Corporal Creed was mortally wounded while crossing an open field swept by machine-gun fire, Hayden unhesitatingly ran to his assistance and, finding him so severely wounded as to require immediate attention, disregarded his own personal safety to dress the wound under intense machine-gun fire, and then carried the wounded man back to a place of safety.

North of Jaulny the 6th Marines were subjected to repeated small-scale counterattacks. It took them two days to completely clear Montagne Wood of Germans. By now the weather had cleared so there was much more German activity in the air: American supply columns were being regularly fired on by German aircraft. However, Allied planes shot down several of them.

The 2nd Division, which had taken 3,000 prisoners and 118 guns of all calibres, was relieved on the night of 16-17 September when the 78th Division took over the line. During the course of the fighting the 2nd Division suffered 1,552 casualties, of whom 195 were killed.

The 5th 'Red Diamond' Division

Maj. Gen. John E. McMahon.

The 5th Division, a Regular Army division, commanded by Major General John E. McMahon, was placed in the centre of I Corps. The 5th Division had been organized as a part of the War Department's programme for the rapid expansion of the Regular Army for immediate service in France. Therefore units that already existed in the army were selected to form the new Division. It was activated on 11 December 1917 at Camp Logan, near Houston, Texas, and immediately began training for deployment on the Western Front. By the start of May 1918 the entire division had arrived in France. An interesting passage in the divisional history notes that

> 'the atmosphere in France was a shock [...] the famine of food was not apparent, but the awful effects of four years of war close at hand had laid its pall on the people. Everyone wore the funeral-air. Scarce a family had not been touched by death of a son or brother or father in battle.'

In June the division trained with the French in the Vosges and was where it suffered its first battle casualties. From 4 to 8 September, under cover of night, the men of the Division moved into the Mihiel Sector and were billeted in the village of Martincourt and the woods around it, about five kilometres south of the front line.

Thursday 12 September
Strong winds and driving rain.

On the night of 11-12 September, after a difficult and arduous march, the first companies of the 5th Division arrived at the front line trenches. The only village in their sector was Regniéville-en-Haye, hardly recognizable and utterly destroyed by four years of shelling. Flooded trenches on the edge of the totally pulverised woods provided the only cover on their front line. The German outpost trenches were located on top of a ridge 400 metres to the north and were protected by a broad zone of barbed wire. A second defence line was built on the top of a ridge, and behind that lay Rappe Wood. The sector that was to be attacked was only two kilometres wide and the mission for that day was to take Viéville-en-Haye, some four kilometres due north. The attack was supposed to have

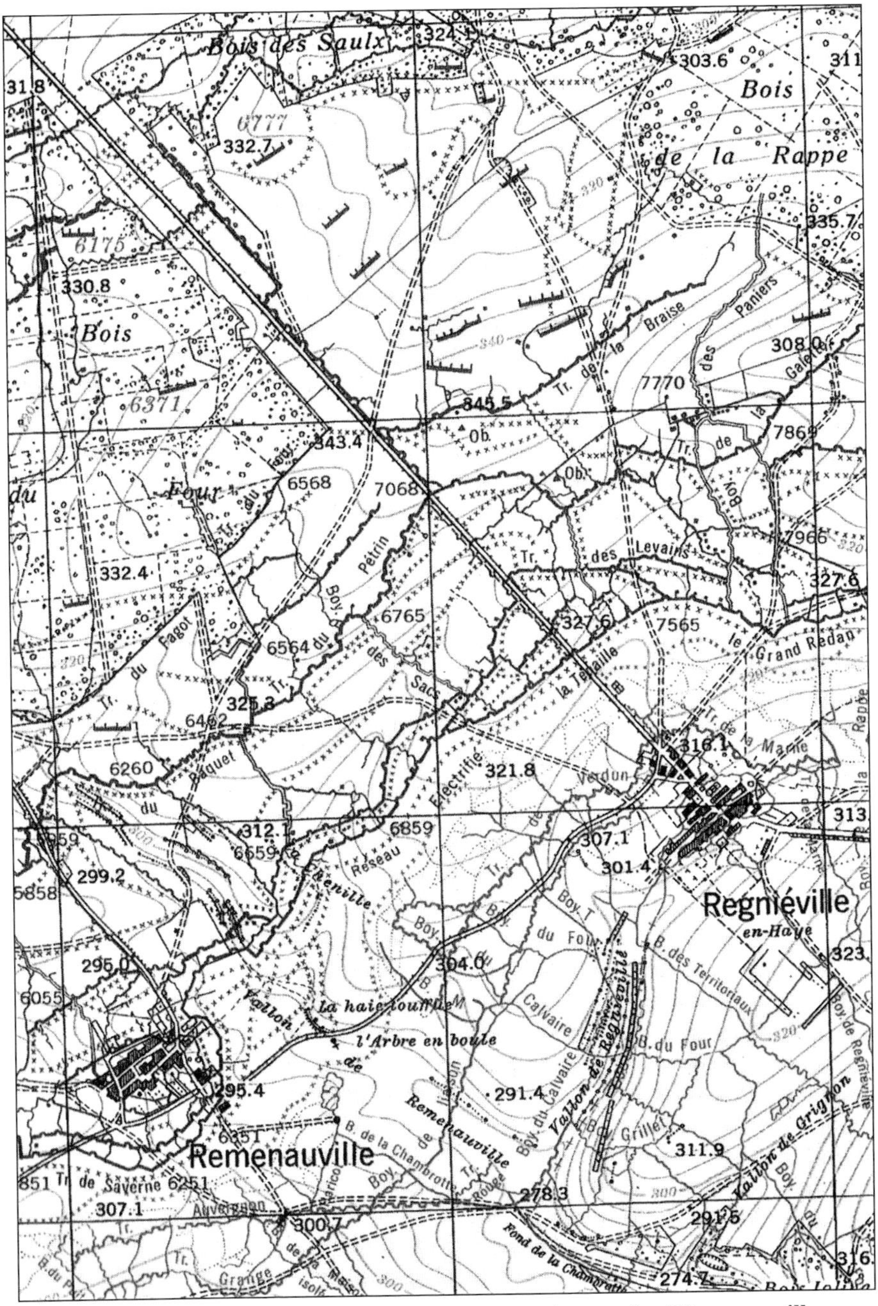

Trench map of the 5th Division sector. The trenches north of Remenauville and Regniéville are German.

been supported by tanks and airplanes, but the weather was too poor to allow the planes to take off.

The preliminary bombardment started at 1.00 am, to be joined by a machine-gun barrage at 4.30 am. Thirty minutes later the barrage lifted and the men went over the top. Unfortunately, the supporting tanks had not reached their start positions due to shell holes and the morass-like ground. When first light broke, the men advanced on the first German outposts under cover of a smokescreen. Most of the outposts had already been abandoned. In spite of the sea of mud and barbed wire the Doughboys had been moving so fast that when they reached the second line of defence they took the Germans by surprise, many still in their dugouts. However, there were some pockets of fierce resistance as the Germans held onto several heavily fortified strong points that were bristling with machine guns. These were outflanked and the occupants bombed out with the help of hand grenades and machine-gun barrages. By 6.00 am, the German first line had been taken. However, the tanks and artillery had problems keeping up as they floundered in the mud and trenches of No Man's Land. Engineers tried to bridge the flooded trenches and to rebuild roads, but to little avail.

In the shattered woods the going was tough; however, for a kilometre or so there was no hostile gunfire and they ended up taking many prisoners. But, when they reached the part of the woods that are known as Saulx Wood and Rappes Wood, the German machine guns started firing again. Companies split up to try to outflank the nests. At the cost of heavy casualties this problem was quickly resolved and the men continued to the northern edge of the woods. The backbone of the German 77th Reserve Division was broken; the pressure of thousands of Americans

One of several German observation posts at Viéville. (Spring 2019)

flooding the sector had been too much to bear; a mere 8,000 Germans had found themselves against three American divisions, namely the 89th, the 2nd and the 5th, some 24,000 men, reserve regiments not counted.

The 5th Division continued on to Viéville, which was heavily protected by wire and machine-gun nests. Coincidentally, the rolling barrage was just leaving Vieville; in the town the defenders remained hidden away in their deep dugouts. Thus when they emerged, they were immediately taken prisoner. Viéville was taken at 10.00 am, and the advance moved on, virtually unopposed, to Gerard Wood, one kilometre north of Viéville. They found the woods deserted; the Germans had fled en masse to the safety of the Michel Zone. Inside the woods, the Americans found a large German hospital and several rest camps.

Sergeant Fred Smith.

Sgt. Fred Smith. (Coll. Peter Wever)

On 12 September 1918, Sergeant Fred Smith, 11th Regiment, 5th Division, led his men towards the small village of Viéville-en-Haye. These actions are described in the history of the 5th Division:

> 'The Eleventh Infantry descended on Viéville, protected by its belt of wire and strong machine-gun nests. They took the town while the barrage was leaving it. The men in steel gray came out of their cellars and deep dugouts to find the olive-drab waiting to receive them. There was resistance only from the isolated machine gunners.'

Early that morning, Sergeant Smith had been gassed and shot through the shoulder near Viéville-en-Haye, but throughout the day continued to lead his platoon, refusing to return to a first aid station for treatment. For these actions, Sergeant Smith was later awarded the Distinguished Service Cross, the second highest military award in the American army.

Sergeant Smith was listed as severely wounded. Yet, after a month in hospital, he returned to his unit and participated in the Meuse-Argonne Offensive. As the oldest man in his company, he was usually asked to lead patrols as 'the kids looked up to him to bring them back'. After the war, Fred Smith remained in the service but eventually thought he 'would not live long enough in the army'. Therefore he left the army in 1923 and became an employee of the Erie Railroad. On 12 December, 1969, at the age of eighty-five, Fred Smith died in the Veterans Administration Hospital in Dayton, Ohio. He is buried in Enon Cemetery in Enon, Ohio.

Because of the terrible weather conditions, even flying ace Sergeant Eddie Rickenbacker (1890-1973), of the 94th Aero Squadron, could not get airborne until noon, by which time visibility had improved sufficiently. Flying at an altitude of 200 metres, he saw *many fires burning … villages, haystacks, ammunition dumps and supplies were being set ablaze by the retreating Huns.* During the afternoon there was much more activity in the air than there had been during the morning; Rickenbacker managed to shoot down four German aircraft before returning to his airfield. In 1931 he was awarded the Congressional Medal of Honor for his actions in the war.

Sergeant Eddie Rickenbacker.

At noon the tanks were still held up at the start line, but by then they were not needed anymore. The road leading from Regniéville to Thiaucourt had been repaired for a distance of two kilometres, but now there was another problem: traffic jams. It was almost impossible to make use of the road because of traffic congestion. However, tracks had been rapidly laid across No Man's Land and along which, not without difficulty, kitchen and ration carts wheeled their way north.

By 1.30 pm, the northern edge of Gerard Wood had been reached, and the advance was halted. The 5th Division had moved so quickly that its left and right flanks had become exposed to the enemy and they were in danger of losing contact with the neighbouring divisions. Nevertheless, patrols were sent out to see what the Germans were doing. Some patrols made it as far as a kilometre south of Rembercourt-sur-Mad, which lay just behind the Michel Zone. However, later in the afternoon German resistance stiffened; they had thrown the relatively fresh 174th Regiment of the 31st Division into the fight; they now occupied Bonvaux and Hanido Woods, just across the fields opposite Gerard Wood. At nightfall, American platoons were sent out to outposts to keep watch on No Man's Land. The Division's casualties on the first day were 144 killed and 450 wounded.

Friday 13 September
Overcast and rainy weather.
During the night the front line companies were relieved by the reserve companies. Fresh troops were needed as it was feared that the Germans were planning to launch a counterattack. During the night, after establishing contact with the neighbouring divisions, it became clear that there were several gaps in the new American front line. It had been a tough advance for the 90th Division and it was lagging two kilometres behind, thereby seriously exposing the 5th Division's right flank. Part of the morning was used to reorganize and prepare the troops for an attack on Venchères Wood to close the gap. However, things did not go as planned.

The arrival of reinforcements renewed the Germans badly disturbed confidence and their artillery fire grew both stronger and more effective. As a result of the terrible conditions underfoot, the American gun batteries still had not been able to take up their positions. At 1.00 pm, it became clear the Germans were preparing a counterattack. The shelling coming from Bonvaux and Hanido Woods was growing heavier and troops were seen massing. The Americans called on their artillery; however, only a few guns had been supplied with ammunition and they just could not provide enough firepower to give effective support to break up the attack. At 4.30 pm the attack started, commencing with a short, violent barrage that inflicted serious casualties among the Americans manning the outpost positions. Shortly afterwards the German attack advanced on Gerard Wood, supported by heavy machine-gun fire. The attacks went on continuously and by about 8.00 pm the Germans had managed to get a toe-hold in Gerard Wood; they were finally repulsed by a large-scale machine-gun barrage. The immediate threat had been overcome at the cost of an estimated 200 American casualties; but the attack carried on until 10.00 pm, when the last fighting spluttered out. At 11.00 pm, the tanks arrived; they had been called up to assist three hours before but now they were no longer needed. In spite of the German counterattack, the 5th and 2nd Divisions had managed to close the gap in the front line at Jaulny. The right flank of the 5th Division was still in danger, but the 90th Division was gradually moving forward to its allocated position.

Saturday 14 September
Clear weather, good visibility.
During the night strong patrols were sent out to close the gap between the 5th and 90th divisions: by 1.15 am the 5th Division had reached and occupied La Souleuvre Farm. The gap between the divisions was still 700 metres wide and, to make matters worse, the Germans started shelling the area with mustard gas. Skirmishes in Venchères Wood and the Trou de la Haye continued throughout the night and several times the Germans launched powerful counterattacks. At daybreak contact with the 90th was finally established but by then the 5th had suffered over 300 casualties. On the right flank, Bonvaux Wood had been entirely cleared of Germans and new American defences were built from Jaulny, to the left of the woods, and through to La Souleuvre Farm, on the right. Despite continuous heavy shelling throughout the day, the Americans managed to reinforce and hold on to their new positions.

Americans killed by German shellfire.

Sunday 15 September
Fair weather, good visibility.
As the weather was clear, the sky was now buzzing with German and Allied planes. Both American and German observation balloons and planes were shot down; dogfights continued throughout the day.

The tanks were relieved from further duty and sent back to the rear; they had been utterly useless to the Division as they had failed to be of any assistance during the operation. They had continually disrupted lines of communication and hindered movement on the roads. Most of the tanks did not even make it as far as the front line due to mechanical breakdown or mud.

In the afternoon, the American 6th and 9th Regiments (10th Brigade) were relieved by the 60th and 61st Regiments (9th Brigade). The Germans continued to harass the American engineers who were building wire defences with light artillery fire.

Monday 16 September.
Clear weather, good visibility.
In contrast to most other divisions, the 5th Division had been engaged with the enemy since the beginning of the offensive. Their task that day was to go forward and capture a ridge in Grand Fontaine Wood; the possession of this ridge was vitally important in case of a future attack as it bordered on the outposts of the Michel Zone. The timing was right for just such a move; the patrols that had been sent on a recce mission discovered that at that time the ridge was only being lightly held. It was feared that before long the Germans would retake it and incorporate the ridge into the Michel Zone.

At 7.00 am Companies G and H of the 61st Regiment moved forward and continued to the crest of the ridge; there was no visible sign of any German defenders. Suddenly, seven Maxim machine guns opened up; each of these nests had to be eliminated one by one. With the aid of hand grenades the strong points were cleared and their crews killed; a few Germans managed to escape in the chaos of battle. Companies E and F, attacking on the right, had been less fortunate; after they reached the desired lines, the valley that they occupied was drenched by gas and they were forced to pull back. Time and again, the Americans tried to reach their goal but on each occasion the attack was repulsed by 77mm, 105mm high explosive and gas shells. Finally, at 6.20 pm, they made it onto the ridge and established contact with G and H Companies on their left and with the troops occupying Souleuvre Farm on their right. The Division had achieved all its objectives. On the night of 16-17 September, the 5th Division was relieved by the 78th Division. During five days of fighting, the Division had casualties that included 318 dead and 1,167 wounded.

The 90th 'Alamo' Division

The 90th Division, a National Army Division, was commanded by Major

General Henry T. Allen. Together with the 82nd Division, the 90th Division was placed on the right flank of I Corps.

Maj. Gen. Henry T. Allen.

The Division, activated in August 1918, was organized with draftees from Oklahoma and Texas and trained at Camp Travis, San Antonio, Texas. In June 1918, it sailed for France. On 15 August, after training with the French for six weeks, the 90th Division arrived in Pagny-sur-Meuse, forty kilometres south of St. Mihiel. Nine days later, they took over a seven kilometres' wide section of front line in the Salient, between Remenauville and Prêtre Wood (Priest Wood) three kilometres west of Pont-à-Mousson.

Preparations were promptly commenced for the coming offensive and front line activities were restricted to a bare minimum so as not to arouse German suspicions. The first casualties of the 90th Division were Lieutenant Richard H. Graham and Sergeant Walter Burke, killed by the accidental discharge of a hand grenade during their first night at the front; the grenade had probably been lost by the French in the sea of mud in the front line trenches.

The 90th Division was on the right of the attacking forces of I Corps. The 82nd Division served as a flank guard between the 90th Division's right flank and the River Moselle. Since the 90th Division was the axis around which the whole offensive revolved, both the 180th Brigade (359th and 360th Regiments) and 179th Brigade (357th and 358th Regiments) played their part. The 180th, in the right subsector, was tasked with holding on to the right part of the divisional front and just had to make a limited advance on the remainder of its front; 179th Brigade was assigned the task of pushing up on the left to help the advance of the 5th Division. The objectives on the first day varied in distance from four kilometres on the left flank to no advance at all on the right.

Thursday 12 September
Strong winds and driving rain.
At 5.00 am sharp, after an artillery preparation of four hours, the four regiments of the 90th Division climbed out of their front line trenches in Prêtre Wood. This forest had been the scene of intensive fighting in the first half of 1915 and there was not much left of the woods; seemingly there was not an inch of ground that had not been ploughed up and the shell-pocked and barren hills looked like a lunar landscape. During the preceding weeks incessant rains had changed the area into a swamp and

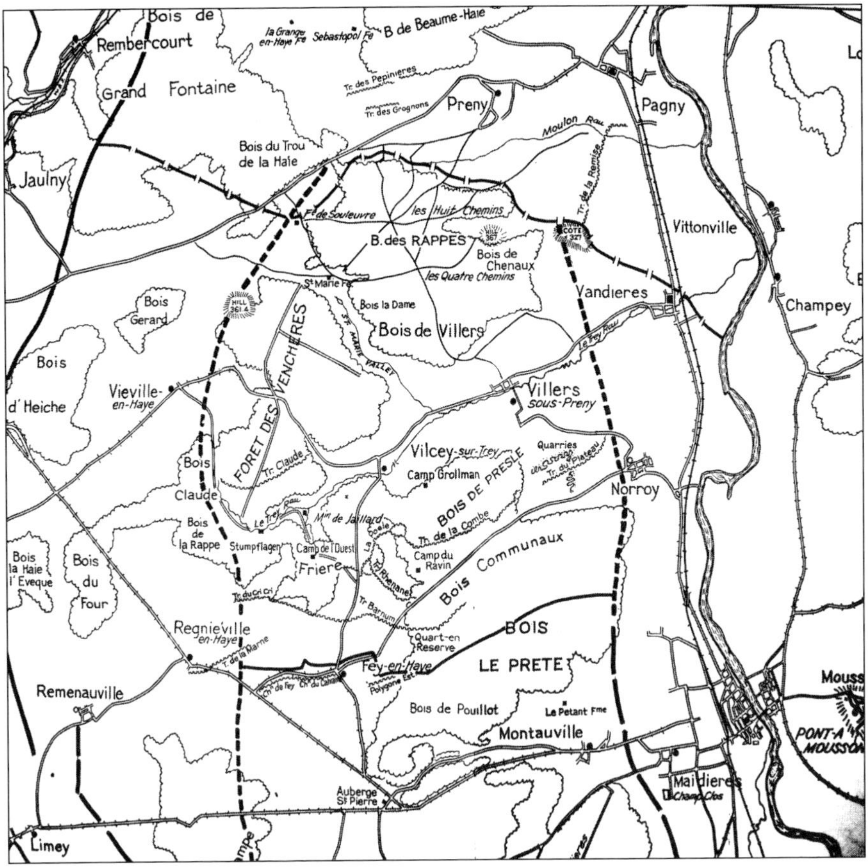

Map of the 90th Division sector.

made the terrain extremely hard to negotiate. For that reason there were no tanks deployed to support the assault.

In spite of this, the leading regiments, the 357th on the left and the 360th on the right, made good progress and kept close to the rolling barrage. Lieutenant Fred Regenbrecht, Company B, 357th Regiment, was mortally wounded when he left the jump-off trench. Hit by machine-gun bullets, he died in hospital several days later.

The supporting battalions, however, advanced far too quickly and got mixed up with the attacking companies. A significant problem was the lack of effective wire-cutters; sometimes only the smallest cutters were all that the Doughboys had to cut lanes through the heavy German wire. A further complication was that, despite the preliminary bombardment, some units came under murderous German machine-gun fire just 500 metres north of their jump-off positions.

German wire found in the Salient in 2019.

US Signal Corps wire cutters for telephone lines were used to cut the German wire.

On the left and right flank, the going was relatively easy as the rolling barrage kept the Germans hiding in their tunnels and dugouts, but in the centre more resistance was encountered. Nevertheless, by 6.30 am the first objective, the German front line trench, had been reached and taken ahead of schedule.

The next objective was to take Venchères Wood in order to keep up with the 5th Division on the left flank. The road running from Vilcey-sur-Trey to Viéville-en-Haye through the Fontaine valley proved difficult to secure. Every approach was covered by machine guns and the valley itself was frequently saturated with gas. By the end of a day of heavy fighting the road was the furthest point of advance of the 357th.

From the start, the 358th Regiment, fighting in the centre, had been caught by German artillery fire. As he was leaving a trench, Major Allen, CO 3rd Battalion, was hit by a piece of shrapnel; the injured man was taken to an aid station. When he came to, he got up and rushed out in search of his battalion. During his search he came across a couple of his men and with them attacked a German machine-gun nest; after emptying his pistol he continued the fight with his fists until once again he was badly wounded. A souvenir hunter, Major Allen picked up a German dog tag on the battlefield. After the fighting died down, he continued the search for his men but somehow became mixed up with a detachment of the 357th Regiment. Without any insignia of rank, they were inclined to suspect him of being a German spy and when they searched Major Allen, they found the German dog tag. Covered in blood and missing a few teeth, it took some persuading on Major Allen's part to convince them that he was indeed an American officer. Once his identity had been established Major

German wire obstacles in Priest Wood, June 2019.

The horrors of Priest Wood.

Allen was evacuated to a nearby casualty clearing station. He was later awarded a Silver Star and a Purple Heart for his actions. He served as a major general in the Second World War, commanding the 1st Division and led it through the North African and Sicily operations.

The going was tough in the advance through the shell-blasted hills and ridges of Prêtre Wood. Units lost fifty per cent of their officers, largely the work of German snipers. The men of the 358th Regiment did not make it to Vilecey-sur-Trey that day, a first day objective. As night fell they had no choice but to dig in on the positions they had reached. Almost everywhere in the 90th Division's sector the Germans were putting up heavy resistance; with the River Moselle on the extreme right, Prêtre Wood and Homécourt Wood, a little to the north, were the only defences before the Michel Zone. Whereas in other sectors the American divisions had to fight their way through twelve kilometres of German occupied area, here it was only a few kilometres before they could knock on the door of the Michel Zone.

In spite of all the problems the inexperienced 90th Division was facing, by 2.00 pm most of the day's objectives had been reached. The rest of the day was used for consolidating their new position and mopping up German stragglers. According to the divisional history, Germans were still emerging from their hiding places several days after the area had been liberated.

Friday 13 September
Overcast and rainy weather.
There was no time to rest for the hungry soldiers; the line had to be consolidated and the men were set to work digging foxholes. In the meantime, the engineers had started to build wire obstacles. Another important task that fell upon the shoulders of the tired soldiers was the establishment of outposts. These positions were to be located about two kilometres beyond the main line reached on the previous day. Strong patrols were sent out and skirmishes continued all through the night. Owing to the nature of the terrain, the machine-gun battalions had not been able to reach the front until after dark. The heavy equipment put a lot of strain on the men, but in spite of their fatigue they set up their guns all along the new front line in anticipation of a possible counter attack. Everybody was feeling tense during the night, while on the left flank there was mayhem as the Germans continued raining shells down on the 5th Division's sector. To the north of the 90th Division the forest seemed to be a hive of activity. The feared attack did not materialize. However, as dawn broke, it became clear that the Germans were massing for a counter attack; German artillery had suddenly become very active on the left flank, north of Prény Wood. At around 1.00 pm the Germans started their attack but the 357th quickly replied with a heavy machine-gun barrage and drove them back.

In the centre of the 90th Division's sector, the attack on Venchères Wood and Vilcey-sur-Trey had been very successful and the 358th Regiment took the woods almost without opposition. Meanwhile, the 360th Regiment pushed on through Prêtre Wood and continued the advance through Norroy Wood. On the right flank, they found the village of Norroy-lès-Pont-à-Mousson deserted. Outposts were quickly established and large quantities of supplies and food were captured. For most of the Doughboys able to feast on the German supplies on this part of the front provided them with their first decent meal for two days.

Saturday 14 September
Clear weather, good visibility.
On this day the 90th Division was reorganized and the lines firmly consolidated. Rations had finally reached the front line troops and by almost super human efforts artillery had been brought forward. Finally, on the left flank, the line was pushed north to close the gap between them and the 5th Division. Strong patrols were sent out to reconnoitre the terrain between the American line and the Michel Zone during which it was discovered that the Germans had deserted Villers-sous-Prény.

Sunday 15 September
Clear weather, good visibility.
Moving forward at 8.15 am, the whole area between Souleuvre Farm and Vandieres was taken by the Division without encountering much opposition; this pushed the front line to the outer limits of the Michel Zone. By now the Germans had practically abandoned the woods south of Prény. Their mission complete, the 90th stayed in the area until relieved by the 7th Division on 10 October, when they were moved to the Meuse-Argonne sector, where they were initially kept in reserve. The 90th Division had suffered 1,972 casualties during the St Mihiel Offensive and in the subsequent days.

Members of the 358th Regiment near Vilcey, 18 September 1918.

Concrete dugouts near Prény.

The 82nd 'All-American' Division

Maj. Gen. William P. Burnham.

From the outbreak of war in April 1917, the American Army rapidly expanded as many new divisions were created. The 82nd, a National Army Division, was one of these new divisions. Formed on 25 August 1917 at Camp Gordon, Georgia, the division was filled with draftees from almost every state, hence the nickname 'All American'. It was commanded by Major General William P. Burnham and sailed for France between the end of April and the beginning of May 1918.

Once in France, the 82nd was transported to the Somme by train to undergo training with the British. Here the troops exchanged the American-made M14 rifles for the British Lee Enfields; each soldier was issued with a helmet and gas mask. On 16 June the division was transported south to Toul, close to St. Mihiel, and the P14 rifles were reissued. On 30 August the 82nd was assigned to I Corps and moved to Marbache, ten kilometres south of Pont-à-Mousson. A few days before the St. Mihiel Offensive was due to begin, the 82nd took over a one kilometre wide stretch of front line a little north of Pont-à-Mousson; the men of the 82nd Division were now positioned between the 90th Division on the left and the River Moselle on the right. The 82nd Division's primary task was to protect the right flank of the 90th Division and to occupy outposts in the direction of Norroy, about two kilometres north of their jump-off line.

Thursday 12 September

Strong winds and driving rain.

Before dusk, the engineers set out to cut gaps in the German wire in No Man's Land, after which the 328th Regiment, joined by Stokes Mortar platoons, moved forward. Because of the 90th Division's successful advance through Prêtre Wood, the Germans had hurriedly abandoned Norroy without offering much resistance. However, before they had left, the village was set on fire. It was quickly occupied and the troops started to dig in on the crest of the ridge a little north of the village. The rest of the day was used to reorganize and to bring supplies to the front line.

Friday 13 September
Overcast and rainy weather.
During the night contact had been established with the 90th Division and strong patrols were sent out to reconnoitre the terrain north of Norroy in the direction of Vandières. During the day the area was secured but the Americans repeatedly came under shellfire from the right bank of the Moselle.

Saturday 14 September
Clear weather, good visibility.
As they had been ordered, the 82nd only sent out patrols to secure and reinforce their right flank. Rations were brought up and trenches were dug. There was considerable aerial activity; both German and American aircraft were busy flying numerous sorties. During the day the Germans relentlessly shelled Norroy and surroundings with a mixture of high explosive and mustard gas, resulting in many casualties.

Sunday 15 September
Clear weather, good visibility.
As the 90th Divison launched an attack in the direction of Prény, it was

Germans posing in front of a dugout in Norroy.

now time for the 82nd to move north to Vandières to prevent the Germans driving a wedge between the two divisions. The advance started at daylight from the high ground north of Norroy. These heights gradually slope away into a level valley where the small village of Vandières is located. The advancing troops had no cover and were in full view of the German gunners; within minutes there were over 300 casualties. In spite of this, Vandières was quickly taken and the Americans continued to a ridge just north of the village. However, not long afterwards they were forced to evacuate the ridge and the village altogether because of the murderous shelling. The 3rd Battalion of the 328th Regiment, which had suffered heavy casualties, retreated to a line south of Vandières and started to dig in. Nevertheless, the 82nd and 90th Divisions eventually managed to link up. Once the German bombardment had slackened off they took possession of Vandières once again; this line was maintained until the Armistice.

Lieutenant Colonel Emory Jenison Pike.

Lt. Col. Emory J. Pike.

Lieutenant Colonel Emory Jenison Pike (1876-1918), 321st Machine-Gun Battalion, was the first member of the 82nd Division to earn America's highest award for valour while in action at Vandières. Unfortunately, he was also one of the hundreds of casualties caused by the incessant German shelling. Having gone forward to reconnoitre new machine-gun positions, Lieutenant Colonel Pike offered his assistance in reorganizing advancing infantry units which had become disorganized during heavy shelling. He only found about twenty of his own men, but with these he continued the advance; they were later joined by several infantry platoons. Pike, encouraging all by his optimism, helped to establish outposts in spite of the extreme danger. When one of the men in the outpost was wounded by a shell, Pike immediately went to his aid but he was severely wounded himself when a shell burst nearby. While waiting to be brought to the rear, Pike continued in command, good-humouredly encouraging all those around him and directing the reorganization so that the position could be held. The entire operation was carried on under terrific bombardment. A day later Pike succumbed to his wounds; he was just forty-one years old. He was posthumously awarded the Medal of Honor.

After the war, his remains were repatriated to the US, where he is buried in Woodland Cemetery, Des Moines, Iowa.

Original 'All-American' 82nd Division uniform grouping. (Coll. Thibault Mansy)

On 21 September, the 82nd Division, relieved by the French 69th Division, was moved to Clermont-en-Argonne to prepare for the imminent Meuse-Argonne Offensive. In its time in the Salient the 82nd had 950 casualties, seventy-eight of them fatal; the casualties were almost exclusively caused by German shelling, mainly on 15 September.

The Second Phase: Monday 16 September to Saturday 9 November

Between 16 September and 9 November, the Americans holding the St. Mihiel front undertook numerous trench raids and small-scale attacks in order to straighten out the front lines so that they would be in more favourable positions should a large-scale attack on Metz be ordered. During this 'second phase' there arose the strange situation that the divisions that had remained in the sector sometimes lost more casualties during this period of occupation than they had during the St. Mihiel Offensive proper. For example, the 89th Division lost 833 men in the battle, but lost 1,351 men during the occupation of the sector from 17 September to 7 October. These casualties were mainly the result of German shellfire and the Spanish Flu; it was at this time, from September to November, that the often fatal second wave of the 1918 pandemic influenza spread globally.

Third phase: Sunday 10 November to Monday 11 November

The last two days of the war saw a lot of activity in the Salient as several divisions prepared for a major push. All along the American front line attacks were launched against the outposts of the Michel Zone. During this period armistice negotiations were in progress; in order to keep pressure on the German negotiators, there was to be no respite in the allied attacks.

The 7th 'Hour Glass' Division

On paper, the 7th (Infantry) Division, a Regular Army Division, commanded by Brigade General Charles H. Barth, was activated at Camp Wheeler, Georgia on 6 December 1917. However, headquarters troop, the four regiments, the machine-gun battalions and all the other units that together form a division, were all trained in separate camps. Between July and September 1918, the separate units of the division, depending on their state of readiness, departed for France. Approximately fifty per cent of the division sailed to Europe aboard the *SS* Leviathan. By the beginning of September 1918 the bulk of the troops had already arrived in France and were receiving additional training. Between 8 and 10 October, the 7th Division relieved the 90th Division in the Puvenelle sector, the area between Riegnéville-en-Haye and Pont-à-Mousson. Their right flank, on the right bank of the River Moselle, was protected by the African-American 92nd Division. On 27 October, the 7th Division took over part of the front line that had been occupied by the 28th Division. At this time Major General Edmund Wittenmyer took over command from Brigadier General Wahl, who was relieved of his command after just three days.

Brig. Gen. Charles H. Barth.

Maj. Gen. Edmund Wittenmyer.

Early in November the 7th Division began preparations for an assault on the Michel Zone. To keep the pressure on the Germans during the Armistice negotiations, they launched small-scale attacks on the Woëvre Plain, but the main assault was never launched, as hostilities ended on 11 November 1918 with the signing of the Armistice. Nevertheless, the actions of the 7th Division during the last days of the war give us a good insight into the effectiveness of the German defences of the Michel Zone, and show why combined-arms attacks by air force, infantry and armour would play such a major role in future wars.

Saturday 9 November
Overcast and freezing weather.
From 1 to 9 November, the 7th Division was engaged in attacking German outposts almost daily. Orders were issued for major attacks on 10 and 11 November; there were intelligence rumours that the Germans were planning an orderly withdrawal from the Michel Zone to Metz (with its heavily fortified zone) and it was determined that the 7th Division would maintain contact with the Germans. The German line of resistance, from left to right, ran through Charey, Mon Plaisir Farm, the valley of the Rupt-de-Mad Creek north of Rembercourt-sur-Mad and from the spur south of that village all the way to Prény. In some places their line was only fifty metres from the American lines. The American left flank was protected by the 28th Division, the right by the 92nd.

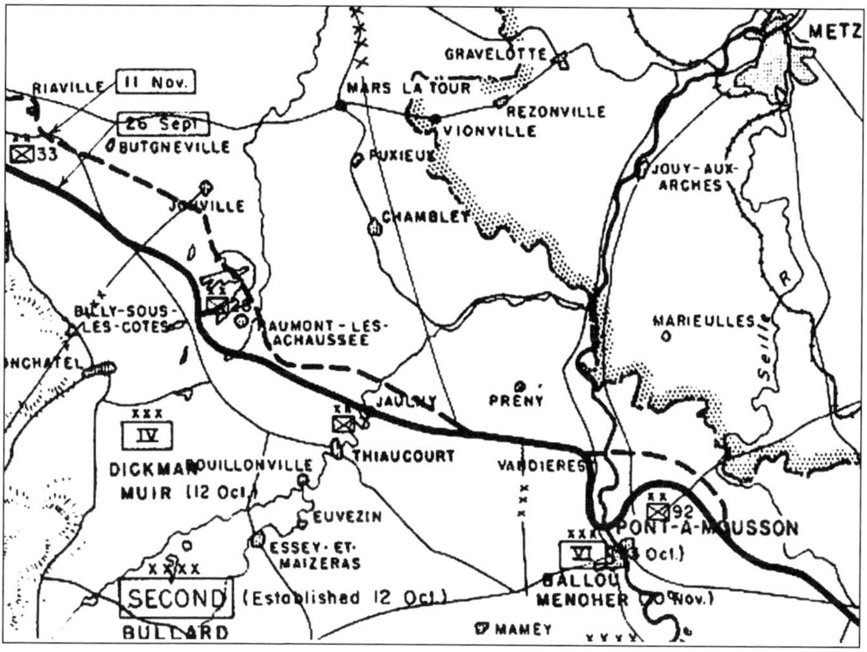

Sector of the 7th Division.

Preparatory attacks, unsupported by either tanks (impossible terrain) or aircraft (unfavourable weather conditions), were made on 9 November, the most significant one being on Prény Ridge. Due to the nature of its topography, these commanding heights were believed to be a key position in the German defences.

The attack started at 8.00 am and was led by the 57th Regiment.

The 7th division resting in Mamey.

Despite occasional sniper and machine-gun-fire, by noon the Americans had made it to the top of the Ridge. Patrols continued to advance and by 3.30 pm, they had reached the outer wire defences of the Michel Zone. As evening fell, the Americans attempted to get through the wire obstacles leading to the German first line trenches. This was exactly the moment the Germans had been waiting for. Caught in the crossfire of machine guns and a thirty-minutes' long artillery barrage, the Americans had no choice but to fall back 300 metres from the Michel Zone.

Sunday 10 November
Overcast and freezing weather.
Major Paul Parker, commanding the 56th Regiment, noted:

> 'Just before daybreak I again gave instructions to enter the Hindenburg [Michel] trenches. This was executed, but by the advance elements only, for as soon as the wire was pierced numerous machine guns, firing from pillboxes, would open up and completely enfilade the trenches and wire. All then fell back to their line and continued to dig. At break of day an enemy plane came over, flew low, and circled over our advanced lines, followed by many flares and rockets. Almost immediately thereafter a very heavy barrage fell on our line and extended to the woods beyond. This included high explosive shrapnel and several kinds of gas. This barrage continued with varying intensity until all companies had withdrawn to their old lines in the woods at 11.45 hours, November 10th.'

No further attempts were made to push forward; without substantial artillery and air support it had proved impossible to break through the German lines.

On the far left of the 7th Division's front, on the heights between Rembercourt-sur-Mad and Trou de la Haye Wood (on modern maps the woods surrounding Côte St-Hubert), it was the same story; after initial gains the attack was broken up by an intense barrage, forcing the Americans back to their start point. The exception was the capture of Hill 323, now in Tête de Buret Wood. Here, with the help of a short artillery barrage, the Americans managed to penetrate the Michel Zone's first line of defences for about 200 metres. In spite of counterattacks and artillery barrages, they managed to hold on to the hill. The 55th Regiment captured five Germans, two minenwerfers (trench mortars) and seven machine guns.

Monday 11 November
Overcast with some rain.
A general attack was planned between Manheulles in the north west and Prény in the south-east. Unfortunately – or, perhaps better, incompetently, there had been no time to thoroughly prepare the infantry units, whilst no preliminary wire cutting had been done. The thinking behind this ill-prepared attack was that the troops would concentrate on weak points in the German defences, catch the defenders by surprise and fight their way through the Michel Zone. It was hoped that by 8.00 am sufficient guns and ammunition would have been assembled to start a three hour barrage. It was decided that the infantry would go over the top at 11.00 am. At 7.40 am the message came through from IV Corps HQ that an armistice

had been signed; hostilities would cease at 11.00 am. With the end of the war imminent, all further operations were cancelled.

It is interesting to speculate – and that is all it is, of course – as to whether the three hour barrage and twice the number of soldiers as previously deployed would have made the crucial difference in helping to achieve a decisive breakthrough in the St. Mihiel zone.

During its thirty-three days on the front line, the 7th Division suffered 1,709 casualties, including 204 killed and 1,505 wounded; the History of the Seventh Division notes that the Germans sent over an average of 720 shells per day on their front (which is not an enormous number by the standards of the Western Front at that time). The Spanish Flu also took its toll on the 7th Division and a number of men died from the disease.

Soldiers of the 7th Division celebrating the Armistice in Jaulny, 11 November 1918.

The 92nd 'Buffalo' Division

The 92nd Division, a National Army Division, commanded by Major General Charles C. Ballou, was organized in October 1917 at Camp Funston, Kansas and Camp Dodge in Iowa. Segregation and racial prejudice were a reality in much of American society and the US Army was certainly no exception. At Camp Dodge a separate Negro Zone was built at the east end of the camp. Black American soldiers were recruited from all over the southern States. To lead this 'all black' division, and as something of an experiment, 104 black captains, 397 first lieutenants, and 125 second lieutenants were trained at a separate 'Negro officers' camp' in Des Moines, Iowa.

Maj. Gen. Charles C. Ballou.

The 92nd Division sailed for France in June 1918; after arriving in France they began ninety days'

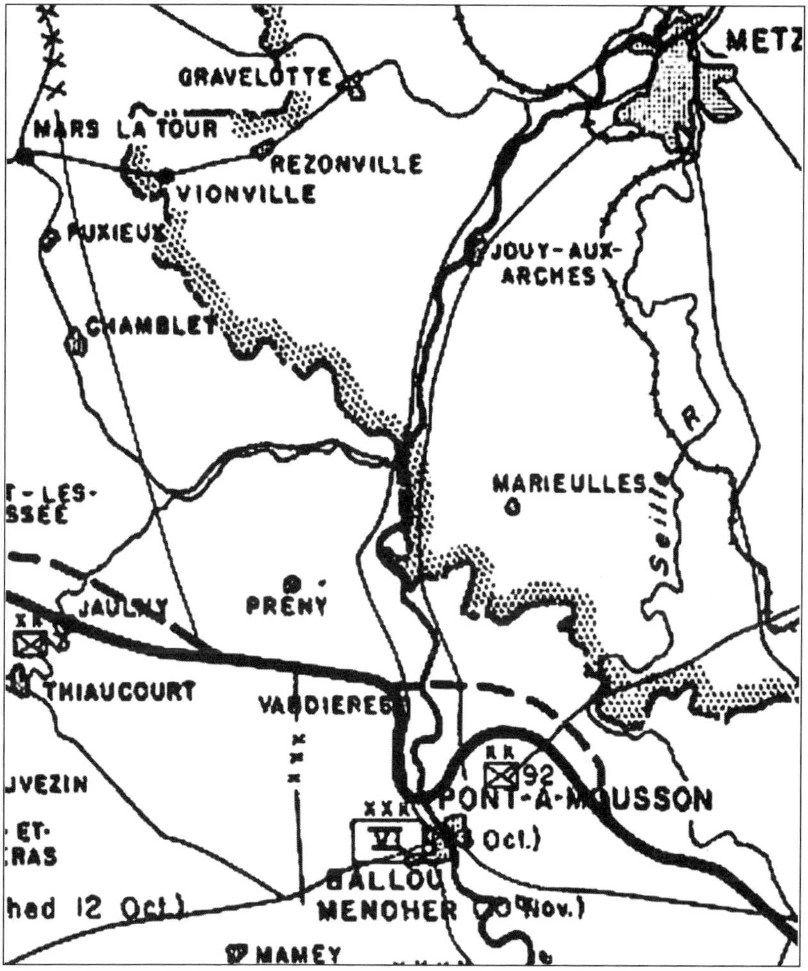

Sector of the 92nd Division.

No. 2498-S-5.

AMERICAN
EXPEDITIONARY FORCES

Corps Expéditionnaires Américains

IDENTITY CARD

CARTE D'IDENTITÉ

Name *Nom* James B. Morris

Rank *Grade* 2nd Lt. Inf.

Duty *Fonction* 3rd Bn Hdqrs. 366th Infantry

Chas. S. Parker

Acting Adjutant General 366 Inf.

Signature of Holder

Signature du Titulaire James B. Morris

ID card of James B. Morris Sr., who was assigned to the 3rd Battalion HQ, 366th Regiment, 92nd Division.

training, thirty days of which were spent with French and British divisions. On 12 August the division was moved to the Vosges region, not far from the Meuse/Woëvre area. The AEF gave the African-American troops all kinds of menial tasks to do (for example, large numbers of them were deployed as labourers in the AEF's ports) but it was very disinclined to allow them to go into action on the field of battle. However, the French and British were crying out for troops and so it was decided the men of the 92nd Division would fight but under French command. As colonial powers, both the French and British armies had a long history of incorporating coloured troops into their orders of battle; many of these colonial troops had the reputation of being fierce fighters.

The 92nd was first deployed in the Argonne. On 26 September 1918, the first day of the Meuse-Argonne Offensive, the men of the 92nd fought their first battle under the command of a French Corps in the area of Binarville. It was far from being a happy experience and the Division was soon withdrawn from the offensive. The reasons for this relative failure are not hard to find and most of them would seem to relate to prejudice and the badly handled matter of officer training. On 9 October, after a period of rest and training, the Division was moved to the St. Mihiel area, where it took over the Marbache sector, a little north of Pont-à-Mousson.

Sunday 10 November
Overcast and freezing weather.
The previous day, at 8.55 pm, the 92nd Division received a telegram from Pershing's HQ that called for immediate action:

> 'The enemy, disorganized, is withdrawing along the entire front. All corps would advance at 7.00 [am], 10 November, and follow the retreating enemy closely. VI Corps (92nd Division) is to push forward west of the [River] Seille along the heights on both banks of the [River] Moselle in the direction of Bouxières, maintaining liaison with the French Army on its right.'

From 3.00 pm and during the night of 9 to 10 November, the troops moved up to their jumping-off lines. Before setting out for the trenches their gas masks had been carefully inspected, as during the previous four weeks the Germans had been liberally shelling the area with mustard and phosgene gas. The 183rd Brigade, composed of the 365th and 366th Regiments, was ordered to advance along the right bank of the River Moselle, to capture Fréhaut and Voivrotte Woods, their first objective, and to continue the advance to Bouxières, Champey-sur-Moselle, Vitonville and Corny, about eight kilometres from their starting point. Contact was to be maintained with the French 165th Division to the right.

At 7.00 am, the African-Americans went over the top. As soon as they started to go down from the hills it became apparent that the German artillery was going to be the main obstacle. In spite of fierce shelling, the 366th managed to take Cheminot Wood, the present-day St. Martin Wood, and prepared to push onto Fréhaut Wood. On the right, the 365th Regiment quickly took Voivrotte Wood but incessant shelling and machine-gun fire forced them to retreat to the southern edge of the woods. At 12.30 pm, when enemy fire slackened off, they made another attempt to take the woods. This attack was more successful; but at 4.30 pm they were blasted out of the woods by effective shelling once more and were again forced to retire to its southern edge. In the meantime, the 366th Regiment on the left had succeeded in taking Fréhaut Wood. Around 4.00 pm orders were received to consolidate their positions; neither regiment made any further attempt to push on. During the evening, patrols were sent out to secure the Champey-Bouxières line and to take advantage of the limited German withdrawal to the Michel Line. Companies were relieved and supplies brought forward.

That night news reached the Allied Headquarters that Emperor Wilhelm II had fled to the Netherlands; Germany was on the brink of collapse. In early November 1918, Wilhelm II was at the military

Jump off positions of the 366th Regiment.

headquarters of his troops in Spa, Belgium. He was unable to return home because of rebellion and revolution in Germany but at the same time was unable to stay in Spa due to the advancing Allied forces. He was advised by those closest to him to flee to a neutral country. The nearest neutral country was the Netherlands. At 6.00 am on 10 November 1918 Wilhelm II arrived at the train station in Eysden on the Dutch border. During her lifetime, Queen Wilhelmina of the Netherlands always claimed (even in her diaries) that the whole affair had been a complete surprise and an embarrassment to her and the Dutch people, but as a neutral country there was no other choice than to grant political asylum. Recently, evidence has emerged that strongly suggests that the whole thing was pre-planned, between the late summer of 1918 and Wilhelm's arrival on 10 November. After the war, Dutch and German diplomats were sensible enough to destroy potentially incriminating evidence, a proverbial smoking gun.

Monday 11 November
Overcast with some rain.
At 3.00 am, the Second Battalion of the 365th Regiment renewed the attack on Voivrotte Wood. This time they managed to take the woods, not encountering opposition. At first light the attack pushed on to Bouxières; but at the southern edge of the village they got caught in a German machine-gun barrage. It appeared that the Germans had worked their way around the flank of the division's attack so that the 2nd Battalion was forced to retreat to the northern edge of Voivrotte Wood. At 9.30 am, they attempted to take the village a second time but were again forced back to the wood; within metres of leaving their trenches the gas alarm was sounded. Gas! Gas! Masks were donned but the attack had lost its momentum.

By now it had become clear that without the aid of substantial artillery and aerial support the heavily garrisoned villages of Champey and Bouxières could not be taken. Serving as outposts of the Michel Zone, the villages were protected by pre-arranged artillery and machine-gun fire. The Germans regularly saturated Fréhaut and Voivrotte Woods with poison gas, which made the going almost impossible; however, this did not stop the African-American soldiers from trying. The fighting went on until 11.00 am and then gradually died down.

Major Warner Ross, 2nd Battalion, 365th Regiment, kept notes about the last hours of the war in his diary:

> 'Not until 10.30 on the morning of 11 November did I receive orders relative to an armistice. The third runner sent out got through to me with a division order. I was in direct command of the principal advancing done in attempts on the tenth and eleventh toward Metz and this was the first definite word I had about the armistice. We had heard that such a thing was expected but I supposed it would be several days, maybe weeks, before it went into effect. We knew that German officers had gone through the lines under a flag of truce to meet representatives of the High Allied Command, but we did not know what the result of those parleys had been. Some thought hostilities would not cease for months. Therefore, imagine our joy in that unbearable shell hole when we found out the war had but thirty minutes to last. Of those with me at that time some shouted for happiness and some stared in amazement, fearing it was too good to be true. I sent the word out to my leaders and sat looking at my watch. Artillery fire increased in intensity and enemy machine gunners elevated their pieces and were spraying the wood with bullets. It would have been hard luck to be hit then. Promptly at

eleven o'clock all fire began to lessen and in a few minutes ceased. The World War had stopped. Not only our men but the Germans also seemed overjoyed. Soon after the buglers had sounded to cease firing the Huns rushed out of their positions and our men met them between the lines. They actually shook hands and slapped each other's backs. I wouldn't believe it if I hadn't seen it.'

In its time in the sector the 92nd Division suffered 959 casualties.

Painted M1917 helmet with the 92nd Buffalo insignia. Very fashionable at the time, insignia were exclusively painted on helmets etc. *after* the war in preparation for the victory parades of 1919.

Car Tour 2

I Corps Area

Duration: A full day's tour
Distance: sixty-five kilometres
Map: IGN 3314 SB - Pont-à-Mousson

This circular tour starts and ends at the church in Thiaucourt (N48°57.263′ E005°51.922′). Petrol stations, supermarkets, restaurants and lunch facilities can be found in Thiaucourt and Pont-à-Mousson. There are no public rest rooms along this route. However, the Thiaucourt American Cemetery is only one kilometre away from the first stop of this tour, and has excellent toilet facilities.

IMPORTANT NOTE: Stop 14 can only be reached by car if it has sufficient bottom clearance, or on foot. Otherwise, continue to stop 17.

NOTE: The Musée du Costume Militaire (N48°57.171′ E005°25.000′) in Thiaucourt is not included in the tour because if its restricted opening hours. Nontheless, it is very worthwhile to visit. Open from 1 April to 11 November, only on Thursdays and every second Sunday of the month from 10 am to 4 pm. Free admission, but please donate generously to make sure the collection stays open to the public. Contact: musee.thiaucourt@pages14-18.com

The tour is designed to cover the general area of the attack as fought by I Corps, commanded by Major General Dickman. From left to right, the 2nd, 5th, 90th and 82nd Divisions were involved. I Corps was part of the First Army, commanded by General Pershing. The 7th and 92nd Divisions occupied the sector during last weeks of the war. From 12 October, the divisions occupying the Mihiel sector became part of the Second Army, commanded by Major General Bullard.

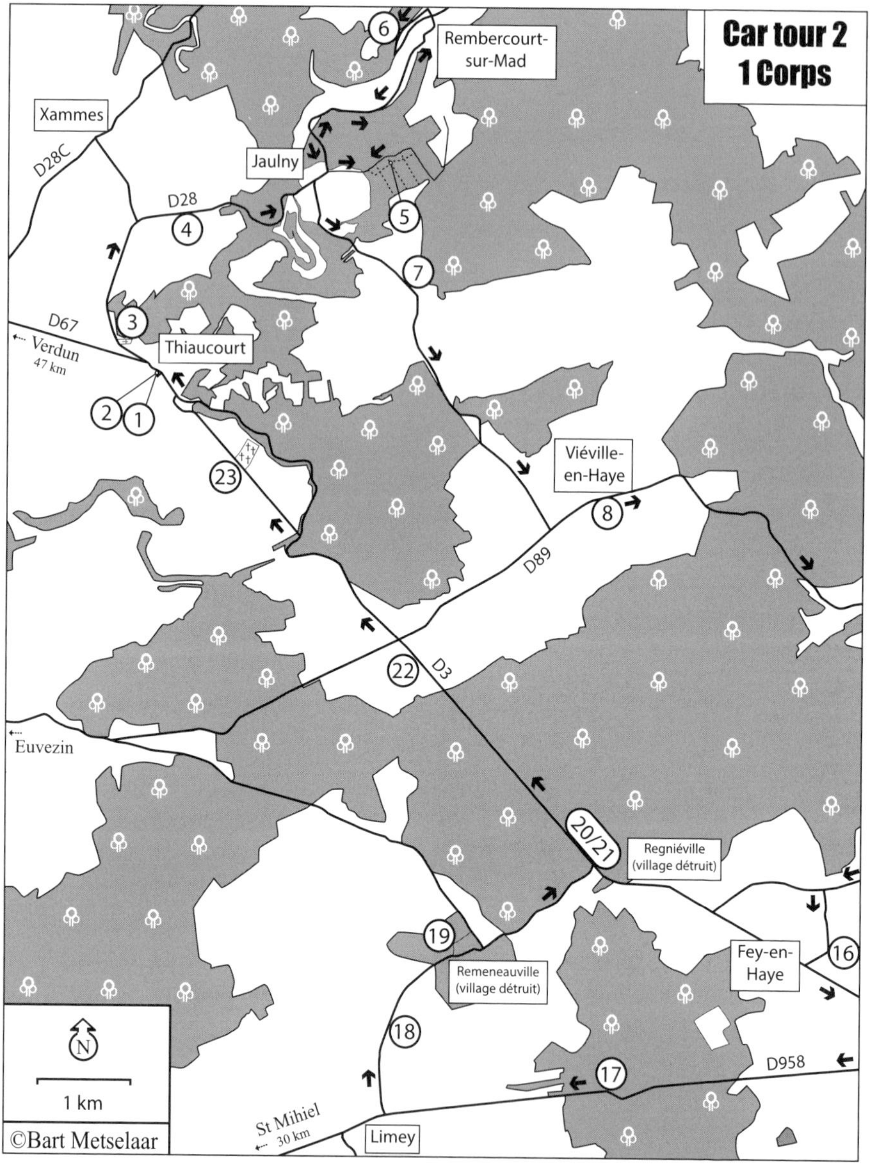

GPS coordinates Car Tour 2

(1) Captain Cunningham Memorial (N48°57.263′ E005°51.922′)
(2) Monument aux Morts (N48°57.243′ E005°51.934′)
(3) Thiaucourt Communal Cemetery (N48°57.424′ E005°51.661′)
(4) US 2nd Division Boulder (N48°58.126′ E005°52.179′)
(5) Cunningham temporary grave site (N48°58.401′ E005°53.913′)

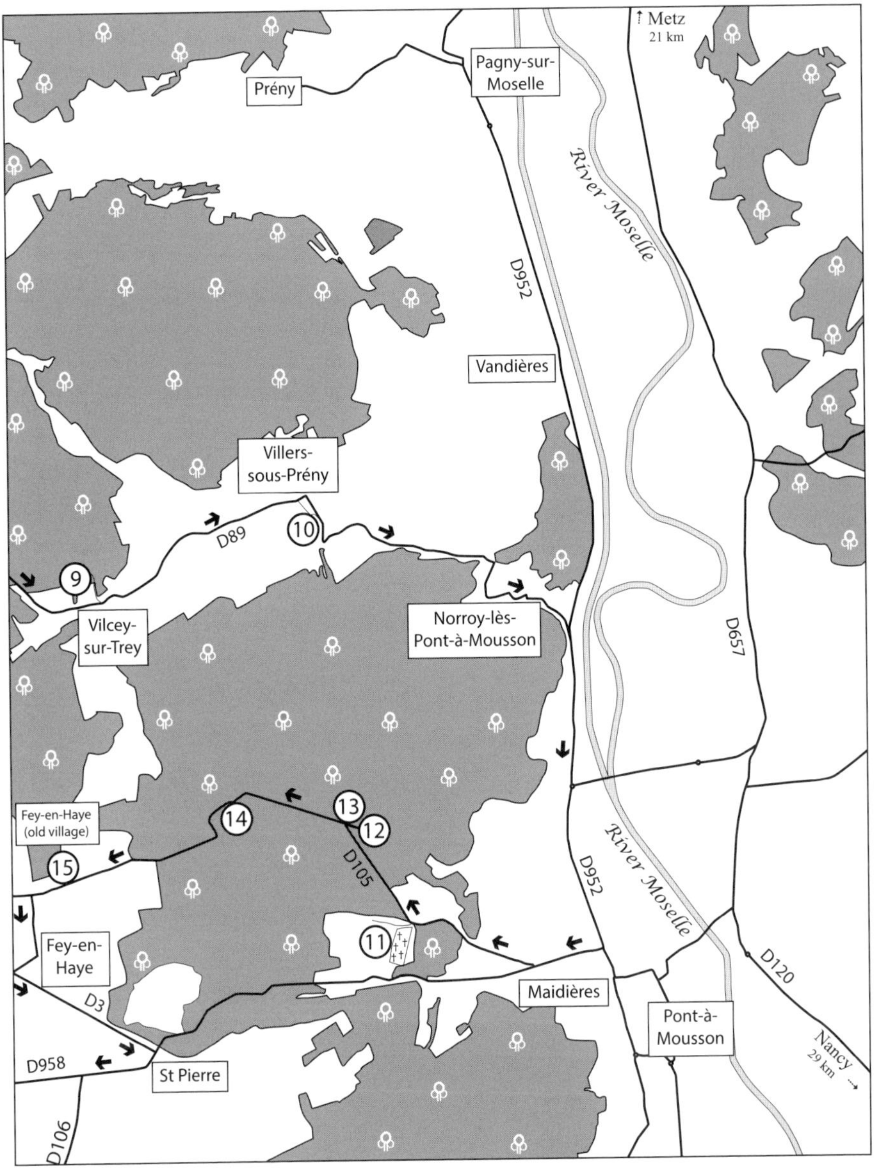

(6) German Cemetery Rembercourt (N48°59.105′ E005°53.980′)
(7) Panorama Jaulny (N49°57.781′ E005°54.009′)
(8) 5th Division Monument (N48°56.591′ E005°55.741′)
(9) German Lion Monument (N48°56.333′ E005°58.360′)
(10) Dominion Airmen (N48°56.517′ E006°00.068′)
(11) Montauville French Cemetery (N48°54.299′ E006°00.829′)
(12) Père Hilarion (N48°54.829′ E006°00.444′)

(13) Borne Vauthier (N48°54.856′ E006°00.327′)
(14) Croix des Carmes+trenches (N48°54.979′ E005°59.339′)
(15) Feye-en-Haye, village detruit (N48°54.530′ E005°57.872′)
(16) Feye-en-Haye, church (N48°54.177′ E005°57.703′)
(17) US 5th Division Monument (N48°53.383′ E005°55.833′)
(18) US 2nd Division Boulder (N48°53.797′ E005°53.953′)
(19) Remenauville distroyed village (N48°54.134′ E005°54.483′)
(20) Regnièville village detruit (N48°54.626′ E005°55.676′)
(21) US 5th Division Monument (N48°54.626′ E005°55.676′)
(22) German bunker (N48°55.753′ E005°54.104′)
(23) Thiaucourt German Cemetery (N48°56.755′ E005°52.648′)

Captain Cunningham.

Park in the parking space on the right side of the Thiaucourt church but note that you are only allowed to park for five minutes. On the right of the church doors, a bronze plaque has been dedicated to **Captain Cunningham (1)** (N48°57.263′ E005°51.922′). Besides the plaque (note the WW2 shell damage), business colleagues of Oliver's father provided funds for a special set of bells, hung in memory of Captain Cunningham. The original bells had been melted down by the Germans for metal during the war. The new bells were dedicated on 30 May 1924. The church was rebuilt in 1918 after suffering significant damage. A metal plaque inside the church states the bells dedication to the memory of Captain Cunningham. Mrs. Cunningham donated money to the town and for 'the reconstruction of the town hall that had been reduced to rubble.'

Church at Thiaucourt. Note the WW2 shell damage.

Captain Oliver Baty Cunningham, 15th Field Artillery, 2nd Division, was born on 17 September 1894 in Chicago, Illinois, the only child of Frank Simpson Cunningham and Lucy Eleanor Baty Cunningham. In 1913, Oliver Cunningham entered Yale University. He also served as a member of the Yale Battery and as an artillery private in the Connecticut National Guard in 1916. Before the first selective service registration took place on 5 June 1917, Cunningham had already enrolled in an officers' training course at Fort Sheridan, Lake County, Illinois and received a commission as a second lieutenant in the Field Artillery. He would later rise to the rank of captain. On 12 December, 1917, he sailed for France with the 15th Field Artillery, a unit of the 2nd Division. After training in France, the unit took part in several major battles, including Château Thierry and Belleau Wood, before being deployed in the St. Mihiel Sector. On 17 September 1918, on his twenty fourth birthday, Lieutenant Cunningham was killed by mortar fire near the village of Jaulny, France. The day after his death his captain's commission arrived, dated 11 September. Cunningham was hastily buried in a makeshift grave near the scene of his death. In 1922, his body was exhumed and reburied in Thiaucourt American Cemetery, plot C, row 13, grave 18. Cunningham was posthumously awarded both the Distinguished Service Cross (DSC) and the Silver Star.

To the left of the church stands the **Monument aux Morts (2)** (N48°57.243′ E005°51.934′). Monuments like this usually depict a French soldier in a heroic pose and commemorates the people that died for France. The monument in Thiaucourt, however, is dedicated to the people of Thiaucourt and to the American 2nd and 89th Divisions who liberated the town. The bronze statue shows a French as well as an American soldier (allegedly Cunningham) shaking hands, symbolizing the friendship between the two nations. The shell damage, clearly visible at the bottom of the monument and on the church walls, dates from September 1944, when the Germans were retreating to the River Moselle. The monument was dedicated on 8 November 1925.

Peter's headstone at the St. Mihiel American Cemetery, plot C/29/5.

Take the D3, the Rue Carnot, in the direction of Verdun. After about 100 metres, take the right fork onto the D28, direction Jaulny. Take the second road on the right and park in front of the **Thiaucourt Communal Cemetery (3)** (N48°57.424′ E005°51.661′). There are two interesting headstones in this cemetery. The first is of Eleanor Bradley-Peters, who has been buried to the right of the entrance gate. After the war, she and her husband moved to France. They lived six months of the year in Toul, some forty kilometres from

Thiaucourt and the other six months near Saint Tropez. Born on 6 July 1855, (incorrectly engraved 1865) in Southborough, Worcester County, Massachusetts, USA, Mrs Bradley-Peters stated in her will that after her death her body should be buried in Thiaucourt, Communal Cemetery in France.

The reason for this is that her son, First Lieutenant Edward McClure Peters Jr., commander of the Company B, Machine Gun Battalion, 16th Regiment, 1st Division, had been killed during a reconnaissance mission in Seicheprey on 11 March 1918. Born on Christmas Day 1892, he was only twenty-five years old when he was killed. He is buried in Thiaucourt American Cemetery, Plot C Row 29 Grave 5. First Lieutenant Peters and his mother have a cenotaph at his father's grave at Forest Hills Cemetery in Jamaica Plain, Suffolk County, Massachusetts.

War Memorial in Thiaucourt.

First Lieutenant Edward McClure Peters Jr.

First Lieutenant Peters and his mother have a cenotaph at his father's grave at Forest Hills Cemetery in Jamaica Plain, Suffolk County, Massachusetts.

Headstone of Eleanor Bradley-Peters.

The second headstone, situated along the central path, is that of a British soldier, Private Thomas John Kite, 1st Grenadier Guards. Son of William and Mary Jane Kite, he was born at Marshfield, Cardiff. Kite died on 8 December 1918, a probable victim of the Spanish flu pandemic of 1918-1920, which killed from two to five times (estimates vary widely) as many people as the war in a much shorter time. After the Armistice a British division, the 9th (Scottish), moved through the American line to get to the Cologne Bridgehead as part of the British Army of Occupation. The exact reason why he is buried here, is not clear. However, there are two other British soldiers, Private J. Brown, Royal Scots and Private T. Downie, Durham Light Infantry buried in La Glorieux French National Cemetery near Verdun; both died around the same time in December 1918 and more than likely from the same cause i.e. disease. Since the Guards Division (of which 1/Grenadiers was a part) did not come down this far south, other options, such as the possibility that he was a staff officer's orderly, come to mind. For the moment his presence here remains a puzzle.

Go back to the D28 and make a right turn in the direction of Jaulny. Halfway to Jaulny, on the right side of the road, stands the American **2nd Division Boulder (4)** (N48°58.126′ E005°52.179′). Erected soon after the Armistice, several of these monuments have been placed along the lines of advance of the 2nd Division. Originally, there used to be a copper information panel bolted to the monuments, but they have long gone. This boulder commemorates the furthest point of advance on 12 September. The first soldiers of the 2nd Division reached this point at about 1.00 pm and liberated Jaulny. Subjected to German shellfire, Jaulny was abandoned and retaken by the Germans. However, the Germans found the village untenable and retreated to the Michel Zone a day later.

Second Division boulder.

Continue along the D28 and drive to Jaulny. Just at the point of leaving Jaulny, the communal cemetery is right in front of you. Park your car and continue on foot along the track that runs along the edge of the forest. In dry weather conditions and if your car has sufficient clearance, it is possible to drive to where the track disappears into the forest. From here, continue 300 metres on foot until you are at the third trail on your right hand. At the time of writing, a small sign fixed to a tree (see photo) points to the right. Also note the sign '25'. A steep climb leads you to **Cunningham's temporary grave site (5)** (N48°58.401′ E005°53.913′). This is the approximate site where Cunningham was killed on 17 September 1918. Hastily buried in a temporary grave, his body was exhumed in 1922 and reburied in Thiaucourt. The memorial was erected soon thereafter and restored in 1996. An information panel in French explains the origin of the memorial. The site is well maintained, which is quite a surprise given its isolated location.

Cunningham's original grave site.

Stay on the D28 and continue to Rembercourt-sur-Mad. Cross the bridge and take a left at the T-junction, the Rue du Moulin. After about 300 metres take the right fork and drive uphill to the **German Cemetery (6)** (N48°59.105′ E005°53.980′), which is immediately adjacent (on the far side) to the communal cemetery. This cemetery, unique on the Western Front, still holds more than fifty per cent of its original

When you see this rather hidden indicator, turn right.

headstones and the original concrete borders are still in place. The son of the original owner of the land said the Germans paid fifteen centimes for every grave.

The village lies right in the middle of the Michel Zone and, because of its sheltered position in the valley, the proximity of the German border and its railway connection, was an ideal site for an army camp. The headstones in the cemetery date from 1915 to 1917 and indicate that the dead came from a variety of units.

Period photo of Rembercourt German Cemetery.

Conveniently for the present-day visitor, the cemetery has recently (2015) been cleared of many trees and undergrowth by local Great War enthusiasts; however, the entrance gate is locked. There is a solution: facing the cemetery, walk along the left wall; the left corner at the back the wall is low enough, with a little effort and care, to step over. Although the bodies have been removed and reburied in Thiaucourt German Cemetery, remember that you enter consecrated ground and that it should be treated as such.

Rembercourt was not taken during the St. Mihiel Offensive. The Mad Valley, from Rembercourt to the River Moselle, served as an outpost for the Michel Zone. After the offensive, this area was regularly subjected to shelling. Consequently, by 11 November, the village had been partly destroyed by the American artillery.

Drive back to Jaulny. After a 90° bend to the right in the D28, you see the first houses of the village appear. Take the first road on the left, the Grande Rue, and make a note of the beautiful war memorial. Take the third road to the left and continue uphill. At the highest point, stop at the side of the road. Step out of your car and turn around, direction Jaulny. Look at the **Panorama (7)** (N49°57.781′ E005°54.009′) of the battlefield and the useful orientation points.

Carry on to Viéville-en-Haye and turn left onto the D89. On the right, standing on the pavement beside the road, just before you leave the village, you will see the **5th Division Memorial (8)** (N48°56.591′ E005°55.741′). Like the 2nd Division, the 5th Division placed several monuments along their route of advance. The obelisks were also fitted with a copper information panel that, like the ones on the boulder, have disappeared over time in most cases. However, the one in Viéville has retained its panel, probably because the obelisk is within the village. *Captured by the 5th US Div in the St. Mihiel drive* [the Americans rarely, if ever, refer to an 'offensive' but rather talk of a 'drive'], *Sept 12th 1918. On this day the front line of the 5th Div was established about three kilometres north of this point.*

Fifth Division Memorial.

Leave the village and drive to Vilcey-sur-Trey. About one hundred metres before you enter the village, on the left side of the road, stands a sign that reads: *14-18 Monument du Lion*. Turn left, and follow the track until you see a big barn. Park here and continue on foot; the trail is signposted and starts on the right of the track. After about 500 metres (much of which is bordered on the right by a wire fence), you will

come to the **German Lion Monument (9)** (N48°56.333′ E005°58.360′), up on higher ground to the left. Inaugurated on 21 November 1915, the monument is dedicated to the 241th Infantry Brigade, which lost 7,000 men killed during the fighting in Priest Wood (Bois du Prêtre) between October 1914 and August 1915. The monument was designed by Lieutenant Wortmann and Corporal Schrader of the 60th Machine Gun Company. It has been said that Brigade General von Eberhard's (1855-1939) speech was barely audible because of the roar of the guns and exploding shells in Priest Wood, only 1,500 metres away. There are useful explanatory panels.

Brigade General von Eberhard.

Period photograph of the German 241st Infantry Monument.

Return to the D89 and continue via Vilcey to Villers-sous-Prény. Here, behind the church, lie the graves of four **Dominion Airmen (10)** (N48°56.517′ E006°00.068′) who were killed in the Second World War. On the evening of 24 February 1944, RAAF (Royal Australian Air Force) Lancaster bomber J for Jig took off from an airfield in Lincolnshire. On board was a crew of seven young men: five Australians and two

WW2 Commonwealth headstones in Villers-sous-Prény.

Scots, whose mission was to bomb ball bearing factories that were concentrated in Schweinfurt, Germany. These factories were very important for the German war effort as ball bearings are used for almost anything that has an engine or wheels. But J for Jig never reached its target. It was shot down in the night skies over France and crashed not far from Villers. Three airmen survived the crash and went into captivity; the rest of the crew were buried by the Germans. In 2018, Mike Colman wrote a book about these airmen: *Crew: The Story of the Men Who Flew RAAF Lancaster J for Jig*.

Continue along the D88 (this road is in bad condition and very narrow, however, this does not seem to impress the locals, who still often drive excessively fast) via Norroy-lès-Pont-à-Mousson to Maidières (D952). Once in Maidières, take the D958, direction St. Mihiel. After about one kilometre, take the D105 on your right. The exit is indicated by the sign *Secteur de Fey-Bois le Prêtre.* The route takes you through the suburbs of Madières. After two kilometres you reach a T-junction; the left fork takes you to the **Montauville French Cemetery (11)** (N48°54.299′ E006°00.829′). This concentration cemetery was originally started at the end of 1914 during the terrible fighting in Bois de Prêtre, Priest Wood, but now holds burials from both world wars. The cemetery was extended between 1920 and 1936 to accommodate the remains of soldiers exhumed from isolated graves and temporary military cemeteries. Between 1963-1965, the site was redeveloped for French prisoners of war who had died in Germany and Austria. In all, 13,519 soldiers are buried here, in individual graves or in mass graves. There are also a number of Russian (Second World War) burials.

French cemetery in Montauville.

Continue along the D105 to Priest Wood. After two kilometres, you will see on your right **Père Hilarion's house (12)** (N48°54.829′ E006°00.444′). Park in the parking area next to the house. The house and spring owe their name to a hermit that lived on this site between 1830-1840. The hermit inherited the name from St. Hilarion, an ascetic from the 3rd and 4th century who was a disciple of St. Antoine, a religious hermit living in Egypt.

Père Hilarion's house in Priest Woods, 1915.

The Père Hilarion house in 2019.

From 1915 to 1917, Hilarion's house was home to the preparation of a trench newspaper, *Le Mouchoir* (The Handkerchief). Many of the men who wrote for the paper were stretcher bearers; they were amongst the best informed on the battlefield because of the nature of their job; they maintained contact with both soldiers and officers. By 1917 the house was completely destroyed by shellfire. NOTE: The water from the well is drinkable and very pleasant; many people come here with water containers to take it home. It also makes a pleasant spot for a picnic.

Borne Vauthier marking the Germans' furthest point of advance.

Leave Father Hilarion's house and drive uphill. At the T-junction there is a brown stone memorial on the right, a demarcation stone, the **Borne Vauthier (13)** (N48°54.856′ E006°00.327′). It marks, give or take, the furthest point of the German advance in this sector. Many of these monuments can still be found along the Western Front. It was the French sculptor, Paul Moreau-Vauthier, who served in the French army during the war and who saw action at the Battle of Verdun, who came up with the idea of these monumental marker stones in 1920. Ninety-eight of them were put in place in France but twenty-four have been destroyed, mainly casualties of the Second World War; a large number of the others have been moved nearby as a result of road improvements or layout changes.

OPTIONAL EXTENSION

Not included in the tour, but well worth the time to take a look if you have the time. The fork to the right leads to the 356th Regiment Monument, a pillbox, several large craters and a trench system. If the barrier is open, you can go by car (but it can be a rough track in places); otherwise, be prepared for a 700 metre walk. What is important is that it is yet another indicator, if one were needed, of the intensive fighting that took place in the wood.

NOTE: Stop 14 can only be reached if your car has good ground clearance; on the other hand the track is solid, if very – and often deeply - potholed. Otherwise, continue on foot for one kilometre, and walk back to your vehicle. Back at the car, continue to stop 17, and visit stop 15 and 16 after stop 21, see map.

The left fork takes you to the **Croix des Carmes (14)** (N48°54.979′ E005°59.339′). The Cross of the Carmelites was erected by veterans who

Monument to the French 351st Infantry Regiment.

fought in Priest Wood and was inaugurated by former President (1913-1920) and then Senator Raymond Poincaré (1860-1934), on 23 September 1923. The monument is dedicated to the French soldiers who were killed in the woods during the terrific fighting of 1914 and 1915. The estimates are that on top of this ridge and in a period of eight months a stupefying 14,000 French and German soldiers were killed and 44,000 wounded; 3,500 soldiers just disappeared, atomised by shellfire. Fortunately the fighting gradually died out after August 1915. Like elsewhere on the Western Front, fixed lines were established and for the rest of the war this hell on earth became a relatively quiet sector. On both sides, deep underground shelters were built and No Man's Land was defended by massive belts of barbed wire.

President and then Senator Raymond Poincaré (1860-1934).

Tenches, bunkers and barbed wire in Priest Wood.

Croix aux Carmes Monument remembering the French that were killed in Priest Wood.

Behind the Carmes Monument you can still find impressive trench systems, tunnels, bunkers and barbed wire defences. If you have some time to spare and at your own risk, it would be well worth your time to explore the area more extensively. **NOTE**: Do not pick up anything that do not recognize as harmless and certainly do not touch unexploded ordnance. Rusty metal, such as barbed wire, is also an ideal breeding ground for tetanus.

Continue for another 200 metres; at the T-junction turn right. After two kilometres, you will come to **Fey-en-Haye, a *village détruit* (15)** (N48°54.530′ E005°57.872′). Dating from 856AD, the village was completely razed to the ground during the fighting of 1914 and 1915, one of three villages in the area that suffered the same fate. In 1914 Fey had 132 inhabitants, coming from forty-two families and occupying fifty-seven houses. The village had a hotel, a bar and a church; ninety-five per cent of the land was used to grow cereal crops, potatoes and beetroot.

On 5 September 1914, the French defenders were overrun by the

Feye-en-Haye, destroyed village.

Feye-en-Haye, early 1915.

German 8th Bavarian Brigade. On 20 September, the Germans launched a new offensive with the aim of taking the Woëvre Plains and the Meuse Heights. This offensive was very successful, but also marked the start of numerous military operations. The French wanted to take back the lost ground, while the Germans were looking for more favourable positions to establish their defences. At the end of 1915 the villages of Fey, Remenauville and Regniéville simply had ceased to exist. In 1918, engineers of the 5th and 90th Divisions used the stone from the villages as raw material for road works. The last remains of Fey were reused in the construction of the new village, some distance off, in the early 1920s. Today, a few stones mark the site of the belfry, whilst a monument,

Stained glass window of the rebuilt church of Fey-en-Haye.

War Memorial in Fey-en-Haye.

unveiled on 22 September 1924, to remember the fallen stands on the former village square.

Keep the monument on your left and carry on to Fey, which is located at about a kilometre from the old, destroyed village. Park at the Mairie, opposite the **Fey-en-Haye Church (16)** (N48°54.177′ E005°57.703′). The beautiful stained glass windows depict the inauguration of the Carmes Monument in Priest Wood; the Carmes Monument is on the left and former President Raymond Poincaré is on the right window. Inside the church stands a remarkable monument; a six metres high bullet and shell riddled **tree from Priest Wood.**

This three hundred year old oak tree is the last remaining tree from Priest Wood. Since

The last original shell-damaged tree still standing in Priest Wood in 2007.

1918 a monument in its own right, it stood behind the Carmes monument (see Stop 14) until 2005 and has been visited by tens of thousands of people. By 2005 the condition of the tree was such that it was decided to cut it down and to preserve it. After the tree had been dried out for over a year, the conservation process started and took several months to complete. Finally, in a huge padded wooden crate, the six metres long mastodon was transported to the church in the new village, the only one in the Priest Wood sector that has been rebuilt although not on its original site. Finally, on 30 June 2007, the tree was placed in a niche at the back of the church. The whole operation was financed by the city of Pont-à-Mousson. To the left of the tree, an altar is dedicated to the French 73th and 128th Regiments, who suffered terrible losses during the fighting in the Wood.

The preserved tree in the church of Fey-en-Haye.

NOTE: The church is locked, but local historian Jean Paul David is the key holder. He lives in Fey and, at the time of writing, can be reached by a cell phone, 0033-662056064.

Take a right turn onto the D3b. At the T-junction, take a left onto the D3. Turn right at the next T-junction. After five kilometres, situated on the right side of the road, you see the **US 5th Division Monument (17)** (N48°53.383′ E005°55.833′). Carry on for about fifty meters and park your car. This obelisk was erected in the 1920s to mark the spot where, on 12 September 1918, one of the Division's brigade headquarters was located. The start line of the 5th Division is approximately along the D958. There were no trees left standing in this No Man's Land and there were blasted trenches and rusted belts of barbed wire everywhere. It was here that companies were to assemble before the attack. Because of the terrible weather the whole area was changed into a morass; it proved impossible to bring tanks to the front.

Fifth Division Monument.

About a kilometre north the Germans were hiding in their shelters; in spite of the terrible conditions underfoot, the Americans quickly overran their positions.

Continue along the D958 to Limey, another village that was completely destroyed during the war. Limey was the starting point for the 2nd Division; their first goal was to take Eiche Woods, about five kilometres to the north. The ultimate objective was the village of Thiaucourt.

On 12 September, Warren R. Jackson, 6th Marine Regiment, noted

> 'Day was now breaking and we began moving up the road toward a village. When we drew nearer we found it to be only the remains of a village. As well as I remember now, there was not a house that had all of its roof, and many walls were blown away entirely. This little town of Limey had been on the outer edge of the line that had not shifted for four years of war. Other troops besides us were in the shattered village, and the ground was covered with raincoats that had been dropped by men preparing to go over and who wanted to rid themselves of all surplus baggage. Now and then a shell came over, striking some distance from us in, perhaps, a distant part of the village. Just ahead, at the front head of a shattered wall, was an entrance to an 'abre'[*abri*, a shelter] with a Red Cross above it. The place was doubtless already crowded.'

Once in Limey, take a right turn onto the D75. After about a kilometre, you will see the (recently repainted, 2019) **US 2nd Division Boulder (18)** (N48°53.797′ E005°53.953′) on the right side of the road. As usual, the

Second Division boulder.

copper plaque has been removed by vandals. However, this spot marks the German first line, taken at first daylight on 12 September by the soldiers of the 2nd Division.

A little bit further along the same road there is a signpost that directs you to **Remenauville destroyed village (19)** (N48°54.134′ E005°54.483′). This is one of the three villages (See Stop 14) that were blown from the face of the earth during the fighting in 1914-1915. Between 13 and 16 September the Americans used the rubble of the village to repair the roads so that supplies could reach the front.

Destroyed Remenauville under German occupation, 1915.

An interesting point, detailed on one of the excellent explanatory plaques, is that this area was classified as lying in the Red Zone by the law of 17 April 1919, because the cost of rehabilitating the land was greater than its pre-war value. The land was bought back from the local population in 1923 by the French Government and was handed over to the Forestry Commission in 1925. The hand-over was subject to a set of

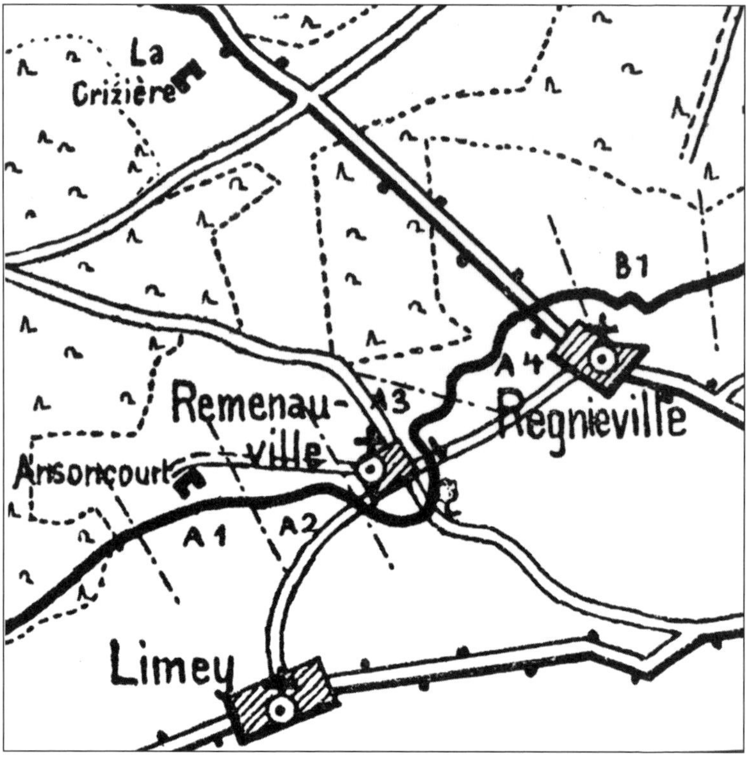

Front line in 1915, Regniéville and Remenauville.

restrictions that obliged the Forestry Commission to retain the foundations of the buildings, trenches and shelters. The chapel was built over the ruins of the old parish church in the 1930s. As late as 1998 the village streets were marked out and cleared of undergrowth. At the time of writing (June 2019) a series of well-made information panels explain the history of the old parish church.

Return to the main road, the D75, and carry on to **Regniéville destroyed village (20)** (N48°54.626′ E005°55.676′). Park on the other side of the D3. There are several monuments on this site. A short walk (ten minutes) along the ruins of Regniéville starts from here. The villages share the same

Regniéville before the war; it was never rebuilt.

Monument to the French 302nd Infantry Regiment.

history as explained at Stops 14 and 18, and its history is very well explained (in English) on information panels on the site.

A special monument, although not unique in design, is the US **5th Division Monument (21)** (N48°54.626′ E005°55.676′) that stands at the side of the D3. Like the other 5th Division monuments, the obelisk was erected in the early 1920s. However, this one has plaques remembering two world wars. The small marble square plaque, a replacement for the original copper information panel, simply reads '5th Infantry Division US Army 12 September 1918'. It commemorates the fact that on the morning of 12 September the 5th Division's jump-off line started from this point.

Unfortunately, Europe needed a Second World War to reach some sort of stability and again the Americans were involved. In September 1944, the 5th Division, now part of Patton's Third Army, once more liberated

Fifth Division Monument in Regniéville.

this part of France from the Germans. This plaque reads: *September-October 1944. 5th Infantry Division assigned this sector after 700 mile drive from Normandy beaches. First breach of Moselle River defenses made by 5th Infantry Division, September 1944.*

Continue along the D34 in the direction of Thiaucourt. Just before the point where the D3-D89 cross stands a **German observation bunker (22)** (N48°55.753′ E005°54.104′). If you decide to visit the bunker take a right turn onto the D89, direction Viéville-en-Haye, and park at the side of the road – there is usually firm ground on the right. The observation bunker is part of the outer defences of the Michel Zone; another one can be seen in the middle of the field on the other side of the D3.

There are apertures in all directions and it has a clear field of observation. Remember, in 1918 there were no trees left standing and because of its elevated position (+320 metres) it could observe the American lines with ease. Limey, for example, was built on a ridge that was twenty metres lower. The observation posts were camouflaged and had heated living quarters below ground level. This particular one shows serious shell damage on the southern aperture. Endless reconnaissance sorties had been flown by French and American pilots to document the German defences and artillery positions, so looking at the damage done it is not unlikely that this bunker was hit in the course of the preliminary bombardment during the night of 11-12 September 1918.

Return to your car and take the D3 to Thiaucourt. After two kilometres, take a left turn onto the D3c; the exit is marked by the sign **Thiaucourt German Cemetery (23)** (N48°56.755′ E005°52.648′). Park in front of the cemetery. This concentration cemetery was started by the Germans in 1914 and was extended by the French military authorities after the war. It became the last resting place of German war dead exhumed from sixty-five temporary cemeteries in a radius of some thirty

German observation bunker.

kilometres. Landscaping was carried out from 1926 to 1928. In this period, 340 trees were planted and the cemetery was surrounded by a stone wall.

German dead from the 1870 war were reburied here. They are buried at the left back corner of the cemetery. In 1974, the original wooden crosses were replaced by the present metal crosses. In total there are 11,685 German dead buried in the cemetery.

The German cemetery at Thiaucourt.

Walk 2

Vilcey-sur-Trey, Stumpf and Quelle Lager

Duration: Half a day's tour
Distance: four kilometres
Map: IGN 3314 SB, Pont-à-Mousson

The tour starts and ends in Vilcey-sur-Trey, and concentrates on a German convalescent and rest camp for soldiers located in a valley in Vanchères Wood. From 14 September 1918, after the area was cleared of Germans, the camp was used as a regimental HQ by the 64th and 56th Regiments of the US 7th Division. The first two stops can be reached by car, the other stops on foot only.

Certain parts of the route are likely to be **extremely muddy and wet** throughout the year. Wellington boots as well as a good flash light are advised. In Vilcey there are no shopping or refuelling facilities, nor public toilets. Make sure you that you bring everything you need for a picnic e.g. food, water, snacks.

NOTE: Entering holes and tunnels can be **extremely** dangerous. The two large bunkers at stop (6) and (7) are easy accessible, but are entered at your own risk. Keep away from unexploded ordnance.

GPS coordinates Walk 2

(1) Kühlewein Brunnen	(N48°55.742′ E005°57.580′)
(2) Moulin de Jaillard	(N48°55.655′ E005°57.498′)
(3) German Altar	(N48°55.591′ E005°57.257′)
(4) Dugout	(N48°55.688′ E005°57.180′)
(5) Dugout	(N48°55.638′ E005°57.044′)
(6) Command Post bunker	(N48°55.580′ E005°56.875′)
(7) Medical bunker/Kandler Brunnen	(N48°55.570′ E005°56.849′)
(8) Pütter Quelle	(N48°55.566′ E005°56.772′)
(9) Oidtmann Quelle	(N48°55.612′ E005°56.564′)
(10) Dreieck Brunnen	(N48°55.637′ E005°56.500′)
(11) Underground shelters	(N48°55.819′ E005°56.201′)

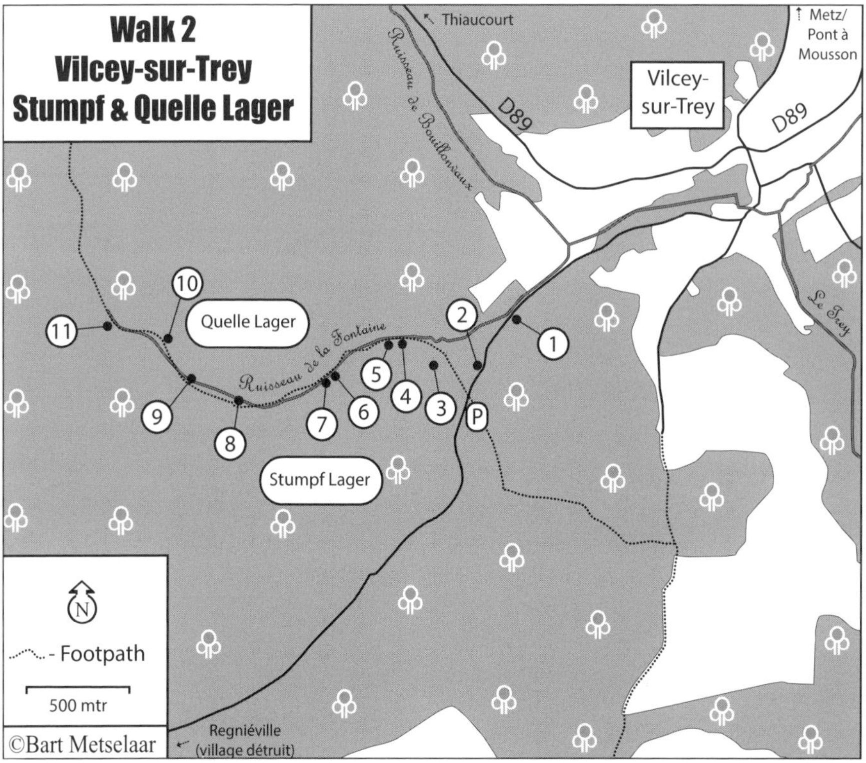

All along the Western Front, on both sides of the wire, hundreds of thousands of soldiers needed billeting. In 1914, in the Meuse and Woëvre area, the inhabitants of the villages close to the front were simply evacuated and their homes taken over by German officers. Barns, shacks and tents became the billets of the ordinary foot soldier and gunner. As villages close to the front became more and more subjected to shellfire, barrack camps were established a few kilometres behind the front. Closer to the front, sheltered valleys were transformed into rest camps. An important condition in determining the location of a camp was accessibility to running water, ie a creek or a well. Over the years, especially on the German side, these camps became more elaborate, often with richly decorated bunkers and dugouts; they even grew vegetables and flowers. The dwellings were fitted with window panes, electric lighting and wood burners. Soldiers not only used china and cutlery taken from the deserted villages, but also cupboards, beds, tables and armchairs; even pianos were lugged in to the camps.

A good example of a German rest camp, although now in ruins, is the Stumpf Lager or Quelle (Source/Spring) Lager. The camp is built in Vanchères Wood, renamed Stumpf Wood by the Germans. The origin of

Germans in Vilcey; note the French trench mortar round in the foreground.

American Signal Corps photo of the Stumpf Lager, September 1918.

this name remains unknown. Quelle Lager was built opposite Stumpf Lager and was named after the seemingly countless springs. One well-known visitor to the camp was the famous post-war German writer, thinker and journalist Ernst Jünger (1895-1998). *Storm of Steel*, his book about his experiences in the war, became world famous. It was the second time Jünger was in the area; in 1915, the 73rd Fusilier Regiment, 111th Division, suffered serious losses during the fighting at Les Éparges. From 20 August to 14 October 1917 the division was rested and reorganized and it was during this period that Jünger paid a visit to the Quelle Lager.

Coming from the direction of Vieville-en-Haye along the D89, drive to the village centre of Vilcey. The road to the camp is signposted by 'Cantonnement'. Turn right onto the Rue Principale; after you leave Vilcey take a right turn. At the next fork, turn right again onto the Rue Moulin de Golange. Drive past Gaulange Farm and, after about a hundred metres, on the left side of the road, you will see the **Kühlewein Brunnen (1)** (N48°55.742′ E005°57.580′). This water trough was built towards the end of 1915 and early 1916, after the heavy fighting in Priest Wood had petered out. The well was dedicated to Lieutenant von Kühlewein, commander of the 2nd Company of the 80th Reserve Battalion. This brigade was part of the 8th Ersatz (Reserve) Division and was formed in 1914 on the mobilization of the German army. The division initially fought in the Battle of the Frontiers in 1914,

The Kühlwein Quelle in 2019.

German shelter in the ruins of Jaillard Mill.

Temporary German cemetery close to Jaillard Mill.

including the battle of Nancy-Épinal. From September 1914 to October 1916 the regiment was stationed in the Pont-à-Mousson sector and consequently was heavily involved in the fighting for Priest Woods.

Return to your car and continue for about a hundred metres. On the right side of the road you will see an information panel and also the entrance of a cellar that once was part of the **Moulin de Jaillard (2)**

(N48°55.655′ E005°57.498′). For centuries, two water mills were operated along the Ruisseau de Fontaine, Fountain Creek. Both were destroyed during the war, but only Gaulange Mill, now a farm, was rebuilt on its original site. Behind the cellar/shelter lie the remains of walls and even parts of the waterwheel can be seen. The creek was narrowed before the wheel to speed the water flow, which turned an overshot wheel, the most economic way to power a waterwheel. Close to Jaillard Mill the Germans started a temporary cemetery to bury their dead comrades who had been killed in Priest Wood. After the war the bodies were exhumed and reburied in Thiaucourt German Cemetery.

Continue for another hundred metres until you come to a crossing and park. The track on the right leads you to the German camp. After fifty metres a trail starts on your left hand. The trail is indicated by a sign that reads 'autel 14-18, 0,1 km'. This leads you to a magnificent **German Altar (3)** (N48°55.591′ E005°57.257′). With the front line only two kilometres to the south, church services were mainly open air services. Remains of trenches and dugouts can be seen all around.

Walk back downhill and turn left at the main trail. After about 150 metres, you will come to the outer walls of a **shelter (4)** (N48°55.688′ E005°57.180′). Often these were built from wood and tar paper, rather like log cabins; but here they were built from stone and concrete. Stone

The altar of Stumpf/Quelle Lager.

The altar in 2019.

A German religious service at Priest Wood.

structures like these are relatively rare in the Meuse-Argonne area but are common in the Salient. Often they were connected to underground shelters. Ernst Jünger wrote an interesting entry in his journal. Whilst staying in a dugout not far from Quelle Lager, he noted that his

> '… dugout was deep and drippy. It did have one quality I didn't much care for: instead of the lice we were used to, this area offered its more mobile cousins. The two sorts apparently stand in much

the same adversarial relationship to one another as black rats and Rattus norvegicus. In this instance, even a complete change of undergarments didn't help, as the thoughtful parasites would stay behind in the straw bedding. The sleeper on the brink of despair would be driven to unmake his bed, and have a thorough hunt.'

There are several remains of other structures along this route, but 400 metres further from here there stands another reasonable intact **shelter/dugout (5)** (N48°55.638′ E005°57.044′).

Remains of German dug outs in Stumpf Lager.

As you carry on along the muddy and winding trail, you come at what was possibly the nerve centre of the camp, the **command post bunker (6)** (N48°55.580′ E005°56.875′) and, fifty metres further on, the **medical bunker,** with the **Kandler Brunnen (7)** (N48°55.570′ E005°56.849′) built against the wall of the latter. Both bunkers are partly build in the side of the

Remains of dug outs.

German headquarters bunker.

Detail of the Kandler Brunnen.

Ernst Jünger (right) at the entrance of the HQ bunker.

German medical bunker.

The medical bunker during the war. Note the red cross.

hill. This way, the roofs were protected by a thick layer of earth and were also camouflaged from reconnaissance planes. Inside the bunkers, tunnels, now collapsed, were dug into the hill. Note the beautiful caduceus on the front wall of the medical bunker. During the war, the Germans had more or less canalized Fountain Creek, but at many places the stream proved too wild to control. Therefore, several raised wooden causeways were constructed.

Water reservoir.

The next three stops are all situated on the right hand side of the trail. After 300 metres you will reach the **Pütter Quelle (8)** (N48°55.566′ E005°56.772′). Originally the reservoir of the well was covered by a wooden roof protected by tar paper to prevent dirt and leafs from spoiling the water in the reservoir. The well was constructed in 1915 or 1916, and was dedicated to Major Pütter, medical officer of the 80th Reserve Infantry Brigade, 8th Ersatz Division.

The Pütter Quelle.

Ernst Jünger (L) and Lieutenant Kienitz at the Pütter Quelle, September 1917.

On 23 September 1917, Lieutenants Jünger and Kienitz led a trench raid in the Regniéville area, not far from Quelle Lager. In *Storm of Steel*, Jünger describes the kit that he took with him during such raids:

> 'I had got together some kit appropriate to the sort of work I meant to be doing: across my chest, two sandbags, each containing four stick bombs, impact fuses on the left, delay on the right; in my tunic pocket a 08 pistol on a long cord, in my right trouser pocket a small Mauser pistol, in my left tunic pocket five egg hand grenades, in the left trouser pocket luminous compass and whistle, in my belt spring hooks for pulling out the pins, plus bowie knife and wire cutters. In my inside tunic pocket I carried a full wallet with my home address, in my right back pocket, a flat flask of cherry brandy. We had removed shoulder straps and Gibraltar badges [worn on the lower sleeve, a reference back to when Hanoverian troops often served with the British and their Hanoverian kings], so as to give our opponents no clue as to our regiment. For identification, we had a white band around each arm.'

A photograph of Jünger and Kienitz, taken in front of the Pütter Quelle, shows a striking resemblance with his description, but it is not clear if this was taken before or after the action had taken place, ie staged.

A little further along the trail lies the beautiful **Oidtmann Quelle (9)** (N48°55.612′ E005°56.564′). Built in 1915 by the 2nd Engineer Reserve Company of II Bavarian Corps, the fountain is dedicated to Major General Ernst von Oidtman (1854-1937). He started the war as the commander of 42nd Reserve Infantry Brigade but was transferred to the 80th Reserve

Oidtmann Quelle in 2019.

Detail of the fountain; note the iron crosses.

Major General Ernst von Oidtman (1854-1937).

Dreieck Quelle.

Infantry Brigade as soon as October 1914. Three of his brothers were also generals in the Prussian Army; one died in 1903, the other two in 1914. Oidtman stayed with the 80th throughout the war.

Some 300 metres after the Oidtman Quelle you will come to the **Dreieck Quelle (10)** (N48°55.637' E005°56.500'). This fountain, not in working order, has only recently been cleared from undergrowth. Presumably it dates from 1915, the same period as the other fountains were built.

Shell fragment at the Dreieck Quelle.

Keep following the trail along the valley floor. After 600 metres, on the left side of the trail, there are steps that leads down to the entrance of three **underground shelters (11)** (N48°55.819′ E005°56.201′). In wet conditions the wooden steps can be very slippery. Tunnels like these had many functions; among other things, they served as shelters, workshops, hospitals and kitchens. **NB!** Entering the tunnels is extremely dangerous.

The walk back to your car takes about twenty five minutes.

Underground shelters.

Car Tour 3

Bouxières, 92nd Division

Duration: A half day's tour
Distance: 15 kilometres
Map: IGN 3314 SB, Pont-à-Mousson

This non-circular tour concentrates on the exploits of the African-American 92nd Division, commanded by Major General Charles C. Ballou. In November 1918, the 92nd Division was part of VI Corps, Second Army, also commanded by Major General Charles C. Ballou.

Provisions, lunch facilities and petrol stations can be found in Pont-à-Mousson. There are no public rest rooms along the route. The tour starts at the Côte-du-Xon (N48°55.818′E006°05.115′). For your own safety, a good quality torch is recommended if you intend to visit the bunkers. **Note: Bunkers are entered at your own risk.**

GPS coordinates Car Tour 3

(1) Côte du Xon	(N48°55.818' E006°05.115')
(2) Bel-Air Farm	(N48°56.237' E006°04.264')
(3) Panorama 11 November	(N48°57.102' E006°05.484')
(4) Monument aux Morts	(N48°57.353' E006°05.411')
(5) Mass Grave 1914	(N48°57.359' E006°05.104')
(6) Froidmont Hill	(N48°57.415' E006°04.762')
(7) Grauer Bär bunker	(N48°57.488' E006°04.456')
(8) Hospital bunker	(N48°57.546' E006°04.450')
(9) Krähen Hütte	(N48°57.881' E006°04.561')
(10) Frontier boundary marker 1870-1918	(N48°57.991' E006°04.773')
(11) Pouget Cross	(N48°57.885' E006°05.281')

It is interesting to note that a regular Army Corps usually comprises at least two and usually several divisions; however, the 92nd Division was the only division of VI Corps. Surprisingly, in this case the corps and division commander were commanded by the same person, namely Major General Ballou. Another exception to the rule was that the 92nd Division

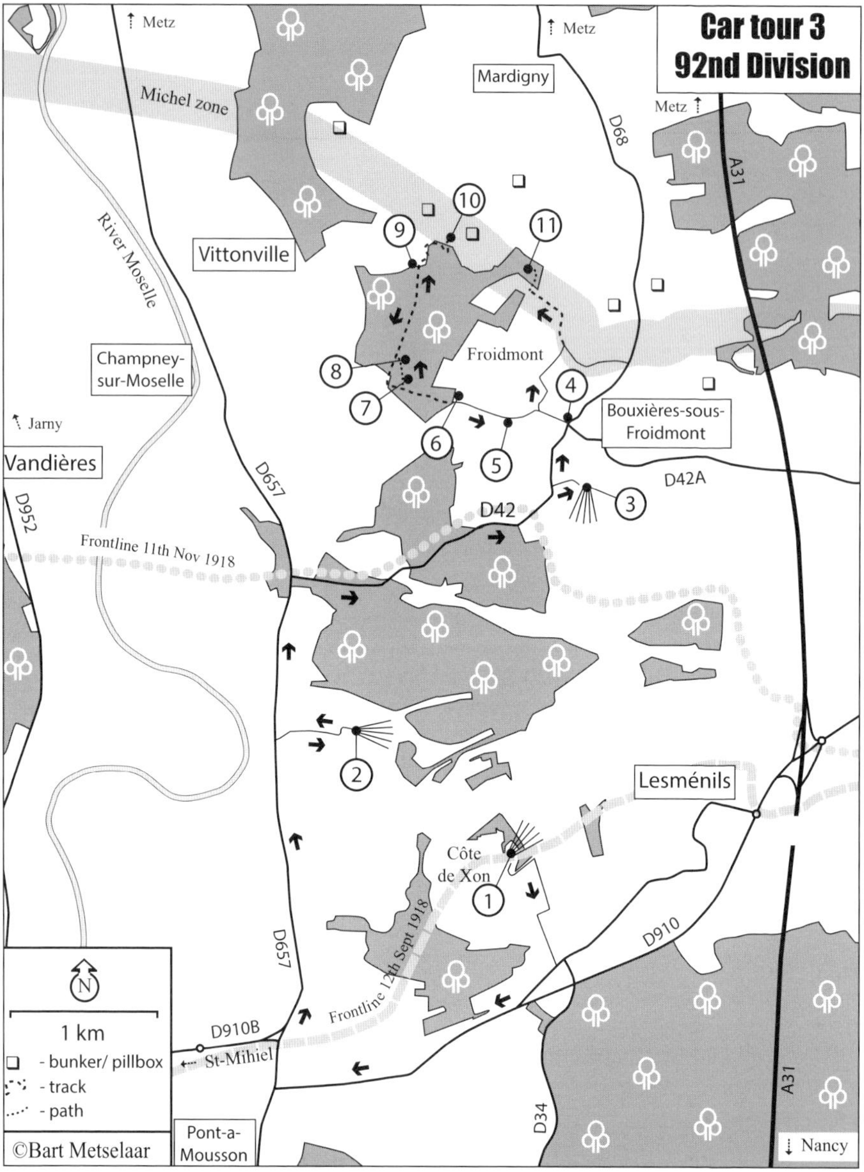

had no support on its right flank. Here, the troops of the French Eight Army were under their own command and not subjected to American orders. When during the last two days of the war the 92nd Division was ordered to advance, the French were not, leaving the African-American right flank unprotected. The fact that the Division was separated by the River Moselle from the rest of the American Second Army did not help much either; if anything went wrong they were on their own, cut off from the rest of Second Army. A third indication that the men of the 92nd seemed to have drawn the shortest straw was the geography. Besides the River Moselle, the Norroy Sector featured the highest hills (over 400 metres) of the area, with large and wide valleys that offered the Germans an excellent field of fire. The very poor infrastructure was almost a guarantee of disaster; if a breakthrough could be achieved there was no way that supplies could reach the front or that the wounded could be evacuated in a timely fashion, to name but a few consequences. Last, but certainly not least, the forested and hilly area to be attacked sheltered outposts of the Michel Zone and were heavily protected by the German artillery situated on Froidmont Hill. It should come as no surprise, therefore, that the African-Americans from the Buffalo Division (who had been badly handled already at the opening of the Meuse-Argonne Offensive) only managed to occupy partially the outpost zone in front of them and never made it to the Michel Zone.

French Monument at the Côte du Xon.

The **Côte du Xon (1)** (N48°55.818′ E006°05.115′) can be easily reached by car, although the track up to it is a little rough. At 358 metres above sea level, the hill offers great views of the surrounding area. Situated close to the Franco-German border of 1871-1918, it is no surprise that the hill was heavily contested in 1914. The Crucifix Monument that was built amidst the old trench system commemorates the fighting for this hill. Situated only a stone's throw from the former Franco-German border, Xon served as an important observation and signal post for the French Army. On 5 September 1914, one month after the German invasion of Belgium and France, the Germans took Xon Hill and quickly started to rework the French positions into an artillery bulwark. Not long thereafter, the shelling of the surrounded villages started. According to the available information, one of these villages was hit by 4,000

Jump-off positions of the US 93rd Division.

shells. In December 1914 the hill changed hands several times, but the biggest fight over Xon Hill started on 13 February 1915. After a surprise attack, in which the hill was taken by the Germans again, the French launched a massive counter attack. On 18 February, the Germans were finally repulsed and Xon Hill remained in French hands until the end of the war. The monument was erected in 1922 and commemorates the approximate 2,000 casualties that fell in these surroundings. It is interesting to note that the monument was destroyed in September 1944 during the fighting around Pont-à-Mousson when the Germans were retreating to the River Rhine. It was rebuilt and rededicated on 22 September 1963.

To get a better understanding of the starting position and the goals of the 183rd Brigade (365th and 366th Regiments) of the 92nd Division, walk through the opening in the trees behind the monument. If there are no crops in the field, turn left and walk along the hedges and trees for about fifty metres to obtain an even better view. Look at the panorama photo to see where the jump-off positions of 10 and 11 November used to be. Note also the complete lack of cover.

Return to your car and drive back to the D910. This road leads you to Pont-à-Mousson. At the main crossroads, take a right turn onto the D657,

direction Champey. After about two kilometres, take a right (note the billboard and a the *Ferme Bel-Air* sign) onto the track that leads you to **Bel-Air Farm (2)** (N48°56.237′ E006°04.264′). Follow the track to the left; do not drive to the farm itself but follow the (narrow) road around it. Where a track meets the road, stop your car. Look at the panorama photo in the book. From where you are standing now, you can appreciate the difficulties the men of the 366th Regiment experienced when on 10 November at 7.00 am they descended from Xon Hill, looming on the right in the distance, to launch the attack on the Germans that were sitting in Fréhaut Wood on the left. The valley was under constant artillery fire and was regularly saturated with gas. With the Germans retreating back to the Michel Zone, Fréhaut Wood was captured around 4.00 pm but lay under constant German shellfire until hostilities ended the next morning. Drive back to the D57 and turn right. At the Ferme de Poncé turn right onto the D42, direction Bouxières. This road runs approximately along the furthest point of advance of the 366th Regiment at the moment the Armistice commenced on 11 November, 11.00 am. After the road leaves the forest, take the second track on your right (the track opposite the crucifix/*calvaire*). Stop after fifty metres. This is a good spot to see where

View from Bel Air Farm to the east.

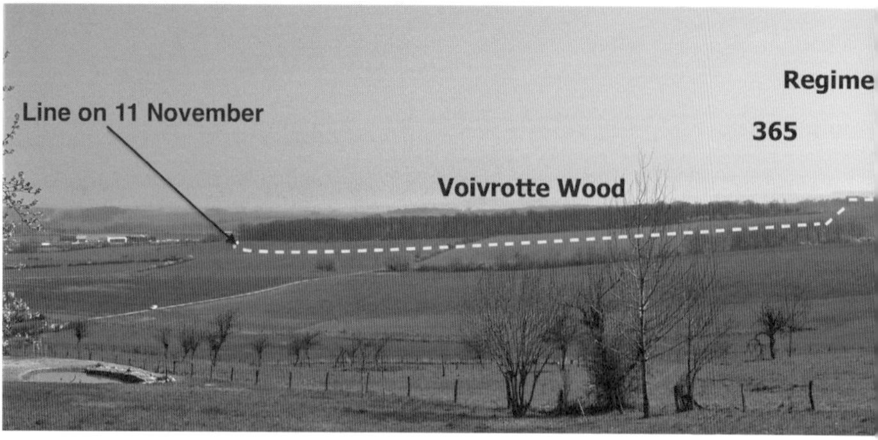

View from the orchards south of Bouxières to the line of 11 November 1918.

the war ended for the Buffalo Division on **11 November (3)** (N48°57.102′ E006°05.484′). See the panoramic picture.

Major Warner Ross, 2nd Battalion, 365th Regiment, noted:

> 'Promptly at eleven o'clock all fire began to lessen and in a few minutes ceased. The World War had stopped. Not only our men but the Germans also seemed overjoyed. Soon after the buglers had sounded to cease firing the Huns rushed out of their positions and our men met them between the lines. They actually shook hands and slapped each other's backs. I wouldn't believe it if I hadn't seen it.'

Return to the main road and drive to Bouxières-sous-Froidmont; stop at the church. Next to the church stands an interesting **Monument aux Morts (4)** (N48°57.353′ E006°05.411′). Of the more than 35,000 'monuments for the dead' that have been erected in France since 1871, this one also commemorates Cavalier Fortuné (what's in a name!) Pouget of the 12th Cavalry. Claimed to be the first French soldier that 'died for France' after the German declaration of war, he was killed on the morning of 4 August 1914 on Froidmont Hill, roughly two kilometres north from where you stand. He was shot through the head and died instantly. The twenty one year old Pouget is

War Monument in Bouxières.

buried in Pont-à-Mousson Communal Cemetery. Also commemorated on this monument is Lieutenant Paul Crozet Fourneyron, see Stop (5).

Return to your car and drive up hill along the Rue de Froidemont. At the T-junction, take the left fork. After about 100 metres you will see the **Mass Grave 1914 (5)** (N48°57.359′ E006°05.104′) on the left side of the road. Nowadays, an engraved marble slab has replaced the original monument, but fortunately the original grave marker, dating from the 1920s, has been maintained next to the new one. The first name on the original monument is that of the aforementioned Lieutenant Paul Crozet Fourneyron

Plaque commemorating the first official French casualty of war.

French mass grave of October 1914 with the original monument inset.

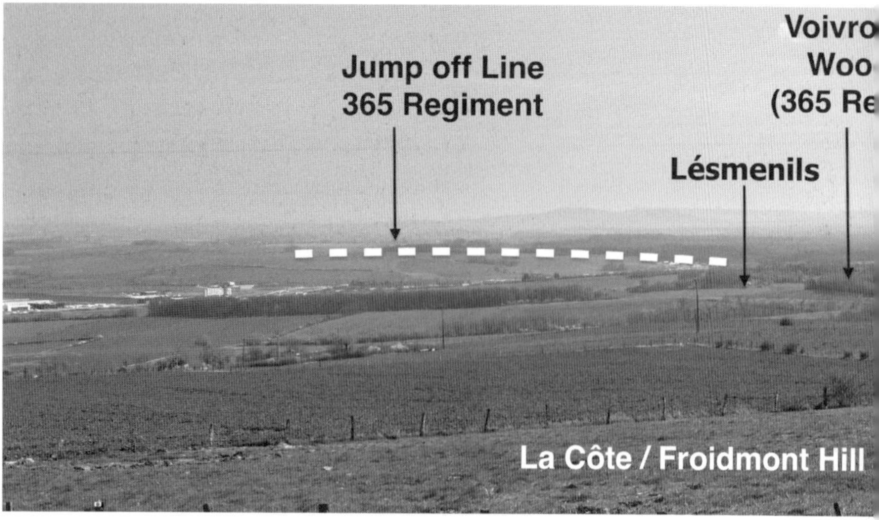

View from Froidmont Hill to the Côte du Xon. Compare with the American view of stop 1.

of the 232nd Infantry Regiment. Born on 1 April 1888 in Paris, Crozet was killed leading his troops in an attack on Froidmont Hill on 7 October 1914. After the battle, Lieutenant Crozet, two non-commissioned officers and thirteen soldiers were buried on this spot. Crozet was only 26 years old.

Continue along the track for about 200 metres and park your car. **Note:** in dry weather conditions and if your car has enough height clearance, it is possible to visit Stops 7, 8 and 9 by car. Since the 12th century, **Froidmont Hill (6)** (N48°57.415′ E006°04.762′) has been the site of various religious buildings; the most recent was constructed in 1973 to replace the chapel that was destroyed during the opening battles of 1914. The well-maintained Chapel of Froidmont is dedicated to Notre Dame de Froidmont and, according to the information panel, many pilgrims still visit the site annually.

For history enthusiasts this site is extremely attractive. After France lost the 1870 war against Germany, the French provinces of Alsace and Lorraine became German territory. Interestingly, border boundary stones of the 1870-1918 era can still be seen on the eastern side of Froidmont Hill; two are included in this tour.

The western side of Froidmont Hill remained French territory after hostilities formally ended in 1871, but was taken by the Germans as soon as hostilities broke out in August 1914. The Germans wasted little time and immediately started to fortify the hill. Besides a few skirmishes in October 1914 (see Stop 5), Froidmont Hill stayed in German hands until the end of the war. From the start of the occupation many fortified

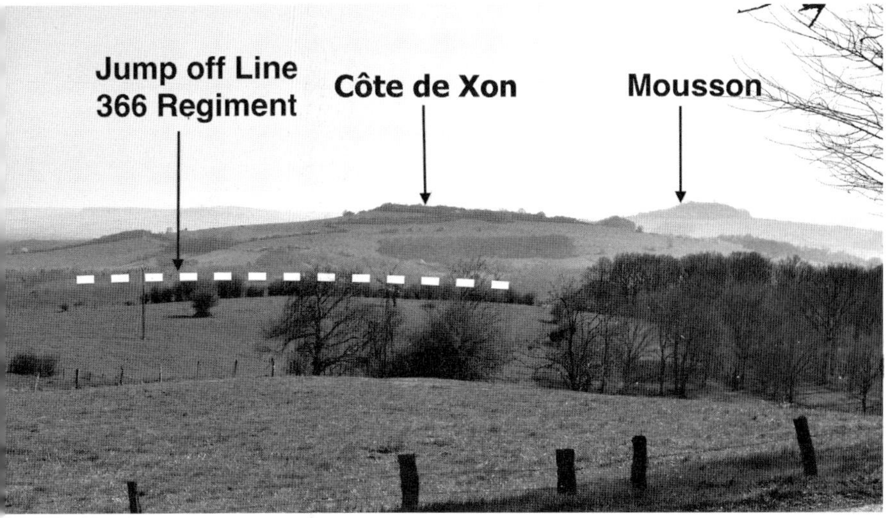

structures were built on and into the hill. Beautiful examples and proof of craftsmanship in building concrete structures are illustrated by the *Grauer Bär* Bunker dating from 1915 and a hospital bunker dating from 1916.

To reach these bunkers, walk along the track (see map) that leads into the forest. Keep the chapel to your left. About fifty metres before the track bends to the right, a trench-trail starts at your right hand. This conveniently leads you to the **Grauer Bär Bunker (7)** (N48°57.488′ E006°04.456′) The reconstructed trenches and approach tunnel (pitch dark!) have been restored by local World War One enthusiasts and lead you to the interior of the bunker. The bunker was built in 1915 by the 4th Company of Landwehr Infantry Regiment 30. Once you have explored the rooms, climb the

German 'Grauer Bär' (grey bear) bunker, built in 1915.

Detail of a German poem cast on the wall of the Grauer Bär bunker. (Collection T. Gudmestad)

stairs to admire the magnificent artwork on the outside of the bunker. On the right wall an inscription is dedicated to *Baumeister* Gansen and *Betonmeister* Valbert and Lange. Follow the right path; about fifty metres behind the Bär bunker, you find the equally monumental, so-called, **Hospital Bunker (8)** (N48°57.546′ E006°04.450′). Built in 1916, it features some beautiful architectural details. It is interesting to see how

The so-called hospital bunker in 1915. (Collection W. Degrande)

The bunker in 2019.

much effort the Germans put in the concrete structures on Froidmont Hill, compared with the underground dwellings and trenches the French lived in on Xon Hill (see stop 1). There is no proof whether this richly decorated bunker really was in use as a hospital; it might just as well have served as a living quarters.

Washing basin.

From here, follow the path that goes to the left. In due course you will reach the main track; turn right. Follow this track for about 400 metres; just before you reach the end of the woods, a path starts on your left hand. Follow this down hill until after about sixty metres you will see the **Krähen Hütte** (Crow's Nest) **Bunker (9)** (N48°57.881′ E006°04.561′), well-embedded into the hillside. This German observation post surveyed the bend in the River Moselle near Vittonville. There are more concrete remains down the hill, but in reality there are bunkers everywhere and one could easily spend a day exploring them. Unfortunately, in 2005, the quarry, which is

German observation post 'Krähen Hütte' , Crow's Nest.

visible on the right (to the east) as you approach the hill and from a distance away, was hugely extended and numerous bunkers have been destroyed since that date.

The reason for the German building frenzy lies in the significance of the topographical position of Froidmont Hill. Twenty metres higher than any other hill in the surrounding area, Xon Hill included, it became an important observation post and artillery position. Froidmont Hill commanded the River Moselle, Pont-à-Mousson, its railway lines and held the French occupying Xon Hill in check. The position also dominated Bois de Prêtre (Priest Wood) on the opposite (left) bank of the river and contributed greatly to the destruction of the extensive wood during the terrible fighting of 1915. On 10 and 11 November 1918, the attacking American 365th and 366th Regiments were ceaselessly shelled by the German batteries protected by this hill. What made it particularly hard for the African-American soldiers was that many of the shells fired were filled with gas – a practice that had been common in the last year of the war.

Go back to the main track and turn left. Leave the forest, but keep the edge of the woods on your right hand. After about 100 metres you will see a fence running along the ridge. The fence runs along the old Franco-German border of 1870-1918. If the grass or crops are not too high, you can see the old **frontier boundary marker 1870-1918 (10)** (N48°57.991′ E006°04.773′) sticking a few feet out of the ground on the other side of the fence. One side is marked with an 'F' (France), the other with a 'D' (Deutschland). Fifty metres to the right, the roof of a Michel Zone shelter is visible.

Remains of the 1871-1918 Franco-German border marker.

Walk back to your car and return to Bouxières. After you have passed the mass grave monument, take a left at the T-junction. At the next T-junction, take a right, and at the third take a left again. This rather deteriorated track leads you to the **Pouget Cross (11)** (N48°57.885′ E006°05.281′). The last seventy metres or so have to be covered on foot. Close to the cross lie the remains of an 1870-1918 border marker. On 4 August 1914, on this spot, the first French soldier of World War One was killed. Officially, Pouget is the first French soldier killed after the German declaration of war; he is buried in Pont à Mousson communal cemetery.

Fortune Pouget.

However, the first deadly casualty of the conflict was Corporal Jules André Peugeot. Peugeot (1893-1914) was killed two days earlier, before the declaration of war, during a skirmish on the Franco-German border at Joncherey, south of Belfort. Lieutenant Albert Mayer of the 5th German Cavalry Regiment, leading a reconnaissance mission of eight men, ran into Corporal Peugeot's little band and in the chaos that followed some sabre cuts and pistol shots were exchanged. Although the first two bullets only scarred his tunic, Peugeot was fatally hit by the third bullet fired by Lieutenant Albert Mayer. The story does not end here; after Peugeot fell from his horse, the French fired a few shots at Mayer. He was hit and promptly became the first German fatality of World War One.

The Pouget Cross. On this spot, the first French and German soldiers of the First World War were killed.

View of Metz in the distance.

Turn around and walk a few metres. through the opening in the trees; note on your left there is a large concrete bunker and plenty of evidence of Great War earthworks and so forth. Metz can be seen in the distance. Many books support the myth that General MacArthur, 42nd Division, saw Metz from a château in St. Benoît en Woëvre. This is not true. In fact, it is impossible to see Metz from there or anywhere on the Woëvre Plain. The reason for this is that the Woëvre Plain and Metz are separated by the hills and ridges that run along the River Moselle. Besides that, Metz sits at the bottom of a cauldron-shaped depression that is surrounded by hills.

CHAPTER 5

V Corps

<u>A short history</u>

The 26th ('Yankee') Division.

Maj. Gen. Clarence R. Edwards.

The 26th Division, a National Guard Division, was commanded by Major General Clarence R. Edwards. A major formation of the Massachusetts Army National Guard, it was based in Boston and was activated at Camp Edwards, Massachusetts on 22 August 1917. Having done hardly any training, the division sailed for France; the men of the 26th Division arrived at Saint-Nazaire on 21 September 1917. Interestingly, it was the second division of the AEF, after the 1st Division, to arrive in France and the first division newly organized in the United States. After arrival the division immediately moved to Neufchâteau for training with the French, as most of the division's soldiers were raw recruits. Later, the 26th trained extensively with the 1st, 2nd and 42nd divisions, organized as I Corps in January 1918, and was moved to a quiet sector on the Chemin des Dames, where it stayed for several months to gain front line experience.

On 3 April 1918 the division arrived by train in the St. Mihiel area and thus were familiar with the terrain over which the offensive was going to take place. They took over the line that extended from Apremont-la-Forêt in the west to Xivray-Marvoisin, Seicheprey, Remieres Wood and as far as Jury Wood, bordering Flirey, on the right, and where the French line joined the American line.

M1917 helmet with V Corps emblem.

The Germans became quite active once they discovered that there were Americans in the sector; the attacks were primarily designed to intimidate the fresh, relatively untrained, American troops; but the Germans also wanted to take prisoners in order to find out what American intentions might be. Once on the front line, therefore, the 26th Division was seriously put to the test by the Germans.

As well as organizing several large-scale raiding parties, they also continually harassed the Americans with artillery fire. Thus during their very first week in the line, the 26th Division was put to the test, but held their ground. Both sides suffered substantial losses. At the end of April the Germans launched an attack on Seicheprey; with the help of overwhelming artillery support, they captured the village. Before the Americans could make a counter attack the Germans had retreated, having inflicted 634 American casualties, including eighty killed. Approximately 130 Americans were captured and taken back to the German lines, a devastating blow to morale.

On 28 June the 26th Division was moved to the Château Thierry sector. Pressure had been exerted all along the central to northern part of the Allied front since the beginning of the German Spring Offensive in March 1918, and this had spread to the Aisne and the Marne line by May. During the fierce fighting in the Château Thierry area, the 26th lost over 4,000 casualties during the fighting in and around Belleau Wood. With the line stabilised, by 31 August the 26th was back in the St. Mihiel sector. After losses in men and materiel were replenished, the Yankee Division was put into the line a little south of Mouilly and Les Éparges. Protecting the left flank of V Corps, it took over a two kilometres' wide line in the north west of the Salient. In the opening stage of the offensive it had the important task of making an unprecedented advance of fifteen kilometres in a south-easterly direction to meet up with the 1st Division to cut off the tip of the Salient. This classic pincer movement was designed to cut off as many Germans as possible. The French, holding the front line trenches at the tip of the Salient, were to distract the Germans by launching demonstrations in order to divert their attention away from what was actually going on.

On 12 and 13 September, the French 15th Colonial Division, under American command and part of V Corps, attacked in a north-easterly direction. Their task was to push the Germans back beyond the Manheulles-St. Benoît-en-Woëvre road, the present-day D904, to prevent the Germans assaulting the 26th Division's vulnerable right flank. In just two days they managed to liberate an area of sixty square kilometres.

Thursday, 12 September

Strong winds and driving rain.

At 1.00 am, the preliminary barrage opened up on the German front line. An officer of the 66th Field Artillery Brigade remembered that:

> 'For the first time the regiment used gas shells and it was with a

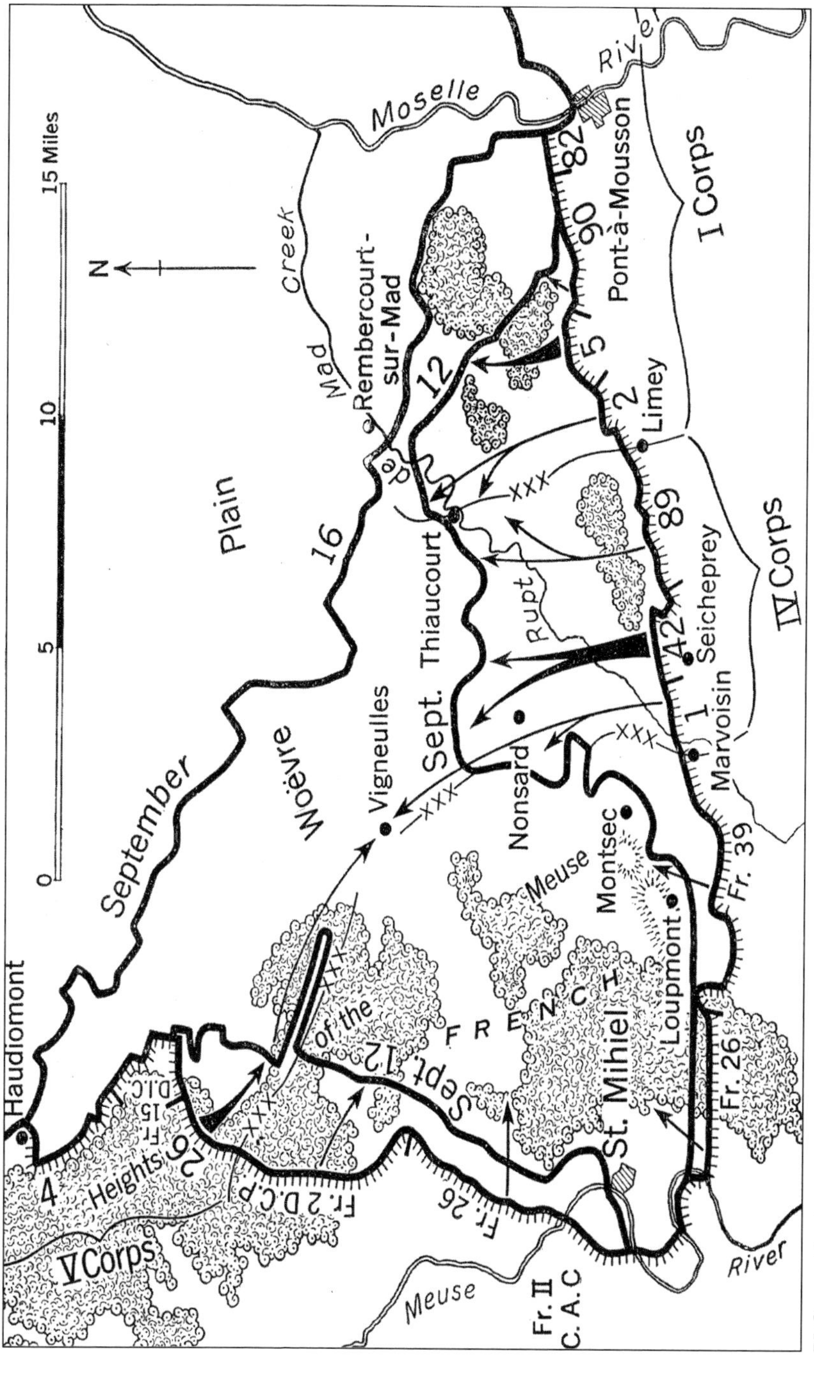

V Corps Sector.

Street view in St. Maurice, September 1918.

> quiet satisfaction that the men rammed these projectiles filled with poisonous gases and sent them forth on their mission into the Boche [German] lines.'

Whereas on the southern side of the Salient the attack started at 5.00 am, the soldiers of the 101st and 102nd Regiments had been ordered to wait until 8.00 am in order not to arouse German suspicion about the impending pincer movement. Thus at 5.50 am just the engineers went over the top to cut lanes in the barbed wire and to mark the routes of approach for the infantry. At 8.00 am the infantry started the assault on an approximately one kilometre wide front. There was no German resistance to check the initial advance, just sporadic German shellfire; soon the first prisoners had been taken. Within the first hour of the attack, Dommartin, the first objective of the day, had been captured. However, it was tough going crossing Montagne Wood, which was interspersed with valleys and gullies. Every now and then German strong points had to be eliminated but, surprisingly, the casualty rate remained low. An officer of the 66th Field Artillery noted that

> 'By midday it was unnecessary to inquire as to the success of the attack, as prisoners commenced to pass our gun positions in great numbers. It was a peculiar sight to see several hundred prisoners marching down the road with one sentinel in advance leading the way and one sentinel in the rear to keep the prisoners in column.'

Burnt-out homes in Vigneulles, 14 September 1918.

German pioneer depot in Vigneulles, 19 September 1918.

The division's final first day objective was the crossroads of Tranchée de Calonne and St. Maurice-sous-les-Côtes, a line that roughly ran along the present-day D101. At 7.30 pm orders were received to continue the attack in a southerly direction in order to close the gap by making contact with the 1st Division. The division moved forward with the aim of cutting off access to the railway and the Vigneulles-St. Benoît Road; this road, now the D901, was the main escape route for the Germans heading back towards the Fatherland.

Friday 13 September
Overcast and rainy weather.
In spite of the appalling weather, the 26th Division made good progress; by 2.00 am they had reached Vigneulles and the D901 and taken about 200 German prisoners. At daybreak American pilots started to bomb the town that was packed with American troops and German prisoners. It was obvious there had been a breakdown in communication; thirty doughboys and an unknown number of Germans were wounded in the air raids on Vigneulles. But this was not the only problem - during the night the advance had slowed down and scores of men had lost their way. Whole squads had become separated from their platoons and hundreds of men were wandering aimlessly through the woods. Communications had been disastrously poor; keeping in contact depended on runners who nearly all lost their way in the hostile and rain-sodden woods. As a result, some companies had been reduced to fifty men from the usual 250. The division was reorganised as best as possible and continued on to Creuë, a village three kilometres to the south-west of Vigneulles. Finally, at 10.00 am, the 1st Division arrived at Vigneulles. For the bulk of the Germans who were still in the nose of the Salient, their escape route had been sealed; however, during the next couple of nights dozens of them managed to escape through the dense woods.

The fighting in the sector of the French, the 26th and 1st Division's was over; the tip of the Salient had been successfully cut off from the main body of the German Army; approximately 16,000 prisoners were taken. The engineer regiments moved in to repair the roads. Supplies were being brought forward but massive traffic jams were blocking the few roads that were in any way serviceable. It was, therefore, fortunate for the doughboys that in the liberated villages they found large supplies of food; the Germans had been preparing for winter so that the warehouses were well filled. Nevertheless, there was still considerable German artillery activity during the day.

Saturday 14 September
Clear weather, good visibility.
During the night a German barrage of high explosives and gas, which lasted four and a half hours, caused substantial American losses. Despite this, just as on the previous day, work on repairing the roads and improving other essential elements of the logistics chain continued.

The 26th Division was pulled out of the line on 8 October and was transferred to the Citadel of Verdun, where it became part of the Army reserve. The Division had suffered 479 casualties during the St. Mihiel Offensive, mainly caused by artillery fire.

Maj. Gen. John L. Hines.

The 4th ('Ivy') Division

The 4th Division, a Regular Army Division, was commanded by Major General John L. Hines. On 10 December 1917 the 4th Division was formed at Camp Greene, North Carolina. Between April and May 1918 the division shipped overseas. After arriving in France they began an intensive training programme, first under British and then French command. In July 1918, during the Second Battle of the Marne, they went into the line in the Château Thierry sector. Due to the number of operations they were involved in, the 4th Division sustained 6,923 casualties during this period. On 27 August the 4th Division was assigned to V Corps and was moved to the Meuse sector. Here the exhausted division received much-needed replacements and equipment. On the nights of 5 to 7 September the division's units relieved the French and took their place in the front line between Haudiomont and Les Éparges. This was an area that had been affected by the fighting in 1914 and 1915, to the extent that the destruction was almost total. In a lot of places roads had completely disappeared and hills were devoid of any form of vegetation.

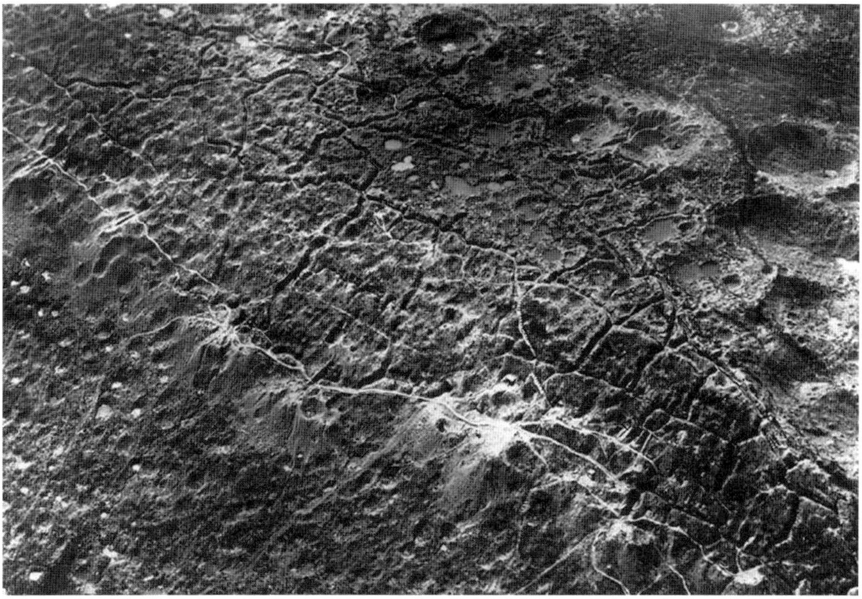

The lunar landscape at Combres Hill/Les Éparges over which the 4th Division attacked.

The 4th Division was the only American division that was in the line but did not join the attack on 12 September; they started on the 14th. On the 12th the French 15th Colonial and the 2nd Dismounted Cavalry divisions were tasked with attacking in a north-easterly direction. However, a five kilometre deep pocket of German held ground remained at the far north of the Salient that had to be eliminated, for which the 4th Division would be responsible. It could only be done after the French had successfully reached their goals and so, in the meantime, the Division acted as a reserve until it was deployed on 14 September.

Saturday 14 September
Clear weather, good visibility.
At 10.00 am, the reserve companies of the 59th Regiment went over the top. Under cover of a rolling barrage, they soon reached the outskirts of Manheulles, which appeared to be deserted. On entering the village they found German field kitchens on which a noon meal was being prepared; a number of the men were able to make the most of a meal of roast beef, fried potatoes, sauerkraut, bread and beer. The advance rapidly moved on to Fresnes-en-Woëvre. As the Americans were entering the village, they were welcomed by a heavy artillery barrage and were forced to fall back. However, by 2.00 pm, they had captured the village and the doughboys started to dig in and build provisional defences. Later that day Champion

The 26th Division passing through a shell swept village, September 1918.

was liberated without any German opposition; the Germans had already evacuated their positions and had withdrawn to the Michel Zone.

Sunday 15 September
Clear weather, good visibility.
During the night, the 4th Division was relieved by the French 15th Division and placed in bivouac in the woods between Haudainville and Sommedieue. During the 16, 17 and 18 September, in preparation for the Meuse-Argonne Offensive, the 4th received special training in liaison. It is not very evident that much good came from this training: during the first few days of the Meuse-Argonne Offensive the Division moved onto their objective too quickly and without regard to their neighbouring divisions, above all on the left. It has been argued that this lack of communication and concern for what might have been happening on the flanks was one of the main reasons for the failure to capture Montfaucon on the first day of that attack. (For a fuller examination of the Division's role in the opening day of that battle, see *Montfaucon* in this series.)

At St. Mihiel, the 4th Division suffered only sixty casualties, mainly inflicted by artillery shells.

Second phase: Monday 16 September to Saturday 9 November
The situation in this part of the St Mihiel front was similar to that of the other divisions in the line here: trench raids, some minor line straightening, some casualties from German shelling and rather more as a result of the effects of the 'flu epidemic.

Third phase: Sunday 10 November to Monday 11 November
The last two days of the war saw a lot of activity in the Salient as several divisions of the US Second Army prepared for a major new attack, in line with Foch's instruction to maintain the pressure on the Germans despite the talk of an Armistice. Consequently all along the American front attacks were launched against the outposts of the Michel Zone.

Maj. Gen. Charles J. Bailey.

The 81st ('Stonewall') Division
The 81st Division was formed as a National Division in August 1917 at Camp Jackson, South Carolina, and was commanded by Major General Charles J. Bailey. In August 1918, after finishing a training programme, this inexperienced division sailed for France. During the

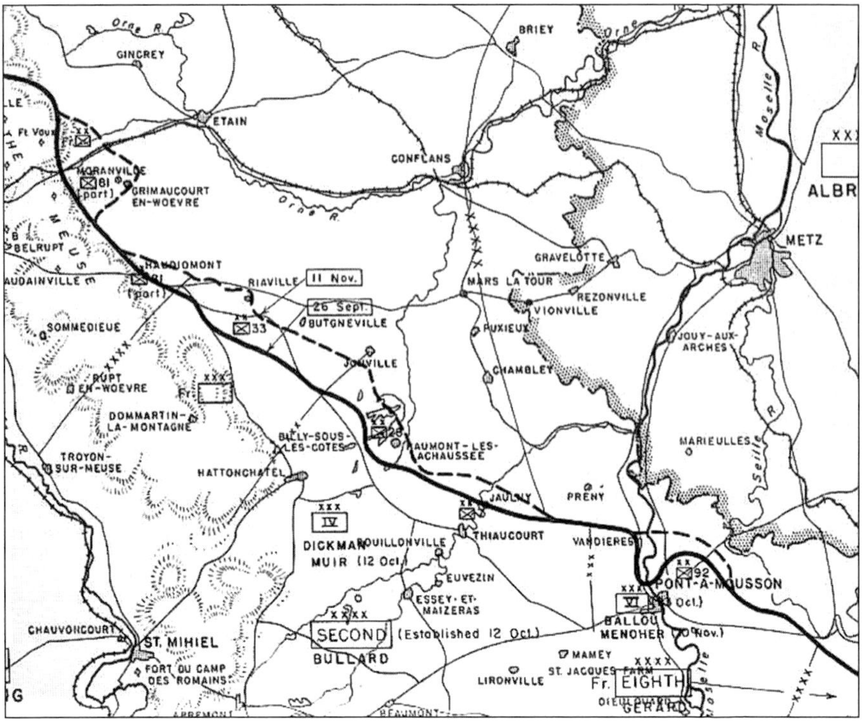

81st and 33rd Division sector, 10-11 November 1918.

defence of the St. Dié Sector, in September and early October, elements of the 81st Division first saw limited action. However, the men of the 81st Division suffered heavy casualties in the St. Mihiel sector in November 1918.

On 5 November the 81st began to relieve the American 35th Division; the following day, on 6 November, they passed through the French II Colonial Corps area. They had taken over the line that extended from Fresnes-en-Woëvre to Ouvrage de Bezonvaux, close to Verdun. The front-line battalions were directed to patrol vigorously and gain as much information as possible. Since the beginning of the Meuse-Argonne Offensive on 26 September, there had been no general offensive action on the portion of the front now occupied by the 81st Division. However, this all changed when on 8 November orders were received from the French II Colonial Corps to launch an attack between Ronvaux and Fresnes-en-Woëvre as early as possible after daylight the next morning. The objective of the operation was to establish a foothold on the plain that would assist later operations in what was hoped would be a war of movement on this portion of the front.

Saturday 9 November
Overcast and freezing weather.
During the night strong patrols had been sent out into No Man's Land and it soon became clear that the German positions were being firmly held. The attack scheduled for the next morning was treated more like the pursuit of a retreating enemy rather than as a frontal attack against a determined enemy. The assault troops in each zone of action comprised one regiment of infantry with machine-gun support, one battalion of field artillery and a detachment of engineers, which acted as the advance guard. The right column was charged with maintaining liaison with the 33rd Division in the vicinity of Fresnes, and the left column with the French 10th Colonial Division.

The artillery barrage started at 7.30 am and lasted for thirty minutes. Under cover of the rolling barrage, the Americans moved closer to the German defences; the rolling barrage continued until 9.00 am. On the left of the sector part of Manheulles Wood was captured. On the extreme right Château d'Aulnois was liberated but in doing so the Americans attracted artillery fire from their front and the right flank. That day's gains were not very impressive but, as explained earlier, these attacks were mainly designed to keep the pressure on the Germans and to straighten out the American front line. By the time evening had fallen the front line companies had withdrawn through the support units and had taken up position on the Fresnes-Manheulles Road. The support units, which by this movement became front line companies, took up positions in the trenches about 400 meters in front of this road.

Sunday 10 November
Overcast and freezing weather.
The Left Flank:
The night was used to relieve the soldiers manning the front line and preparations were made for the attack the next morning. At 6.30 am, the first companies started the attack, but owing to a heavy concentration of friendly artillery fire on Grimaucourt-en-Woëvre, the infantry was unable to enter the village. When the barrage lifted, the attack on Grimaucourt continued. At 8.45 am, Company I advanced about 800 metres to a position on a slope east of Moranville and north-west of Grimaucourt, where it was held up by shell fire. At 9.15 am, two platoons were sent in to storm the town from the north-west, while the 2nd Battalion continued the attack from the south. The town was taken at 9.30 am,

and by 10.15 am the assault waves of three companies were pushing north and east, leaving one company in position on the eastern edge of Grimaucourt. As the assault troops emerged from the eastern edge of the village they met strong resistance in the vicinity of the cemetery and the advance came to a halt. At 11.00 am a German barrage was laid down on Grimaucourt, to the rear of the position of the support company. The doughboys were ordered to withdraw to a position 200 metres south-east of the village.

Centre:
Patrols were sent out but failed to maintain contact with outposts established earlier. This state of affairs continued throughout the day. At 9.00 am, the 1st Battalion, 324th Regiment, attacked the woods at Manheulles (north of the D903) but, after leaving the start line (often referred to as the 'line of departure' by the Americans), the assault companies soon became disorganized; by the time they reached Massenoue Wood they were thoroughly mixed up. Nevertheless, some order was restored and one platoon of each assault company entered Les Clairs Chênes Wood; by 4.30 pm, after intense fighting, the southern edge of Massenoue and Clairs Chènes woods were in American hands but the doughboys could advance no further. German resistance grew stronger as the Americans moved closer to the outposts of the Michel Zone, the defensive tactics including heavy artillery fire on pre-arranged sectors. In spite of only limited success and small territorial gains, on the far left the 81st succeeded in occupying Blanzee and Moranville.

Right flank:
The right flank of the 81st Division, occupying the Fresnes area, was ordered to stand fast; they were only to move forward in liaison with the 33rd Division.

Monday 11 November
Overcast, with some rain.
At midnight orders were received to start the attack on Grimeaucourt and to straighten out the front line in the centre between Manheulles and Fresnes in order to maintain liaison with the neighbouring 33rd Division on the right. The short preliminary bombardment had, not surprisingly, failed to cut the wire and when the assault started at 6.45 am virtually no progress was made on account of heavy German shelling. In spite of this, engineers moved forward to cut lanes in the wire, but still, progress was very slow and in some sectors it was only just a few hundred metres. At 11.00 am several of the front line companies of the 81st Division were

Americans manning their foxholes near Fresnes.

within reach of the enemy outpost trench system; however, there were three separate barbed wire defence systems guarding the Michel Zone that still had to be overcome. The devastating German artillery fire, in combination with the crossfire of machine guns, would not allow the Americans to get any closer.

On the last morning of the war, Grimaucourt had been taken, the front line straightened out and liaison with the 33rd Division was established, but at a terrible cost. The Michel Zone had not been breached. In three days, the 81st Division suffered 974 casualties, mainly to shellfire.

The 33rd ('Prairie') Division

Maj. Gen. George Bell Jr.

The 33rd Division, a National Guard Division commanded by Major General George Bell, Jr., had at its nucleus the former National Guard of the State of Illinois. Supplemented by draftees, the 33rd trained at Camp Logan, Houston, Texas, from September 1917 until May 1918. Most of the troops of the Division passed through Camp Upton, Yaphank, Long Island, and sailed for France at various dates in May 1918, disembarking at Brest. Once in France, it trained with the British on the Somme. On 4 July 1918, four companies, about 1,100 men, had their first battlefield experience in the Battle of Le Hamel, fighting alongside the Australians. In fact their participation almost never happened. Pershing refused to allow the men of the Division to participate in the attack, but he was overruled by General Rawlinson (commanding Fourth Army), supported by Haig, when Monash protested that without them the attack could not go ahead. By the time the 33rd arrived in the St. Mihiel Sector in early September, the division had been involved in several other battles, including the Second Battle of the Somme (21 August - 2 September); after the St. Mihiel drive the 33rd moved on to the Meuse-Argonne.

Upon being relieved in the Meuse-Argonne, the 33rd Division marched off to the Troyon-sur-Meuse sector on the St. Mihiel Front, where during the nights of 23 to 25 October it replaced the 79th Division. The region, a so-called rest area, included Les Éparges, the scene of such desperate fighting in 1914 and 1915. Soon after the arrival of the 33rd Division, the front line in this area became a rather lively spot; the more motivated German troops (who had replaced the Austrians) had been ordered to hold the Michel Zone at all costs as it was considered the key to Metz. The operations of the 33rd Division, beginning with daily and nightly patrols, developed into trench raids, among which were those of the 130th Regiment on Château d'Aulnois on 7 November, the raid of the 131st Regiment on St. Hilaire on 8 November and one more on 9 November. No large-scale attacks were planned, but even so the raids in the sector between Fresnes-en-woëvre and Woël resulted in hundreds of casualties. On the evening of 9 November a message was sent by Foch that directed that vigorous pressure be applied immediately along the whole front. The attacks started on the next day. To keep the pressure on the Germans, who were negotiating for an armistice, the Americans were ordered to launch an attack and enter the German outpost zone in the heavily defended Michel Zone. However, once in the outpost zone, the Doughboys came under such devastating shell and machine-gun fire that it made entry into the Michel Zone impossible. It was the same old story over and over again.

Sunday 10 November
Overcast and freezing.
On 10 November the 130th Regiment attacked and captured the German stronghold of Marchéville and on the same day the 131st Regiment and Companies A and B of the 124th Machine Gun Battalion finally drove the Germans out of Hautes Epines Wood. Later, they captured the southern portion of Harville Wood and managed to break through the wire of the outer defences of the Michel Zone. The capture of Marchéville and Harville Wood were important insofar as, for the time being, the Americans had managed to get a toehold inside the Michel Zone.

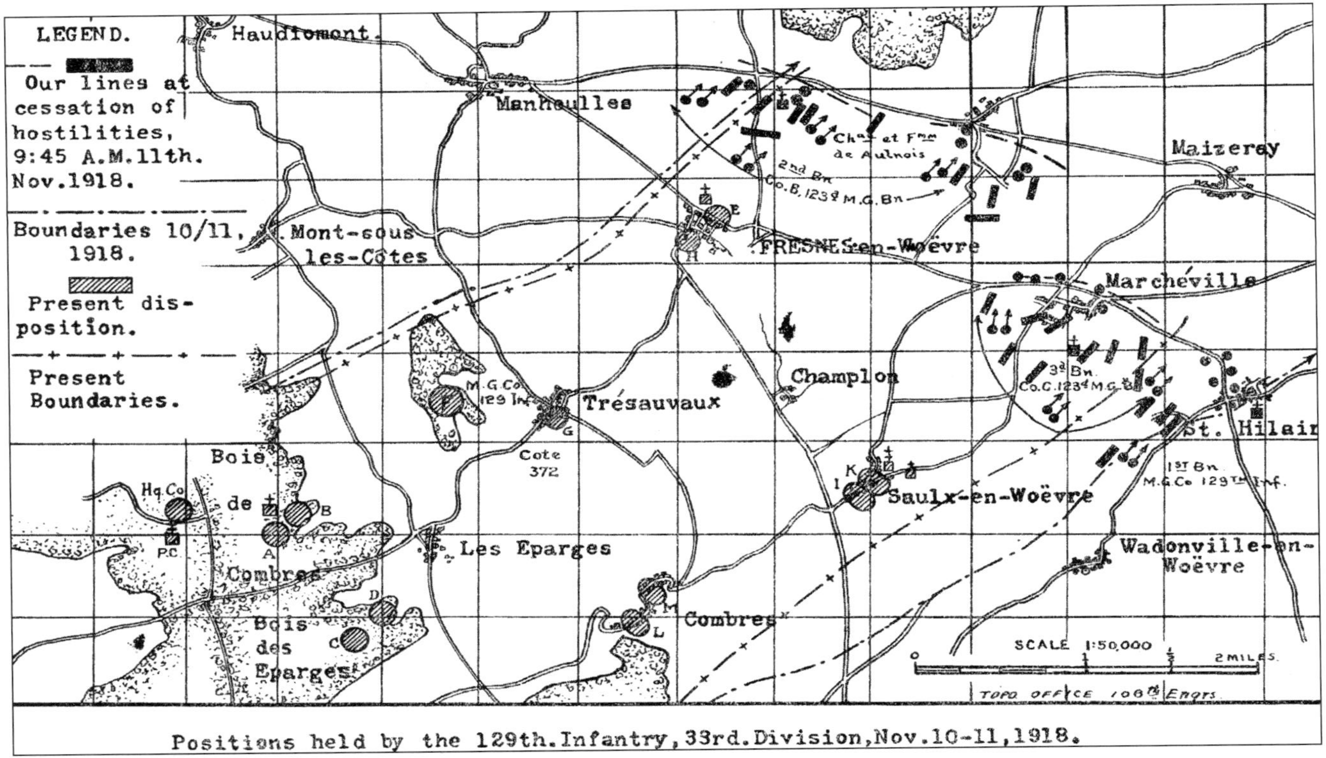

Positions of the 33rd Division on 10-11 November 1918.

Monday 11 November
Overcast, with some rain.
On the morning of 11 November, the 65th Brigade, headed by the 129th Regiment, attacked and captured Château d'Aulnois, Riaville and Marchéville, when at 11.00 am the order to cease hostilities put an end to the advance. That morning, part of the 66th Brigade was being held up in their attack on Butgnéville; they were about to resume the attack on the northern part of Harville Wood and Jonville, in an attempt to smash through the first line of the Michel Zone defences, when hostilities ceased.

During this period of trench raiding and small-scale attacks, the 33rd Division suffered 825 casualties, mainly from shellfire. However, the numbers killed by the second wave of influenza must also be taken into account.

The transport of wounded near St. Benoit, 10 November 1918.

Car Tour 4

V Corps Area

Duration: A half day's tour
Distance: Sixty-five kilometres
Maps: IGN 3213 E, Vigneulles-lès-Hattonchâtel

Infantry collar disc, worn on the right collar.

This circular tour starts and ends in Manheulles (N49°06.718' E005°35.433'). Along the route, petrol stations, supermarkets, restaurants and lunch facilities can be found in Fresnes-en-Woëvre and Vigneulles. Besides the aforementioned places there are no public rest rooms. All sites are easy accessible and can be reached by car, camper van or bicycle. Walking boots are not required. In summer, make sure to bring water.

The tour is designed to cover the general area of the attack as fought by V Corps, (the US 4th and 26th Divisions, the French 15th DIC, 2nd DCP and 39th Divisions) but also includes the advance made by the 33rd Division during the last few days of the war. Besides the stops of this tour, there are many other points of interest, such as Les Éparges and the Alain Fournier Monument. If you have time to spare, these 1915 sites are highly recommended and are easily added to the tour between stop 3 and 4.

GPS coordinates Car Tour 4

(1) Manheulles Bunker	(N49°06.718′ E005°35.433′)
(2) 4th Division Monument	(N49°36.148′ E004°47.869′)
(3) Louis Pergaud Monument	(N49°05.374′ E005°40.005′)
(4) St. Maurice German Cemetery	(N49°00.924′ E005°41.097′)
(5) Viéville-sous-les-Côtes German Cemetery	(N49°00.211′ E005°41.406′)
(6) Crash site Lady Jeanette	(N48°59.364′ E005°42.937′)
(7) Taylor Plaque	(N48°58.846′ E005°42.230′)
(8) 1st Division Monument	(N48°58.703′ E005°42.910′)

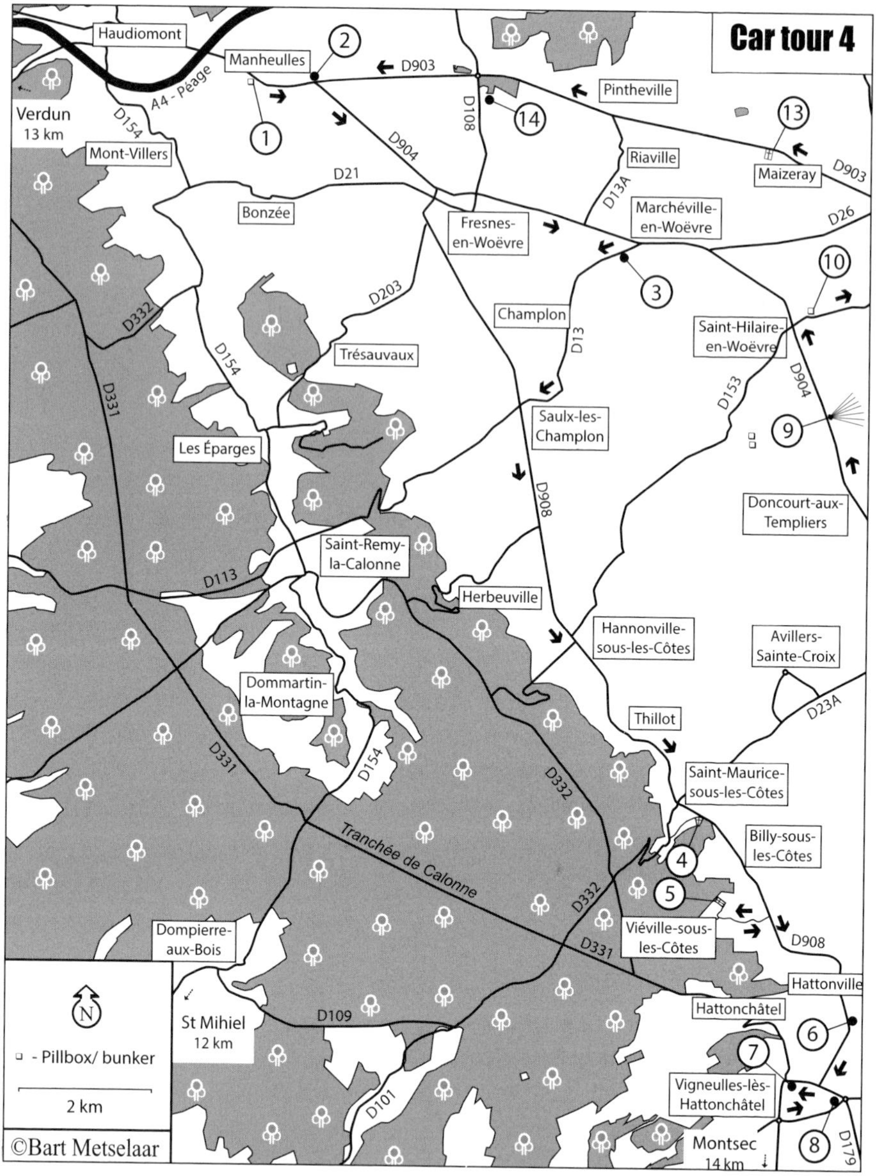

(9) Hautes Épines Woods (N49°04.095′ E005°42.602′)
(10) German MG bunker (N49°04.905′ E005°42.355′)
(11) Harville Carré Militaire (N49°05.912′ E005°43.746′)
(12) Harville German Cemetery (N49°05.956′ E005°43.766′)
(13) Maizeray German Cemetery (N49°06.224′ E005°14.798′)
(14) Château d’Aulnois Ruins (N49°06.597′ E005°38.208′)

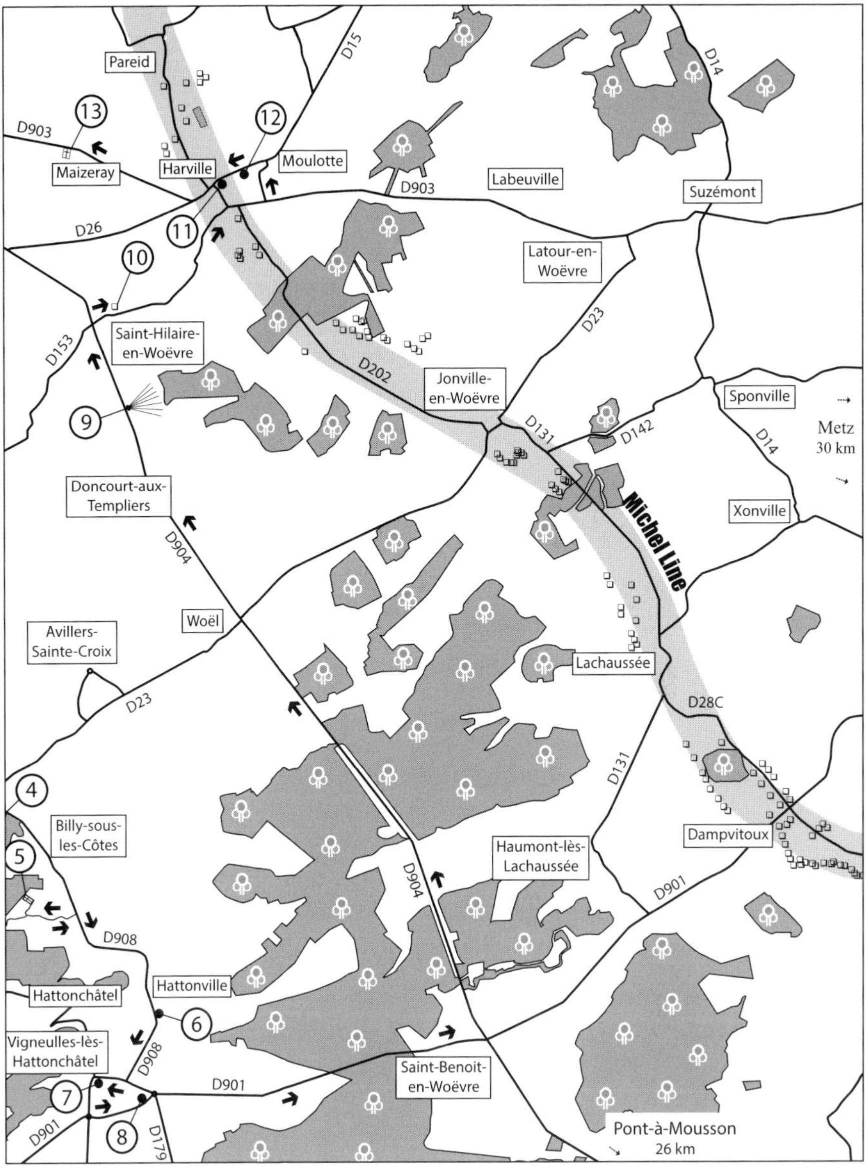

Assuming you come from the direction of Verdun, the **Manheulles Bunker (1)** (N49°06.718′ E005°35.433′) is on the right side of the D903, just before you enter Manheulles. The structure is clearly recognizable as today it supports several billboards. It is not safe to park next to the bunker; continue for about thirty metres and park in front of the first house on the right. This German bunker served as an observation post

German observation post in Manheulles.

and is part of the Hagen Line, the outpost zone of the Michel Zone. The aperture is roughly facing in the direction of Verdun.

Continue along the D903 for one kilometre until you come to a T-junction. The **4th Division Monument (2)** (N49°36.148′ E004°47.869′) stands on the left side of the D903. You cannot stop here (it is a busy junction, often with fast traffic), so turn right onto the D904, park at a safe spot and walk back. The monument marks the furthest point of advance of the 4th Division on 16 September 1918, but also coincides with the furthest point of advance on 11 November 1918. The D904 from Manheulles to Fresnes can be regarded as the line of 11 November.

Return to your car and carry on to Fresnes and Marchéville. Several Hagen Line bunkers are still visible on both sides of the road. Just before

View in the direction of Verdun from the observation post bunker.

you reach Marchéville, turn right onto the D113, direction Saulx. After fifity metres, the **Louis Pergaud Monument (3)** (N49°05.374′ E005°40.005′) is on the left side of the road. Pergaud was born on 22 January 1882, in Belmont, Doubs, Bourgogne (Burgundy). Son of a republican schoolmaster (ie he was politically fairly 'radical' and anti-monarchist, church etc.), Louis was encouraged to excel in his studies. His academic successes earned him scholarships, permitting him to continue school with the intention of following in his father's footsteps.

Fourth Division Monument.

He finished his education in 1901 and became a schoolteacher. In 1903, he married Marthe Caffot. Soon thereafter he started to get into trouble with the local Catholic clergy and several other people in the village where he was teaching. Major political issues of the time, like the separation of church and state to name one, became irreconcilable issues. He separated from

Louis Pergoud (1882-1915).

Louis Pergoud Monument.

his wife and in 1907 he decided to go to Paris to pursue a literary career. In 1910, *Mercure de France* published a collection of Pergaud's short stories; this work was promptly awarded the prestigious *Prix Goncourt*, which also led to modest national recognition. His *oeuvre* comprises four books, of which *La guerre des boutons* became his most famous publication.

At the outbreak of the war he tried to register as a pacifist but was conscripted nonetheless. After the horrific losses of the first six months of the war, the French army was in serious need of replacements. In March 1915, as an educated man and because of a serious shortage of officers, he became a sergeant in the 166th Regiment and was transferred to the Verdun sector. On 7 April 1915, during a peak in the fighting on Les Éparges, Pergaud and his regiment launched an attack at Hill 233 near Marchéville. If you look straight behind Pergaud's monument, you see a line of trees; this is Hill 233. Here, Pegaud was shot and tumbled into the German barbed wire. This is where the French explanatory plaque ends, simply stating, 'killed by the Germans'. However, after the attack had fizzled out the Germans, looking for wounded, rescued him and some other wounded French soldiers and evacuated them to a field hospital behind the German line in Marchéville. Patched up by German doctors, he was killed one day later, on 8 April, by a French artillery barrage aimed at the village. His body was never found.

Go back to your car, pass through Saulx and take a left turn at the D908. Those who want to visit Les Éparges: continue straight on and follow the signs 'Crête des Éparges'.

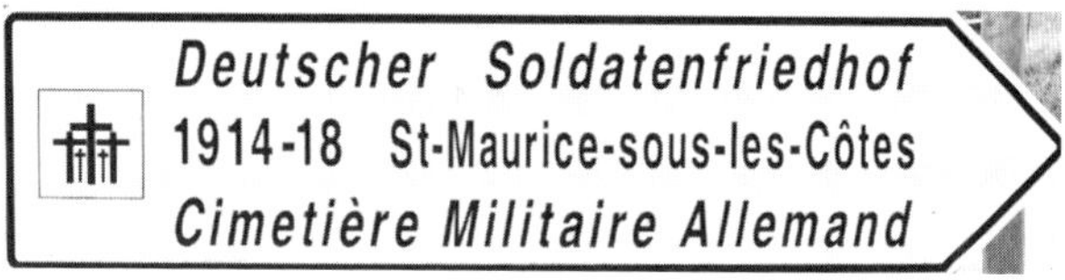

You have just left the 4th Division's sector and entered the French sector. Pass through Hannonville, Thilot and St. Maurice-sous-les-Côtes. Just after you have left the latter village you will come to **St. Maurice German Cemetery (4)** (N49°00.924′ E005°41.097′) on your right. This cemetery contains the remains of 1,775 German and fourteen Austro-Hungarian (KuK) army war dead. Started in 1914, the cemetery was extended several times. After the war, the French Government used the cemetery to rebury Germans found in isolated field graves or in small road-side cemeteries. These hastily dug field graves date mostly from the last week of November and, if you look closely, many of the metal crosses bear the 10 or 11 November date, when the Americans were trying to increase the pressure on the Germans. The Austro-Hungarians that are

Killed on the last day of the war.

buried here were mostly killed during the St. Mihiel Offensive and were members of the 35th *Kaiserlich und Königlich* (reflecting the Dual Monarchy: Imperial – Austrian Empire – and Royal – Kingdom of Hungary) Division. Originally fitted with wooden crosses, the grave markers were replaced by metal crosses in 1970.

A little further along the D908 you will arrive at another German cemetery. What makes the **Viéville-sous-les-Côtes German Cemetery (5)** (N49°00.211′ E005°41.406′) so interesting is that the original German monument that was dedicated during the war is still in its original position. The location of the cemetery is well-indicated and lies next to the village church. Viéville was used for billeting purposes for soldiers that came back from the front. Reasonably sheltered by the hills that surround the village from the west, during the war all kinds of recreational activities were organized for the soldiers. To forget about the

Viéville-sous-les-Côtes German Cemetery during the war.

The original German memorial.

war for a while, sports and games were organized. Viéville even had a cinema and an open air circus.

The cemetery was begun in November 1914, by troops of the German 33rd Reserve Division, and stayed in use all during the war. Also buried here are three Austrian soldiers from the 35th KuK Division; they were killed during the St. Mihiel offensive of September 1918. The original German monument, dating from 1915, was heavily damaged by American shell fire on 12 September 1918, but restored by the French in 1920, who used the cemetery to bury German soldiers that were found in isolated graves in the area.

Return to the D908 and continue to Hattonville. Just before you leave the village, on the left side of the road and next to the last house/barn of

The laundry of Viéville during the German occupation.

Lady Jeanette Memorial.

Hattonville, you will find a monument to the B-17 **Lady Jeanette (6)** (N48°59.364′ E005°42.937′). The monument is erected to commemorate the crew of a B-17 bomber that crashed not far from the monument. During the morning of 9 November 1944, on its way to Saarbrücken, Germany, on a bombing mission, the Lady Jeanette was hit by flak, German anti-aircraft fire. One of the engines was blown off the right wing and the plane caught fire. In an attempt to return to their own lines, the pilots managed to make a 180° turn. Losing altitude, the B-17 crossed the French border and passed Metz. Looking for a place to crash-land the plane, the Woëvre Plain seemed the best option. However, the plane was now loosing altitude fast and before reaching Hattonville three men bailed out and landed in the field behind the monument whilst two others had abandoned the plane a few minutes earlier.

It now seemed as if the B-17 would crash in the town's centre but fortunately the pilot managed to make another 180° turn. Very soon afterwards the plane smashed into the ground, about a kilometre to the east of the monument. Four crewmen were killed in the crash, the remainder survived. The pilot, 1st Lieutenant Donald J. Gott, and co-pilot William E. Motzger were awarded the Medal of Honor. They sacrificed their lives so the others could bail out and prevented the plane from crashing on Hattonville, doubtlessly saving the lives of many of the villagers. In the 1990s, thanks to the detective work of author WS Cole Jr., it became clear that the B-17 was in fact a B-24 on a secret mission; for more detailed information, Google 'Lady Jeanette B-17'.

Pilot 1st Lieutenant Donald J. Gott, MOH.

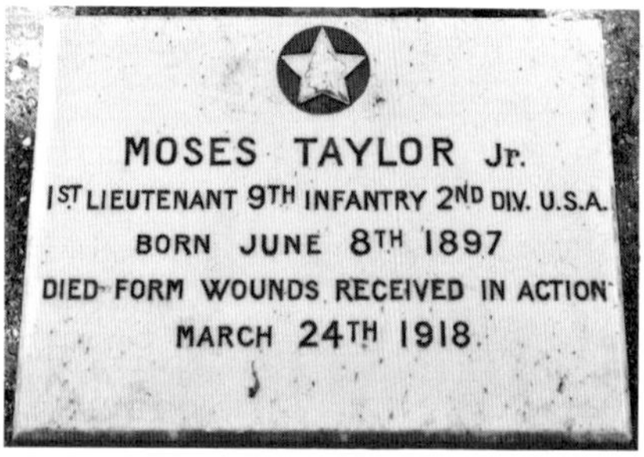

Note the spelling error in the word 'from'.

War Memorial in Vigneulles.

Carry on along the D908 to Vigneulles and take a right turn in the direction of the town centre. Across the street from the Mairie (the Town Hall), on the village square stands the Monument aux Morts. Park here. The statue at the back of the monument is dedicated to 'A young American that [sic] died for France'. At the base of the monument you will see a plaque dedicated to **Moses Taylor Jr. (7)** (N48°58.846′ E005°42.230′). The plaque reads: *'Moses Taylor, Jr., 1st Lieutenant, 9th Inf. 2nd Div. USA, born June 8th, 1897, died form* [sic] *wounds received in action March 24, 1918.'* [This plaque has been recently replaced by one with the correct spelling.]

Moses Taylor Jr. (1897-1918).

Born in Babylon, Long Island, New York, 1st Lieutenant Moses Taylor Jr. arrived in France in December 1917. On 14 March, after additional training, the Indian Head division was moved to the Verdun/Mihiel area, into the so-called Troyon Sector. Taylor and the 9th Regiment occupied the French trenches between Lacroix-sur-Meuse and Vaux. The story goes that on 23 March 1918 Taylor gathered a group of volunteers for a raid in No Man's Land. The objective was to capture a mill housing several German machine guns. With Taylor in command, at 2.00 am the group went over the top and crept towards the German line. Suddenly, shots rang out and Taylor was hit. Alarmed, flares went up and the Germans started shelling the area in front of their positions. Panic-stricken, the Americans hurried back to their own lines, leaving Taylor behind. The Second Division's History continues:

> 'The German 82nd Reserve Division lay opposite the Troyon Sector with headquarters in Vigneulles. In spite of rigorous patrolling, the division commander felt his information was incomplete, especially in view of the evidence that Americans were arriving. It had been reported that men wearing brown overcoats (the French overcoat was blue) were seen. On 23 March, 2nd Lieutenant Moses Taylor of the 9th Infantry, mortally wounded while commanding a patrol, had been captured and identified as an American.'

Taylor's body was buried in Vigneulles by the Germans. After the war his body was exhumed and, surprisingly, re-interred in Romagne-sous-Montfaucon American Cemetery instead of Thiaucourt American Cemetery. The reason for this is unknown. Talyor's grave can be found at plot H, row 44, grave 37.

Taylor's headstone, Plot H/44/37.

Return to your car and drive back along the same road on which you entered the village. Continue onto the D901. At the roundabout, take the first exit on the right and stop at a particularly undistinguished parking area (much favoured by heavy trucks) alongside the road. Here, of all places, stands the **1st Division Monument (8)** (N48°58.703′ E005°42.910′) that commemorates the historic event of 13 September 1918 when the 1st and 26th Divisions met and cut off the tip of the Salient.

On 12 September, at 5.00 am, the 1st Division left Seicheprey. In the early hours of 13 September, after losing ninety-eight men killed and 489 men wounded or missing, the division arrived in Vigneulles. By closing the gap that morning, 16,000 German soldiers were trapped in the pocket and 450 guns and tons of supplies were captured. If you look behind the monument, Hattonchâtel can be seen; this village

First Division Monument; it was here where the 26th and 1st Divisions met and cut off the tip of the St. Mihiel Salient.

and Vigneulles, among others, were captured by the 26th Division.

Return to the roundabout and continue straight along the D901. At the roundabout at St. Benoît turn left onto the D904. Pass through Woël and Doncourt. Once you have passed through the latter village, on the right, you see a wooded area. These are the **Hautes Épines Woods (9)** (N49°04.095' E005°42.602'). Beyond the latter woods lies Herville Wood.

On 16 September 1918, the D904 roughly marked the furthest point of advance of the St. Mihiel drive. However, on 10 November, during the last days of the war, the 33rd Division launched a small-scale attack against the Hagen Line, the outpost zone of the Michel Zone. The 130th Regiment attacked and captured the German stronghold of Marchéville and on the same day the 131st Regiment and Companies A and B of the 124th Machine Gun Battalion finally drove the Germans out of Hautes Épines Wood. Later, they captured the southern portion of Harville Wood and managed to break through the wire of the outer defences of the Hagen Line. The capture of Haute-Épines and Harville Woods were important insofar as, for the first time, the Americans had managed to get a toehold inside the Michel Zone. Harville Wood also marks the furthest point of advance by the Americans within the Michel Zone.

A litte further along the D904 lies the sleepy little village of St. Hilaire-en-Woëvre. Turn right onto the D153 and stop at the back of the parish church. Across the street from the church you can see a **German machine gun bunker (10)** (N49°04.905′ E005°42.355′). Serving as both observation and machine-gun position, this bunker is part of the Hagen Line and also provided basic living quarters. The bunker is a good example of how the Germans made use of existing buildings to blend in their defensive works. Built in 1918, anyone coming from the main road, the D904, in this direction would have been surprised by its presence. As there are not that many lateral roads, a bunker like this could easily hold up the advance. The bunker remained in German hands until the end of the war.

Continue along the D153 to Butgnéville. When you reach the T-junction, take a left turn to Harville. Harville was part of the Volker Line, the main defence line of the Michel Zone. Cellars of houses were transformed into pillboxes and roadblocks and trenches ran across the streets. Drive to the church and stop here. To the left of the church, you see the **French Carré Militaire (11)** (N49°05.912′ E005°43.746′). Although far from unique, it is worth an explanation. During the first months of the war French soldiers were often buried in communal cemeteries close to where they were killed; the same thing happened in 1940. The reason for this is that military cemeteries had not yet been

German observation and machine-gun bunker in St. Hilaire.

established, or, as in this case, the area had been overrun by the enemy before the bodies could be evacuated. Nine soldiers from two world wars have been laid to rest here.

After the sharp bend in the road turn right onto the D26; **Harville German Cemetery (12)** (N49°05.956′ E005°43.766′) is situated on the right side of the road. The cemetery was started in the autumn of 1914, after Harville had fallen into Germans hands on 19 September. The reason

French carré militaire, Harville.

Killed during the St. Mihiel Offensive.

Original headstone in Harville German Cemetery.

for this was that the Germans quickly established several field hospitals in and around the village and a cemetery was needed for the casualties who died there. The hospitals and cemetery stayed in use until May 1916. From May 1916 the hospitals came under regular fire from the French heavy artillery and were evacuated. Partly destroyed, the cemetery was repaired and extended between 1926 and 1932. In 1966, the temporary wooden crosses were replaced by stone and metal grave markers. Interestingly, several of the original German grave markers were placed alongside the hedges that mark the outer boundary of the cemetery. In total, 494 soldiers are buried in this cemetery.

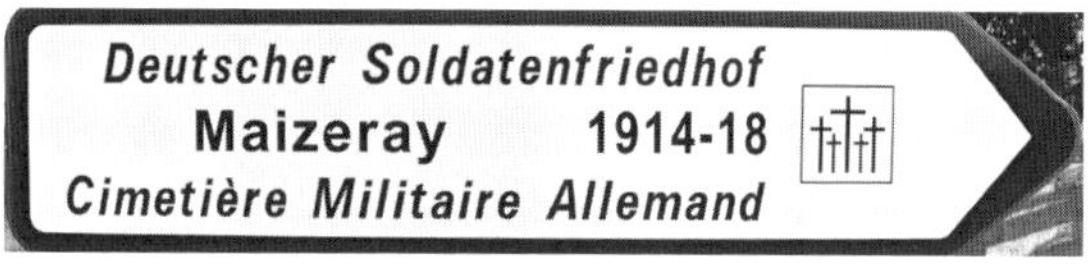

Go back to your car, turn around and drive along the D903 to Maizeray. After you have passed through this hamlet, **Maizeray German Cemetery (13)** (N49°06.224′ E005°14.798′) is on the left side of the road. The cemetery, started in 1914 by the Germans, was transformed into a concentration cemetery by the French after the Second World War. It contains bodies from sixty different burial sites in a radius of twenty kilometres around Maizeray. Many of the crosses bear dates from the start of the St. Mihiel Offensive to 11 November. A number of Austro-Hungarian troops from the 35th KuK Division are buried here. No less than thirty-nine different German divisions are represented. The cemetery was restored in 1966; in 1972 the wall, entrance and stairs were built. In total, 2,876 soldiers are buried in this cemetery.

German shelter.

Go back to your car and continue along the D903 to Pintheville. Pass through the village and carry on until you arrive at a roundabout. Take the third exit. At the moment you leave the forest, park on the track on the left side of the D908. On your immediate right stands a German bunker. Originally, this was part of the gate house of **Château d'Aulnois (14)** (N49°06.597′ E005°38.208′) but the Germans reinforced the structure with concrete to withstand shrapnel.

Château d'Aulnois was built in the 19th century but has its origins in the 14th century when a castle was built on this place. The tower that is

The facade of Château d'Aulnois in 2019.

still visible today was added to the complex in 1810. In 1910 the château was completely renovated.

When the war broke out, the château was situated behind the French lines and was occupied by French troops. It has been said that before his death, in April 1915, the French writer Louis Pergaud spent a few nights at the château (see also Stop 3). When, on 21 February 1916, the Battle of Verdun started, the Germans decided to increase pressure on the French in this area too. During the night of 27-28 February Château d'Aulnois fell into the hands of the 65th Landwehr Infantry Regiment. With the French pushed back, the Germans started to reinforce the line between Ville-en-Woevre and Fresnes-en-Woevre. This line became the new first line of defence. Part of the cellar of the château was fitted with a thick reinforced concrete roof that was poured on top of the floors of the rooms above and which served as a shelter. The new line was called the Auler Stellung, after Lieutenant General Carl Auler-Pascha of the 5th Landwehr Division and consisted of several Stützpunkte, strongholds. Château d'Aulnois served as one of these strongholds. In 1917, the Auler Line was integrated into the Hagen Line, the outer defence line of the Michel Zone and came under the command of Army Group von Strantz.

Severely damaged by fire during the fighting of September 1914, by the end of 1916 the château had been largely destroyed by the French artillery. Interestingly, on several French websites the Germans are solely blamed for the destruction of the château, conveniently ignoring the fact that it was part of the front line for four years and that the building was mainly destroyed as a consequence of being hit by French shells. At the end of the war, Château d'Aulnois and the surrounding area again became

The château in better times.

the scene of heavy fighting, now between the German 13th Landwehr Division and the American 33rd Division. During several trench raids, members of the American 130th Regiment captured and killed soldiers of the German 60th Landwehr Division. The remains of the Château were finally taken by the 129th Regiment, 33rd Division on the morning of 11 November 1918. The fighting ceased at 9.45 am.

Today, only the façade, part of the inside walls and one tower remain. The château stands on private property and permission from the owners is needed to visit the ruins. Do not walk through the field when there are crops planted; always try and keep to field boundaries whenever possible!

Turn your car and go back to the roundabout. Turn left onto the D903 to return to Manheulles and Verdun.

Reinforced cellar of Château d'Aulnois.

Walk 3

Hattonchâttel

Duration: One and a half hour
Distance: Three kilometres
Maps: IGN 3213 E, Vigneulles-lès-Hattonchâtel

This circular walk concentrates on Hattonchâttel, a sleepy little hilltop village that lies in the 26th Division's sector and was liberated during the night of 12-13 September 1918. Occupied by the Germans since autumn 1914, the village was partly destroyed by shelling during the fighting that took place in 1914 and 1915. In September 1918, the village was shelled again, this time by the Americans. Before the arrival of the American 26th Division, Hattonchâtel was set on fire and evacuated by the Austrian 35th Division. This tour tells the remarkable story of the restoration of the village that was financed by American businesswoman and philanthropist Mrs. Belle Skinner.

In Hattonchâtel there are neither shopping nor refuelling facilities. However, there is a café, *L'Air du Moulin*, in the town square where the thirsty battlefield tourist can enjoy a nice quiet drink. Unfortunately, the opening hours are not clear. Apart from the café (if open), there are no public toilets. Walking boots, binoculars and a bottle of water are recommended.

GPS coordinates Walk 3

(1) Château	(N48°59.548′ E005°42.340′)
(2) German grave markers	(N48°59.544′ E005°42.267′)
(3) Cloister, then and now	(N48°59.523′ E005°42.231′)
(4) Church	(N48°59.523′ E005°42.231′)
(5) Mairie	(N48°59.520′ E005°42.176′)
(6) Panorama Montsec	(N48°59.500′ E005°42.182′)
(7) Ludwig Platz	(N48°59.521′ E005°42.141′)
(8) Monument aux Morts	(N48°59.517′E005°42.112′)
(9) Lavoir, washing facility	(N48°59.508′ E005°42.041′)
(10) Cemetery	(N48°59.427′ E005°41.909′)
(11) Former German Cemetery	(N48°59.425′ E005°41.937′)

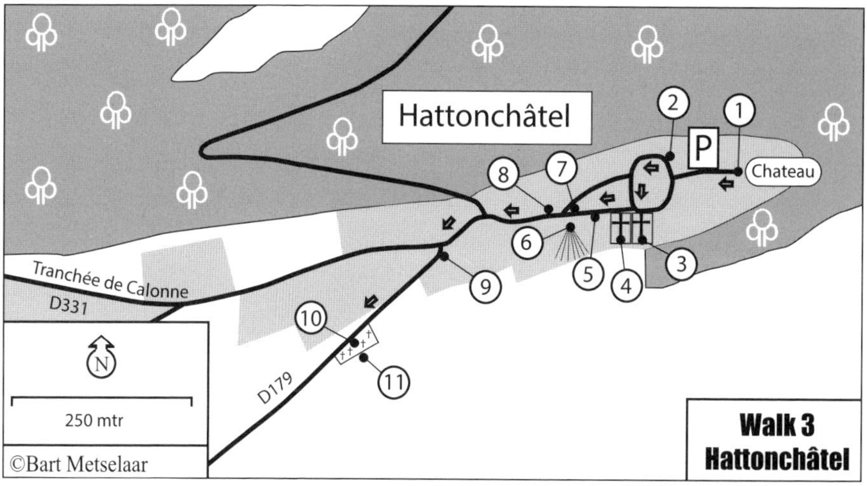

The background to a remarkable story

Ruth Isabelle Skinner (1866-1928).

Ruth Isabelle Skinner (1866-1928) was an American businesswoman and philanthropist. She was born with a silver spoon in her mouth, the daughter of a wealthy silk manufacturer William Skinner and his second wife Sarah Elizabeth Allen. Isabelle 'Belle' Skinner never married and lived most of her life at the family estate, Wistariahurst in Holyoke, Massachusetts, now an historic site. Passionate about music, she renovated and expanded this house, centred on a music room, where she housed her remarkable collection of musical instruments. This collection is now based at Yale University.

In 1902, after her father, William Skinner, died, Belle and her sister Katherine established the Skinner Coffee House in honour of their late father. The coffee house initially hosted women working in the Skinner mills for social, service and educational activities. However, the coffee house gradually became a meeting place for dozens of men's clubs, women's clubs, community organizations, children's groups etc., making it an ideal place for networking.

Shortly after the war ended, Miss Skinner, a Francophile, decided to visit France. After first seeing the French countryside and villages destroyed by the war, she allegedly cabled home: 'War is awful, I can make a difference'. Back in Holyoke and making use of her network, Miss Skinner initiated and led the effort to rally American cities to adopt French villages during the postwar reconstruction, establishing the American Committee of Villages Libérés in New York City in March 1919.

Miss Skinner (r) amidst the ruins of Hattonchâtel.

Holyoke, Miss Skinner's hometown, was the first city to take part in the program, providing a water supply to the village of Apremont-la-Forêt (see car tour 6). She herself decided to adopt the small town of Hattonchâtel, which meant that she provided the money for the restoration of all public services in the village. However, in practice it was her brother William Jr. who administered the immense family capital trust and it was William who officially provided the funds for the restoration of Hattonchâtel.

An interesting, though not unbiased, newspaper article explaining the work of the Committee was published in *The Vassar Miscellany News* of 12 March 1919:

> 'Splendid work in the reconstruction of the devastated villages of France has been done under the leadership of Miss Isabel Skinner, an alumna of the class of '87. The following article describes briefly her own work and that of the society of which she is the head. Miss Isabel Skinner will soon return to France to resume

her work with 'Villages Libérés.' Her adopted village is Hattonchâtel. a ninth century village, not far from St. Mihiel. In the old days it was a favorite retreat of the bishops of Verdun; during the recent war it was captured by the Germans, and used by them as a base from which to shell Verdun [not true; the village was used for billeting German troops]. The destruction of the charming little village, with the church noted for its beautiful cloisters – which fortunately can yet be restored – the homes, the gardens and the vineyards that covered the hill crowned by the tiny village, was so complete that the returning villagers, most of whom escaped [in truth they were evacuated by the French Army in 1914], will need all the assistance, moral and material, that their 'Marrame' can give. The French Government will aid to its limit, and it is hoped that supplies for the reconstruction will be delivered at Hattonchâtel by April first, so that every advantage of the season may be utilized to hasten the rebuilding of the homes. Through Miss Skinner's efforts, as President, an American Committee of the Villages Libérés has been organized and incorporated, and now throughout the country, individuals, groups and even cities are adopting villages, or by gifts of money and materials are aiding the French villager to resume his normal life, industrial, family and religious. The plan of the Committee to have a representative of each of its groups resident in its particular village, through whom passes the desire to help on one side, and gratitude on the other, cannot but increase the spirit of brotherhood felt by the French and American people.'

Miss Skinner in later life.

Besides being awarded several other high French decorations, in 1923, on the fifth anniversary of the liberation of the village by the Franco-American forces, President Millerand (1859-1943) awarded Miss Skinner the *Légion d'honneur* (the Legion of Honour) France's highest and most important award, for her practical devotion to France and her work for the American Committee.

Miss Skinner paid several visits to Hattonchâtel to follow the progress of the rebuilding of the village. Sadly, while traveling to France to oversee the last phase of the restoration project, she contracted pneumonia. Not being able to continue her journey to Hattonchâtel, on 9 April 1928 sixty-two years old Isabelle Skinner died in Paris. Her body was returned to

New York City where a funeral service was held. A few days later a second service was held at the Skinner Memorial Chapel of the Holyoke United Congregational Church. She was interred in the family's plot at Forestdale Cemetery.

Château d'Hattonchâtel in 2019.

The walk

This short walk starts and ends at Château d'Hattonchâtel. There is more than enough parking space in front of the château. The building of the **Château (1)** (N48°59.548′ E005°42.340′), dating from 859, was commissioned by Bishop Hatton of Verdun; then it was a formidable stronghold and housed his own personal mint – Verdun was a Prince Bishopric of the Holy Roman Empire at the time. It stayed in use throughout the Middle Ages; it was badly damaged by Swedish troops in 1638 during the Thirty Years War and its destruction was completed by Cardinal Richelieu soon afterwards. Cardinal Richelieu became the most powerful man in France for a number of years from 1624, when he became the First Minister of King Louis XIII. By reducing the power of the French nobility, he tried to maximize the power of the French state, which at that time meant the king. In this he succeeded; Louis XIII's successor, Louis XIV. 'le Roi Soleil' ('the Sun King'), over the period of his very long reign (1638-1715) became the most powerful monarch in French history. During this period Château d'Hattonchâtel was destroyed; in fact, a number of rich families who had fortified properties saw them destroyed and their wealth and local power significantly reduced. Besides physically destroying the basis of their local power, Louis XIV more or less forced the senior aristocracy to spend much of their time at the royal court, at centres such as Versailles, thereby further weakening their hold in their home territories.

German headstone at the cafe.

Commemorative plaques are fixed on both sides of the entrance gate. Lying in ruins for a few centuries, it was Belle's dream to rebuild the château as the ultimate gift to the French people. In 1927, after most of the work on the village had been finished or was in its final stages, the first stone was laid for the rebuilt château. Following Belle Skinner's untimely death in 1928, her brother William decided to continue the massive undertaking of rebuilding the château in honour of his sister. On 7 September 1933 the building was finally ready, fifteen years after the war had ended. By that time, the Skinner family had spent one million dollars on the rebuilding of Hattonchâtel. In today's money that would be approximately forty million dollars – but in fact a restoration project on such a scale now would probably cost three or four times as much as that.

Today, the château is privately owned and used as a hotel; neither the gardens nor the hotel are open to the general public. The facade looks magnificent but, alas, it is only skin deep. A walk around the building makes it painfully clear that since the building was finished in 1933 there appears to have been little or no maintenance work carried out.

Walk along the parking space in the direction of the L'Air du Moulin cafe, called after the windmill that stood here before the war. In the garden, between the tables, several **German grave markers (2)** (N48°59.544′ E005°42.267′) can be seen. The origin of the stones is unknown, but it is likely that they are from the former German cemetery in Hattonchâtel. Unfortunately, it is impossible to make out any of the names on the stones so it is not an easy matter to make further investigations.

The cloister then and now.

Continue in the direction of the parish church. Just before you reach the entrance, you see the **Cloister (3)** (N48°59.523′ E005°42.231′) on the left. Although the roofs were destroyed of this fifteenth century

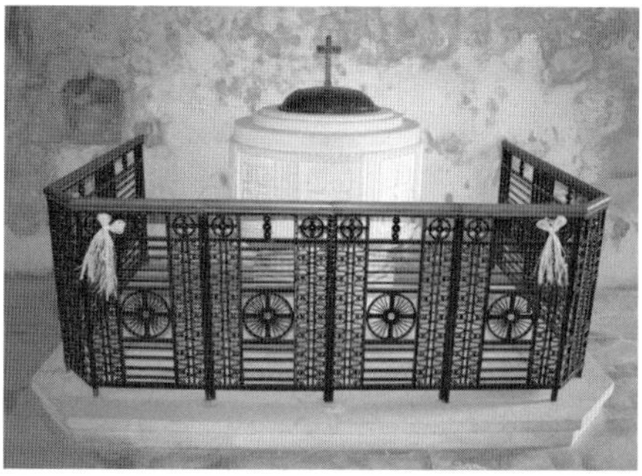

Holy water basin donated by Miss Skinner.

Detail of the Ligier Richier altar piece dating from 1523.

building, the walls and crucifix in the garden survived the war. See the then and now photo in the book.

Next, enter the **Church (4)** (N48°59.523′ E005°42.231′). Besides paying for the restoration of the roofs of the cloister and the two churches (or, perhaps better, the church and a chapel), the holy water stoop in front of you was also donated by Miss Skinner. This church dates from the sixteenth century but itself was built over a ninth century church. The belfry dates from the nineteenth century and was more or less added to the building. The reason for this was that originally a belfry had been built on the other side of the church but no one in the village could hear the bells. At the back of the

The Mairie, town hall, paid for by Miss Skinner.

church, on the left side, there is a door leading to another, fourteenth century, church/chapel. Immediately behind the door there is a beautiful Passion of Christ altar piece, the creation in 1523 of the famous artist Ligier Richier. Also note the date 1920, where the arches of one of the vaults meet. As an integral part of the ramparts and citadel, the outer walls of the church are 1.35 metres thick. The outer wall of the church also doubles as a rampart and here the floor level drops about ten metres.

NOTE: When you leave the church, please close the door!

About a hundred metres further along this street, at Rue Miss Skinner 16, is the **Mairie (5)** (N48°59.520′ E005°42.176′) the town hall. When you enter the building there are several plaques on the wall that are dedicated to

View over Vigneulles with the Montsec Monument on the hill in the distance.

the benefactress of the village. The bronze plaque on the right, inaugurated in Belle's presence on 13 September 1923, commemorates the fact that since the liberation several buildings, such as the Mairie, had been completed.

Enter the courtyard of the Mairie and walk to the back of the garden. From here, you have a superb view of the American Memorial on **Montsec (6)** (N48°59.500′ E005°42.182′). Montsec lies at about eight kilometres distance; the front line of 12 September was two kilometres beyond Montsec.

Walk back to Rue Miss Skinner and turn left. After a hundred metres stop and turn around. You are now looking at a medieval building (see the then and now photographs). The German photograph was taken in 1915 at the *Place du Grand Puits*, which was renamed **Ludwig Platz (7)** (N48°59.521′ E005°42.141′) during the occupation. Fortunately, the building with the arcades that served as a market place for centuries largely survived the war. If you are able mentally to block out the cars it is a scene where it appears that time has stood still, a testimony to the skills of the workers who rebuilt the village by hand, stone by stone.

Turn around again and leave Ludwig Platz behind you. Fifty meters down the road you will come to the **Monument aux Morts (8)** (N48°59.517′ E005°42.112′). This extraordinary monument depicts a mourning woman instead of the usual heroic French soldier. Dedicated to honour the women of France, it is clear that Belle Skinner put her personal mark on the monument. It stands in front of the only building

The Grand Place (Ludwig Platz) then and now.

that apparently had not been included by the building program, the *Maison de la Voute,* literally the vaulted house. This 12th century edifice was originally part of the defences of Hattonchâtel but was later transformed into a house.

One hundred metres further on, on the left side of the same road, stands the **Lavoir (9)** (N48°59.508′ E005°42.041′), the washing basin or trough. Access to fresh water was of the utmost importance and therefore this basin was among

The village war monument depicts Belle Skinner.

The lavoir, wash house.

the first of the facilities that were rebuilt. Dating from 1921, the lavoir, still in working order, can be entered from the other side.

Go back to the Rue Miss Skinner and take the left fork in the direction of Vigneulles-les-Hattonchâtel. The **communal cemetery (10)** (N48°59.427′ E005°41.909′) is on the left side of the road and note that the entrance has not been missed from the Beaux Arts Style, with its Romanesque, Gothic and Renaissance influences. All the public buildings in Hattonchâtel have the

The entrance of the communal cemetery.

same recognizable architecture, which, among many others, can also be seen at the Montsec American Monument and the American Cemetery in Thiaucourt. Walk through the entrance. Although nothing could be found in the literature nor online, the Masonic altar built into the left wall almost certainly dates from the same period the village was rebuilt. The characteristic Masonic triangle, with the Eye of Providence and the rays of light can clearly be seen.

The site of the **former German Cemetery (11)** (N48°59.425′ E005°41.937′) is at the far left corner of the cemetery. It was only a small one and most fatal casualties were buried in Viéville-sous-les-Côtes.

The view from the former German cemetery then and now. Note the roof of the barn, centre left.

Return to the road, turn right and walk back to the castle. This will take about ten minutes.

ALTERNATIVE RETURN ROUTE

There is a short and interesting alternative route. A track behind the lavoir takes you along the ramparts of the village. This trail can be followed to either the church or all the way around the castle. Just before the church a track to the left leads you to Rue Miss Skinner. If you decide to extend the walk for another ten minutes and walk round the castle, you end up at a flight of stairs which leads you to the back of the cafe. From the cemetery, this route takes about thirty minutes.

CHAPTER 6

The Michel Zone

The Hindenburg Line

Bethmann-Holweg.

After the catastrophic battles in 1916 of the Somme and Verdun, the Germans amended their defensive doctrine on the Western Front in line with the new realities. The Germans no longer had sufficient manpower (in particular) and materiel (to a lesser extent) to replace all that had been lost in 1916. The situation, however, looked promising in the east, on the Russian Front; and they had captured the resources of Romania after that country's short lived and ill-fated intervention in the late summer and autumn of 1916. In the west there was a radical rethink of how best to maintain a defensive posture in the light of the massive increase in both the number and calibre of guns available to the artillery.

In view of the worsening situation on the Western Front, on 12 December 1916 Chancellor Theobald von Bethmann-Hollweg delivered a speech in the Reichstag in Berlin declaring Germany's desire to open peace negotiations. However, at this stage of the war, having lost so many lives, France would not agree to anything less than an unconditional surrender – and the Germans certainly had no intention of offering anything like that.

Falkenhayn.

The defensive doctrine at the opening of the Somme ordered by Chief of the German General Staff Falkenhayn, which was embraced with some enthusiasm by some of his army commanders, basically required that the line should be held (or recovered if lost) at all costs. By the autumn of 1916 this approach demanded unsustainable manpower resources; whereas in 1914 manpower was plentiful and weapon systems, such as aircraft, machine guns, mortars and an abundance of artillery, were relatively scarce, by this stage in the war the situation had been reversed. When the duumvirate of Hindenburg and

Ludendorff replaced him at the end of August, they introduced a new strategy for the Western Front. At the Cambrai Conference of Army Group commanders on 8 September 1916 this new strategy was outlined, discussed and important decisions were made. The offensive at Verdun was to be ended definitively (it had, more or less, by mid July, in fact) and soldiers from the Verdun Front were to be transferred to the Somme to bolster the defences in that area. In anticipation of a future Allied offensive, Ludendorff directed military engineers to study the possibility of building two major withdrawal positions behind the front lines of the Western Front. These positions became known as the Hindenburg Line, a name coined in 1916 when the first defensive line was constructed in the British-held Somme region; the name stuck. However, the Germans called it the Siegfried Stellung. After completion of the line in the Somme and Flanders, the German front line was shortened by about fifty kilometres and released at least nine divisions for deployment elsewhere, as well as creating a bigger strategic reserve and allowed for the availability of a sufficiency of *eingreiff*, or counter attack, divisions.

Wilhelm II and Hindenburg.

The implementation of the policy in the St. Mihiel Salient

Although large scale military operations in the St. Mihiel area were limited after 1915 (which had notably involved Les Éparges and Bois du Prêtre), the soldiers in the Salient were far from enjoying a quiet life. The Germans and the French spent the three years of relative tranquillity in developing their positions, making them ever stronger and more robust. Because of the lack of offensive activity, both sides indulged in numerous elaborate building projects to make life at the front as comfortable as possible under the circumstances. Deep shelters and tunnels, well-equipped with beds, electric light etc, were commonplace in the sector; in many cases even front line trenches were lined by concrete or brick walls. Huge underground hospitals were built close to the front line, unheard off in other sectors of the Western Front. All the same, the St. Mihiel Salient was a highly dangerous position for the Germans to occupy; the French held two sides of the distorted triangular shape that it formed and thus their positions were potentially vulnerable to flanking attacks. This never happened, mainly because the French needed a quiet

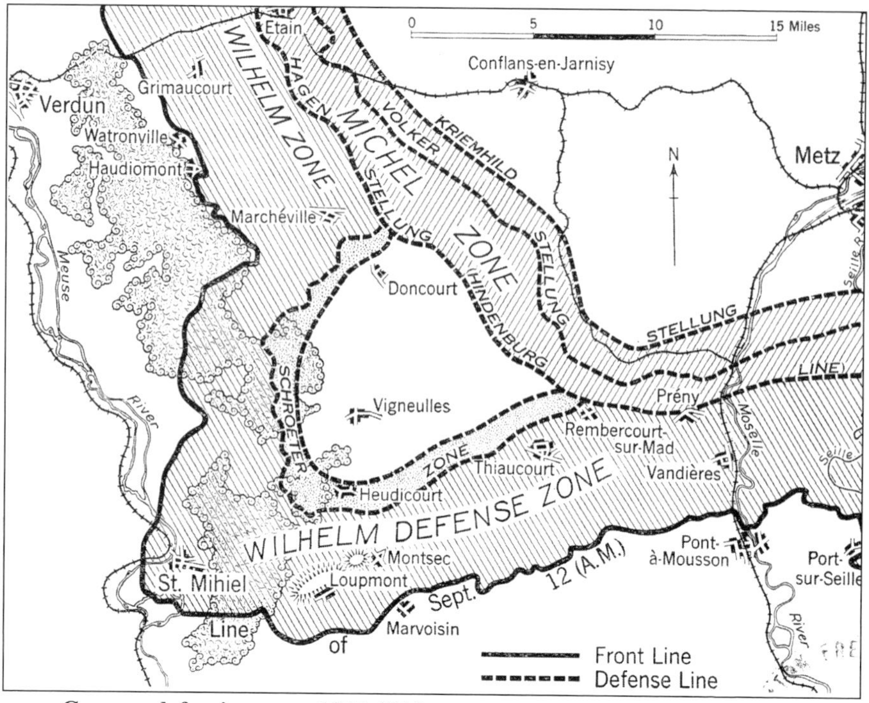

German defensive zones 1917-1918.

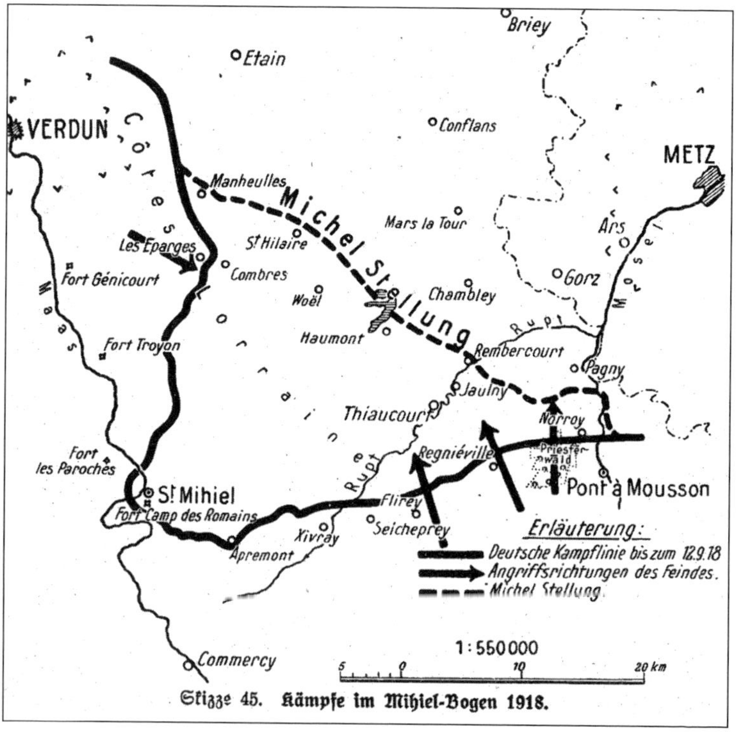

German map of the Michel Stellung.

front for their soldiers to take a breather from the fighting elsewhere. In the great scheme of things the French Army simply lacked resources and manpower to take the Salient as they considered there were greater strategic options elsewhere on the Western Front.

The Hindenburg Line was scheduled for construction in the Salient in the summer of 1917; the main defensive line was called the Michel Zone, instead of the Hindenburg/Siegfried Line. Here, the word 'zone' applies much better to the defences than the word 'line' (indeed, the Hindenburg Zone would have been a better description all along the front) due to the fact that the Michel Zone consisted of three lines, the whole to be designed as a complex defensive arrangement. The Michel Zone was built across the base of the Salient and would ultimately shorten the German front line by sixty kilometres and release just over four divisions from line holding duties, two of the main goals of the building programme.

The outpost zone:
The Hagen/Hindenburg Line

This was the zone closest to the enemy and covered No Man's Land; this sector was usually lightly held by outposts and could easily be evacuated as prescribed by the doctrine of flexible defence that was experimented with in the autumn of 1916. A few hundred metres beyond the outpost zone, two bands of wire defences, three metres wide and one metre high, were built, behind which concrete shelters and strongholds were prepared; the wire entanglements in this area were constantly maintained and developed. Lanes were made in the wire to channel potential attackers to machine-gun killing zones.

There was almost no artillery positioned in the outpost zone except for a few isolated batteries; most of the guns were placed behind the battle zone and even further to the rear. However, individual field guns could be brought forward to bolster defences, especially as a battle developed.

In the Meuse sector the number of German soldiers per metre was significantly less than on other fronts. There were several reasons for this. In the Meuse-Argonne things had been quiet for almost a year, since the Second Battle of Verdun ended on 28 September 1917, and thus fewer troops were needed. After the promising (but ultimately fruitless) German spring offensives of 1918, which were fought in other sectors, the Germans were faced by the Allied counter strokes. Thus from late July and especially by the end of August, the Germans were desperately in need of manpower replacements in areas such as the Somme and Arras. This meant that there were even fewer troops available in the Salient than usual. A few weeks before the Americans launched their offensive,

German intelligence officers suspected that something was going to happen on the St. Mihiel front. They had major concerns about Metz, concerns reinforced by imaginative American deception designed to draw away German attention from the Meuse-Argonne. According to the 7th Division History,

> 'The heavy machine guns were placed in the line of resistance and checkerwise behind the position. Minenwerfers [trench mortars] were also in this position, but were not very active except on the occasions when our forces made decided attacks. The whole scheme of machine gun and trench mortar defence appeared to be one which was constantly shifting, guns and mortars never being definitely located in one place for any length of time.'

The battle zone:

The Volker Line

In front of the main line of resistance, in its outer bands of barbed wire, the Germans placed tank 'traps'. These traps consisted of large calibre shells that were wired together and set so as to explode upon contact; these so-called mines were also placed near main roads and along railroads. The area between the outpost zone and the battle zone was the

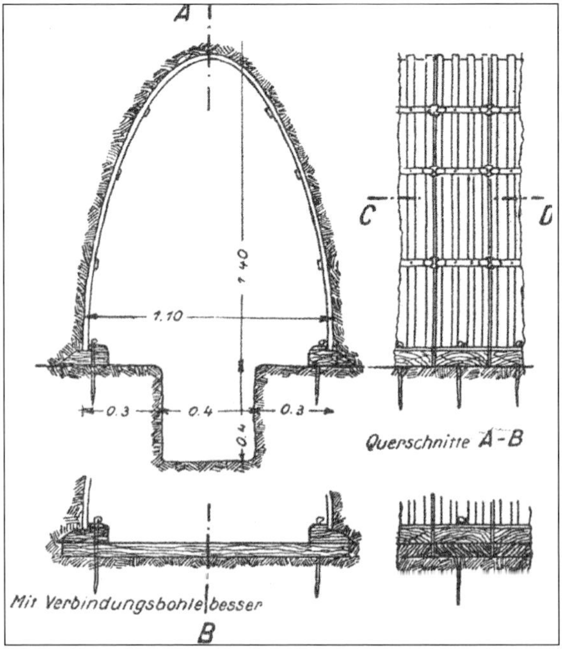

Siegfried sheets. (Seeßelberg)

A collapsed tunnel entrance.

terrain the enemy was to be allowed to take only temporarily. Once the enemy had reached the barbed wire of the Volker Line they were to be annihilated by pre-arranged zones of machine-gun and artillery fire and counter attacks made by specially trained shock troops. The Volker Line, built approximately 200 metres behind the first line of pillboxes, was a stop line, an elaborate line of bunkers spaced eighty metres or less apart, protected by at least three broad belts of barbed wire over one metre high fixed on wooden and iron stakes. A second line of bunkers and strong points were built just two hundred metres behind the first line.

The Volker Line was looked upon as a 'border' line; there were barely any other defences beyond this line at the time of the Offensive; for the most part they had yet to be constructed. The withdrawal zone leading up to the Volker Line pillboxes was a few kilometres wide and the Germans defending this zone were ordered to hold the enemy as long as possible. If necessary, they could retreat to their line of pillboxes to the rear to keep the enemy engaged without the immediate danger of a hostile breakthrough. In theory, this provided the Germans with enough time to start a massive bombardment, to organize a counterattack and ultimately push the enemy back to the outpost zone. As for the machine guns and artillery pieces that had been in short supply in 1914, these were plentiful by 1918. The 7th Division's History notes that

'The outposts and machine guns behind the outpost line had only camouflaged splinter proof shelters, usually formed by digging into the ground three or four feet and erecting a corrugated sheet iron cover on wooden uprights and covering the whole with earth, leaves and branches. Most of these shelters contained a small stove and a mattress, light sleeping bag or other cover taken from French homes. Around the shelter was erected a light barrier of barbed wire. In addition to apertures for machine guns, there were also sometimes small adjacent pits from which hand grenades could be thrown and protection thereby could be given to the machine gun. These shelters were usually occupied by two men.'

However, the overall German plan was based on the premise of major enemy attacks against one or possibly two sectors simultaneously; they did not expect and could not manage a persistent all-out Allied offensive that stretched from the North Sea in Belgium to Verdun and beyond. If the whole German front line were seriously engaged by the enemy, it would be very hard to find the reinforcements to plug the holes in the defence lines and provide sufficient manpower for the Eingreif divisions, the latter the essential element in their defence doctrine. At the end of September 1918 this situation, an all-out Allied assault along much of the length of the Western Front, was exactly what happened.

The withdrawal zone:
The Kriemhild Line

In theory, this part of the zone was designed to be the last line of defence – and the last on this part of the Western Front before the enemy could launch an attack on Germany itself. This line had not yet been built when the American Offensive commenced.

The Michel Zone defences were built in an advantageous position and on high ground. Height provided dominance over the surroundings; you could see greater distances and it had the added advantage of forcing the enemy to attack uphill, thereby wearing him out. The whole line was designed to maximize the firepower of machine guns and artillery with a minimum of manpower. In addition, the enemy had to cross wide, open valleys and then to find a way through the labyrinth of barbed wire entanglements that were constantly subjected to machine gun and artillery fire before eventually reaching the German trenches. Theoretically, the newly adopted concept of elastic defence allowed the Germans to fall back on yet another line of defence from which a counter attack could be launched. The defences were supported by large numbers of guns of all calibres, the 77mm field gun dominating.

Typical Michel Zone bunker. Note the wire defenceless in the background.

Building the Michel Zone

Military engineers were given the responsibility for the construction of permanent and consecutive defence lines or, better, zones. Machine-gun posts, broad belts of barbed wire, deep tunnels and hundreds of concrete pillboxes followed topographical contours and were organized in depth. The main defences were built just over the crest of ridges on the reverse slope to impede enemy observation and to provide better protection during an enemy artillery barrage. Whereas during 1915 pre-cast concrete building blocks were used to construct bunkers, this system was largely

Ready to pour concrete.

abandoned after 1916; those to be found in the Michel Zone today were all made from reinforced concrete and by form work.

The German defences in the Michel Zone extended from Manheulles in the north-west to Pont-à-Mousson in the south-east. The main defence line, the Volker Line, was based on a line of mutually supporting bunkers that had been dug into the ground, staggered in depth in a checkerboard or draughts board pattern. These shelters, built with one metre thick concrete roofs flush to the surface and covered with earth, were nearly impervious to artillery fire and air attacks. On average, the walls were also one metre thick and the ground plan measured five by seven and a half metres. Each shelter had an air vent, a chimney, two exits and sometimes bunkers were connected to deep tunnels. If the enemy did manage to break through the wire, the Germans could rain down artillery, mortar and heavy machine-gun fire, thus clearing the threatened area without endangering their own troops, who were secure in their shelters.

Observation bunkers could be as large as eleven by fourteen metres. Such shelters were built more for protection against shellfire than for defence. The US 7th Division's History recorded that

> 'The enemy relied mainly upon efforts to protect and preserve his full personnel until such time as our artillery ceased, when his machine guns could be brought into action without hindrance. Troops in reserve were either placed in larger dugouts, excavations on the slopes of hillsides or in reinforced cellars of houses in villages.'

To manage the construction programme, a centralized command structure was established. Overall supervision was assigned to General Ludwig Lauter and Colonel Krämer, a staff engineer. On the ground and under direct command of Krämer and Lauter, construction staff oversaw the building of the fortifications. Teams of geologists were brought in to provide information about how to avoid ground water when positioning trenches and pillboxes. They also advised on where to find the necessary sand and gravel for concrete work and road construction. Significant quantities of sand, gravel and cement were also purchased from the Netherlands, a neutral country surrounded by belligerents. Complaints from Britain led to the Germans proving that the cement provided by the Dutch was being used for repairing war damage in Belgium and France. Whatever the truth of the matter, by providing the Germans with raw materials a few unscrupulous 'businessmen' became notably rich.

Logistics, men and building material were needed in staggering quantities for the Hindenburg Line programme and, consequently, new

A well-prepared German trench; these were still largely lacking in the Michel Zone.

engineering camps and workshops were set up and the ones already in existence were enlarged. In the area local rail emplacements like Chapelet Wood, between Puxieux and Chambley-Bussières, were hugely expanded and became a hive of activity. Wooden formwork, used in the construction of bunkers, duckboards (wooden floorboards for the trenches) and other building projects demanded huge quantities of wood; carpenters, lumbermen, metal workers, electricians, plumbers and countless other trades were required to build the defences. Commercial contractors from Germany, as well as from occupied France and Belgium, were used to meet demands; Russian prisoners of war and conscripts, unfit for military service, were used to do the unskilled work. To get an idea of the scale of the operation, in the Somme Sector, from October 1916 to March 1917, about 70,000 labourers worked on the fortifications; about 50,000 standard gauge boxcars were needed to transport the material.

The designated area had to be surveyed and the position of the defences marked out on the terrain. Then roads and railway lines and loops had to be constructed. After that, workshops, lumber mills, depots and generating stations were built, as well as barracks to house the workers. A whole network of narrow gauge railways had to be laid to

German stock of so-called corkscrew pickets used for attaching barbed wire.

deliver the raw materials and concrete mixers as close to the building site as possible. Standardization and mass-production techniques were used to speed up the process; about eighty per cent of the shelters in the Michel Zone are of the same design.

First to be built were the forward positions; once finished the workers immediately started to place the wire obstacles. Trenches and other earthworks were only built after all other work had been completed. Thousands of anti-tank mines were buried in front of the wire entanglements, mostly buried 21cm shells with the primed detonator flush with the ground, though other improvised devices were also used.

Despite all their efforts, the Germans still had not finished constructing the Michel Zone by the time the Americans attacked in September 1918; the actual building programme had started in July 1917. The Michel Zone, though not completed but already of formidable size, was – unsurprisingly – hastily occupied in September 1918.

The US 66th Field Artillery Brigade history notes:

> 'Just why the American Army did not push its advance in the St. Mihiel operation, when the German Army was in a full, disorganized retreat across the plains of the Woëvre was a mystery to the average Doughboy, who had visions of following Old Glory up to the streets of Metz. There is no doubt but that the American Army, within a few days' time could have advanced to the very gates of the city itself and threatened its capture. The men of the 66th Field Artillery Brigade fully expected to assist in a bombardment of that German fortress.'

This passage clearly shows that:

- To insure secrecy, the average American soldier was not informed about the upcoming Meuse-Argonne Offensive;

• American propaganda had done its job; on the Allied side, it was believed that the German retreat was in fact a rout;
• There is no mention of the Michel Line or Zone; the average American soldier probably expected a leisurely walk to the open gates of Metz.

On 12 September 1918, as the Germans hastily vacated the Salient, the Americans encountered minor resistance, in contrast to other large-scale attacks elsewhere, and cleared the Salient within two days. The St. Mihiel Offensive halted just a few hundred metres short of the Michel Zone, sometimes less. The Michel Zone was never really put to the test, but the half-hearted attacks on 10 and 11 November by the 7th, 28th, 33rd and 92nd Divisions clearly show that without a well-prepared, combined all arms assault, the line was all but impregnable.

An American soldier observing the Michel Zone, November 1918.

Car Tour 5

The Michel Zone

Duration: Half a day's tour
Distance: 10 kilometres
Maps: IGN 3313 SB, Ars-sur-Moselle or 3313 O, Chambley-Bussières

The best time to visit the Michel Zone is between October and the start of April. Some ninety per cent of the Michel Zone bunkers are built flush with the ground; if there are crops in the field they are simply not visible. However, in summer time one can still enjoy the views and use the panoramic pictures in the book as a reference.

The non-circular tour begins at a crossroads in the centre of Xammes (N48°58.533' E005°51.372'). From here you drive from the furthest American point of advance through No Man's Land and into the Michel Zone. Here you can see for yourself the enormous amount of energy and material the Germans put in their defences.

There are no shops, petrol stations, restaurants or public rest rooms along this route. However, Thiaucourt and the St. Mihiel American Cemetery are about five kilometres from Xammes. A pair of binoculars and a flash light/torch would be very useful during this tour.

A warning note on bunkers

Entering bunkers and other structures are entirely at your own risk. IF you decide to enter a bunker, use a decent flash light and not, for example, a cell phone. Never go in alone. Once inside, first look at the floor before you continue; sumps, air vents, basements, tunnel entrances – there are countless painful opportunities to acquaint yourself with the German defences. Remember that a cell phone does not have reception inside a bunker. Do not walk on fields where crops are growing; they are the farmer's livelihood.

GPS coordinates Car Tour 5

(1) 2nd Division Monument	(N48°59.321′ E005°52.379′)
(2) Panorama	(N48°59.857′ E005°52.946′)
(3) Observation post	(N48°59.680′ E005°53.326′)
(4) Panorama north	(N48°59.680′ E005°53.326′)

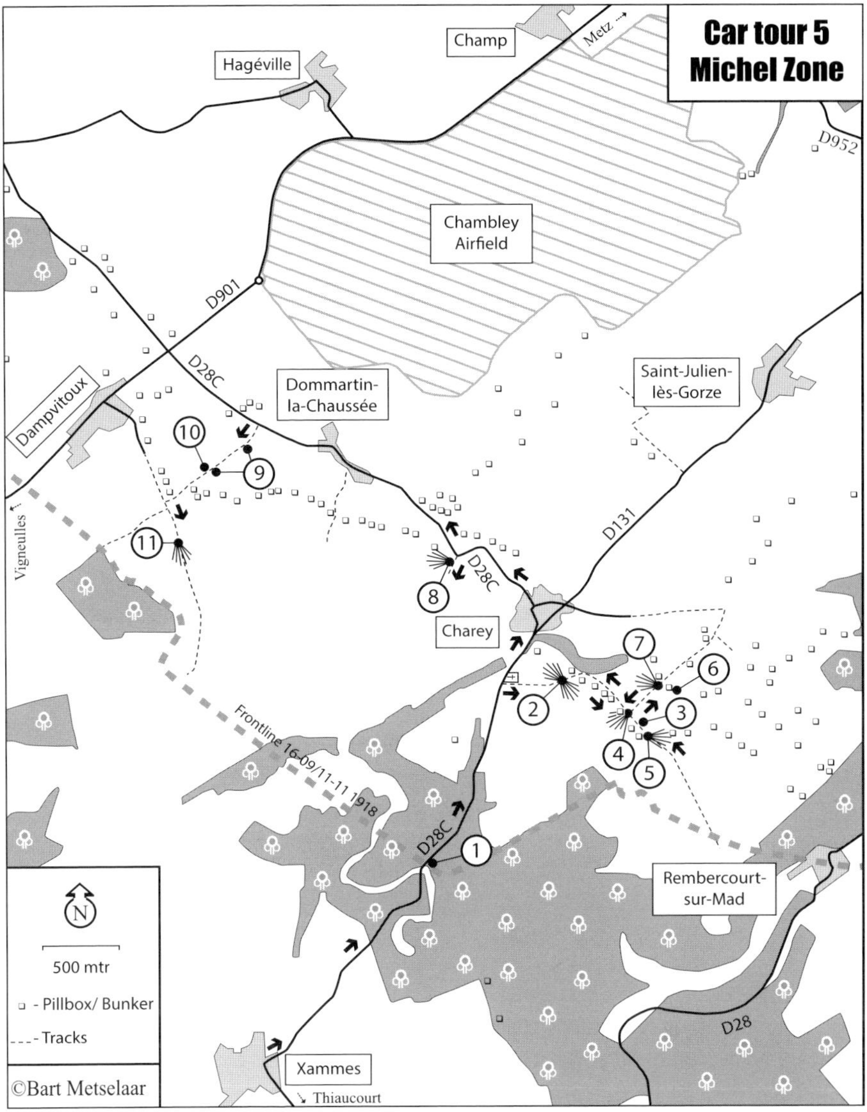

(5) Panorama south	(N48°59.680′ E005°53.326′)
(6) Observation post	(N48°59.843′ E005°53.430′)
(7) Panorama Montsec to Dampvitoux	(N48°59.843′ E005°53.430′)
(8) Dommartin bunkers	(N48°00.304′ E005°52.324′)
(9) Loading docks Dampvitoux railway station	(N48°00.501′ E005°50.973′)
(10) Command post	(N49°50.515′ E005°50.975′)
(11) American front line of 11 November 1918	(N49°00.347′ E005°50.935′)

Starting from the crossroads in Xammes (N48°58.533′ E005°51.372′), you continue via the D28C in the direction of Charey. After a kilometre you cross the bridge over the Rupt Creek. Soon thereafter, you will see a triangular traffic sign on the left side of the road. About two hundred metres further, on the right side of the road, a minor track into the woodland starts. Stop here. Obscured by foliage, the **2nd Division Monument (1)** (N48°59.321′ E005°52.379′) stands on a bank on the right side of the track. The monument marks the furthest point of advance made by the 2nd Division during the St. Mihiel Offensive.

Second Division boulder.

The bottom of the Rupt Ravine remained in American hands until the Armistice. Naturally, the Germans held the high ground. The nearest bunker of the Michel Zone is situated at about 500 metres distance (north) and sixty metres higher than this point. Built on a series of ridges, any American attack would first have to deal with crossing the bottom of a ravine or valley and than continue uphill on foot in plain view of the Germans. Waiting in their well built and sited shelters and with an excellent view across No Man's Land, machine guns, combined with a well-directed artillery barrage, would stop the attackers in their tracks.

Continue to Charey; before you reach the village turn right onto a farm road that starts just before the communal cemetery. Pass the crucifix on your right and follow the road past the bend. Stop three telegraph poles

View over Dommartin.

back from the house in front of you. Close to the pole the roof of a typical Michel Zone bunker is visible. Look to the north-west across the Woëvre Plains and compare your view with the **panorama (2)** (N48°59.857′ E005°52.946′) in the book.

View on observation post Stop 3.

Go back to the car and drive uphill to the **observation post (3)** (N48°59.680′ E005°53.326′) that is partly hidden in the copse on the summit. From here, the Germans had an excellent view over the American hinterland. Inside there is only one room. At the back wall a doorway and a staircase lead to underground shelters which have collapsed.

Observation post.

Tunnel entrance inside the observation post.

Standing in front of the bunker you have a great view along the pillboxes that are part of the Hagen or Hindenburg Line. See **Panorama north (4)** and **Panorama south (5)** in the book. To get a clear view, you might have to walk up and down a bit; the photos were taken from the roof of the bunker. Around the time of the American attack in September 1918, the work on the

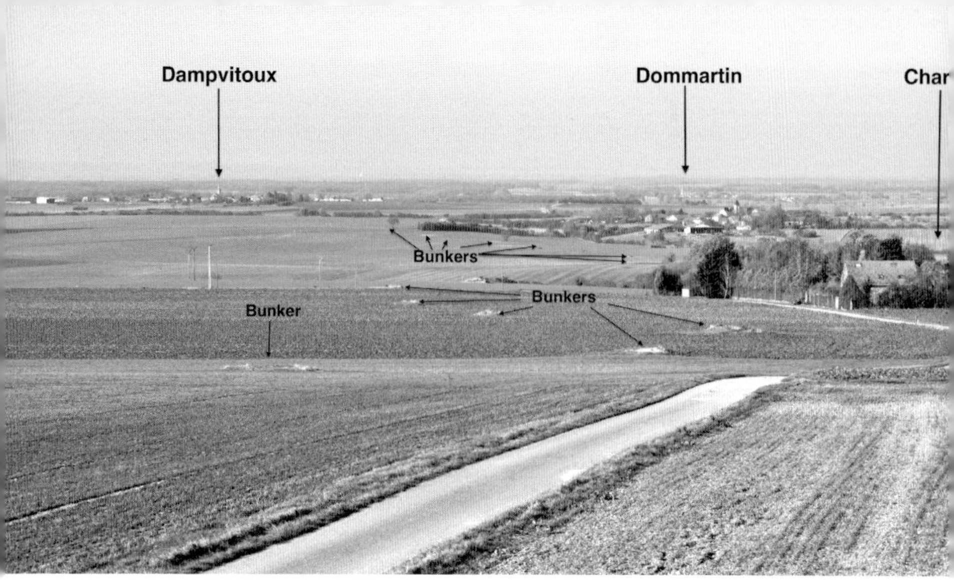

pillboxes was nearly completed but the trenches that were to connect the bunkers were not. Also, the wire entanglements were just eighty per cent completed. This omission was largely made up for during and immediately after the St. Mihiel Offensive. Today, there are no remainders of these field works; the area has been restored and returned to the farmers.

Turn the car around; after twenty-five metres turn right onto another (perfectly driveable) farm track. After about a hundred metres you will see the remains of a concrete **observation post (6)** (N48°59.843′ E005°53.430′) in the field on the right. For the best view of the **panorama from Montsec to Dampvitoux (7),** climb on the roof of the bunker. Note that the metal reinforcement that once protected the observation slit has disappeared. The shelter behind it is still intact, although the entrances are largely filled in. From positions like these,

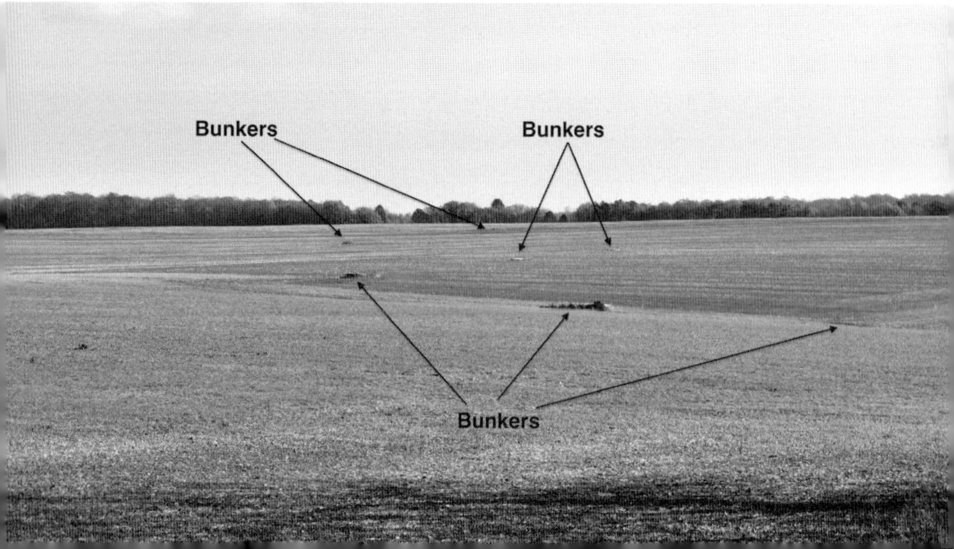

Observation post with a view over the Woëvre Plain; note the Meuse Heights in the back ground.

Detail of a step to reach the roof.

Detail of the observation turret; the roof was demolished after the war for scrap metal.

information about enemy troop movements were relayed (by telephone) to gun batteries that were situated behind the third line of defence, the Kriemhild Line; the enemy was to be destroyed before they reached the Hagen Line.

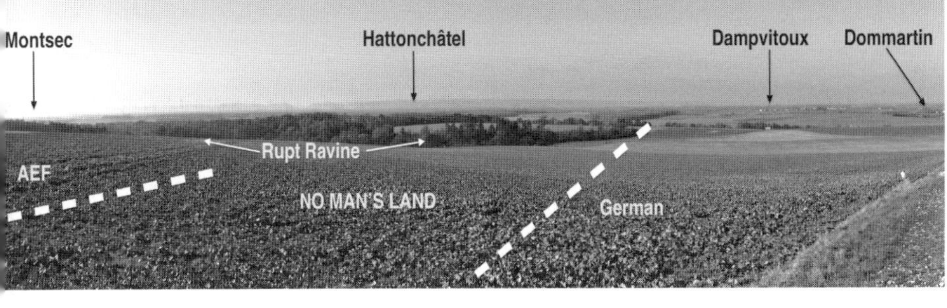

View from Charey to Dampvitoux.

Continue along the track for another 150 metres and turn left. Descend from the hill through the orchards until you are reach Charey. When you come at the crossroads, take the D131 to Dommartin. At the next crossing, take the D28c to Dommartin. As soon as you leave Charey, note the bunkers on both sides of the road. After the second 90° bend turn left onto a farm track; stop here. From this point you have a great view of the **Dommartin bunkers (8)** (N48°00.304′ E005°52.324′).

Return to the road and carry on to Dommartin, which is possibly one of the most unusual villages that you are likely to see in this part – possibly anywhere in France – of France. It is a never ending source of visual surprises, art for art's sake. Once you have entered the village, follow the main road, the D28c to the left, and leave this remarkable place behind. After you have crossed the bridge, turn left onto a farm track. Originally this track was a railway embankment built by the Germans. After a couple of hundred metres note the top of a concrete wall or buttress that runs alongside the track. These are the remains of the loading docks of **Dampvitoux railway station (9)** (N48°00.501′ E005°50.973′). Stop where the concrete wall ends.

A few metres further on down the track you will find the former German **command post (10)** (N49°50.515′ E005°50.975′) of the railway station. Obscured by shrubs and foliage, it is possible to enter the bunker

Loading docks at Dampvitoux.

Entrance of the command post at Dampvitoux station.

from around the back. The original wooden steps are still in situ. Apparently, the bunker has been used by local youth; inside you will find old furniture and empty liquor bottles. It seems that the command post once was part of a larger structure, possibly made of wood, as several concrete foundations suggest. The station was part of a loop line that delivered building material for the fortifications in the Michel Zone.

Carry on along the track until you come to a T-junction. Turn left and stop next to the pylon. From here, you have an excellent view across No Man's Land and the **American front line of 11 November (11)** (N49°00.347′ E005°50.935′). See the photograph in the book. To return to the main road, the D904, along which the American cemetery is located, you can drive to Dampvitoux. At the crossroads, take a left turn onto the D901 in the direction of St. Benoit. Take a left turn at the roundabout onto the D904 and after a few kilometres you are back at the cemetery.

CHAPTER 7

Car Tour 6

The All-American Tour
Monuments and Memorials of the United States

Duration: A full day's tour.
Distance: Seventy kilometres.
Maps: Michelin Sites de la Guerre 1914-1918 en Meuse OR IGN 3213 SB, Vigneulles-lès-Hattonchâtel, 3214 SB, St-Mihiel and 3314 SB, Pont-à-Mousson.

This circular car tour is especially designed for people who only have one day to spend in the area. It should be of special interest to American visitors as it covers sixeen American monuments and memorials in the St. Mihiel area. All monuments are easy to reach by car and there is not much walking involved; walking boots are not needed. However, a pair of binoculars, a bottle of water and some provisions are recommended.

Any visitor to St. Mihiel will be drawn to Montsec American Monument. General Pershing, the Commander-in-Chief, determined that the major memorial to the American Expeditionary Forces in this region should be located at this site. Erected on the summit of Montsec Hill, the impressive classical temple-like structure can be seen from many parts of the battlefield. However, the monument is actually located in the sector of the Salient that was liberated by the French 39th Division and has therefore not been included in any of the previous tours.

So, for practical purposes, the 'All-American' tour starts at Montsec; but you can start the tour at any given location and follow the route around. Along the route, there are shops, petrol stations, café and toilet facilities in Vigneulles and Thiaucourt. Visitors coming from Verdun, St. Mihiel or Pont-à-Mousson will find everything they need in town. Good toilet facilities can also be found at the St. Mihiel American Cemetery Visitors Centre in Thiaucourt, see stop 12.

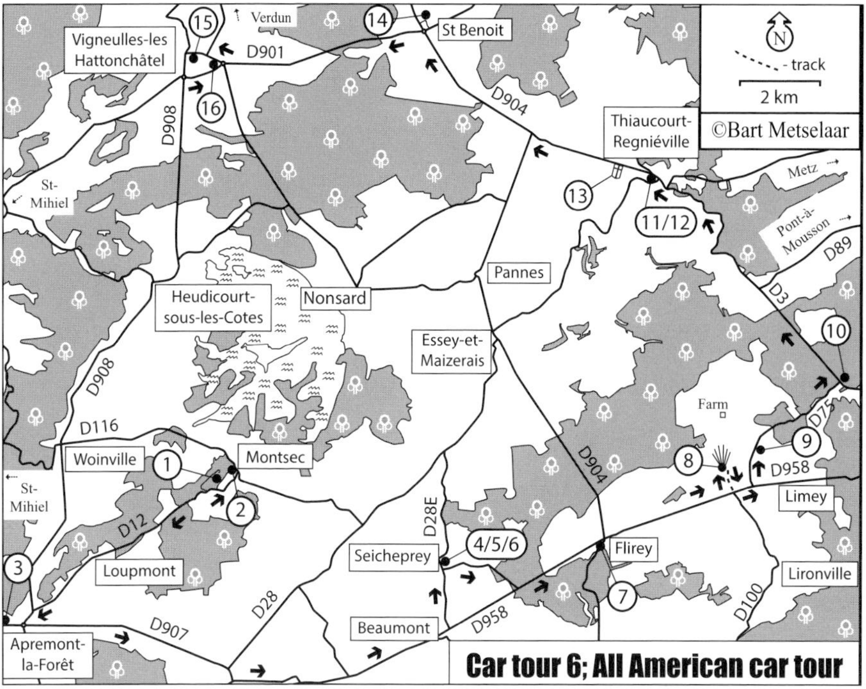

GPS coordinates Car Tour 6

(1) Montsec American Monument	(N48°53.402′ E005°42.803′)
(2) Montsec then and now	(N48°53.418′ E005°42.839′)
(3) Apremont-la-Forêt, Massachusetts Monument	(N48°51.302′ E005°38.426′)
(4) 26th Division, 102nd Regiment Memorial Fountain	(N48°52.169′ E005°47.456′)
(5) Seicheprey, Memorial plaque on church	(N48°52.179′ E005°47.439′)
(6) Seicheprey, Plaque on French War Memorial	(N48°52.194′ E005°47.441′)
(7) Flirey, Lorraine-USA Monument	(N48°52.508′ E005°50.841′)
(8) Ansoncourt Farm, Medal of Honor, H. Wickersham	(N48°53.526′ E005°53.371′)
(9) Limey-Regniéville, 2nd Division Monument	(N48°53.797′ E005°53.953′)
(10) Regniéville, 5th Division Monument	(N48°54.626′ E005°55.676′)
(11) Thiaucourt, Monument aux Morts	(N48°57.243′ E005°51.934′)
(12) Thiaucourt, Captain Cunningham Plaque	(N48°57.263′ E005°51.922′)
(13) St. Mihiel American Cemetery and Memorial	(N48°57.417′ E005°15.133′)

(14) St. Benoit, 42nd Div/MacArthur (N48°59.261′ E005°47.069′)
(15) Vigneulles, Le jeune Américain (N48°58.846′ E005°42.230′)
(16) Vigneulles, First Division Monument (N48°58.703′ E005°42.910′)

1. Montsec American Monument (N48°53.402′ E005°42.803′)
This is one of eleven monuments erected in Europe by the United States of America to commemorate the services of the American Armed Forces in World War One. Inaugurated in 1932, it recalls the achievements of the more than 550,000 American troops (reserve divisions included) who were involved in the St. Mihiel offensive, from 12 to 16 September 1918. The St. Mihiel offensive was the first operation in World War One carried out by an American Army under the independent control of the American Commander-in-Chief, General Pershing.

Montsec American Monument dominates the surrounding territory, which was known during the war as the St. Mihiel Salient. Occupied by

Montsec Mamerican Monument.

the Germans for over four years, the Salient was heavily fortified. Montsec provided excellent observation behind French lines and was tactically crucial to pass on information to the German gun batteries. In 1914 the French had made a number of unsuccessful attacks against this veritable fortress. It was finally taken on 12 September 1918 by the French 39th Division.

Of the three American corps and the fourteen American divisions that took part in the attack, two of the corps and four of the divisions had never before been engaged in offensive combat. Therefore, First Army had the 35th, 80th and 91st Divisions in reserve for use in case of necessity. The US Army's need for additional planes, artillery, machine guns and tanks was largely met by the French and, much more limited, by the British.

More than 500,000 Americans (216,000 in line) and about 110,000 French (48,000 in line) were involved in the offensive – from muleteers, clerks, engineers, to the soldiers in the front line. Apart from the Springfield and M17 American Enfield rifles and small arms like the Colt 1911, most of the equipment of the AEF was supplied by the French. For example, the American Air Service, commanded by Colonel William 'Billy' Mitchell, was supplied with 1,481 airplanes of French manufacture. In addition to this, the commander of the Independent Air Force – effectively a branch of the RAF, Major General Trenchard, supplied the Americans with eight night bombing squadrons for the forthcoming offensive. As well as supplying fuel for the aircraft, the Americans also contributed a handful of American-built De Havilland DH-4 planes, nicknamed 'flying coffins' because they were notorious for catching fire.

The Americans were also provided with about 400 French tanks, 350 of which were the light Renault FT17s, mainly operated by French drivers; 144 were operated by Americans. About 2,700 French artillery pieces of all calibres were used and approximately 3,300,000 rounds of artillery ammunition were brought into the area in preparation for the offensive. The secret movement of such a large number of troops to the battle front and the many details involved in planning the operation and in providing the necessary special troops put a tremendous strain on the AEF's staff. However, they faced up to the task given to them with great enthusiasm. George Marshall later wrote that

> 'It was growing increasingly difficult to conceal Pershing's intentions. Everyone was enthusiastic and each felt that his individual part was of momentous importance and, therefore, an exception to the rules or regulations, with the result that, despite drastic orders to the contrary, the traffic on the roads in the daytime had grown to such proportions as to ensure its observation by the enemy. Every officer desired to make a personal reconnaissance of the ground over which he was to operate, and there were frequent violations of the orders against promiscuous reconnaissances in the daytime.'

Opposite the Americans lay the German Army Detachment C, composed of eight divisions and two brigades of mostly second rate troops in line and five divisions in reserve. Their defences, however, were formidable.

The preliminary bombardment of hostile positions began at 1.00 am on 12 September 1918. At 5.00 am the main infantry attack jumped off, hidden by a smoke screen placed in front of the American trenches. The Americans moved up behind the protection of a rolling barrage and encountered little resistance. At noon on 12 September, the Germans were ordered to withdraw behind the Michel Zone, three prepared defence lines of at the base of the Salient. On 13 September, just after 2.00 am, patrols from the two axis of advance, the 26th and 1st Divisions, met just north-east of Vigneulles, thereby cutting off the tip of the Salient. With this action, the Salient was pinched out. Although the offensive officially ended on 16 September most of the heavy fighting was over. More than 15,000 prisoners and 450 cannons were captured. The number of Germans killed remain unknown. Estimated American losses were 8,600 killed, wounded and missing; 4,153 are buried in St. Mihiel American Cemetery.

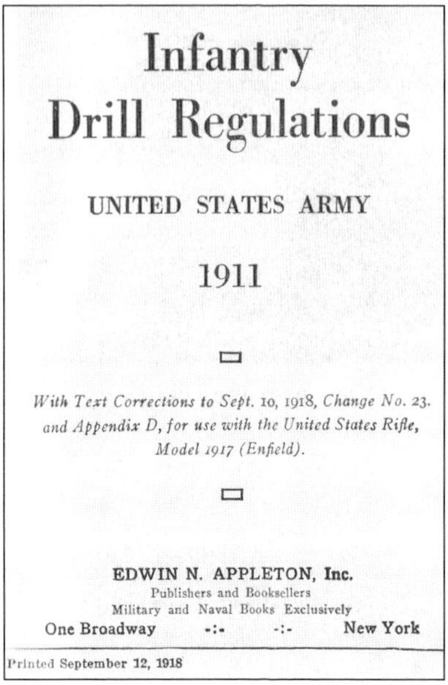

Infantry
Drill Regulations

UNITED STATES ARMY

1911

With Text Corrections to Sept. 10, 1918, Change No. 23. and Appendix D, for use with the United States Rifle, Model 1917 (Enfield).

EDWIN N. APPLETON, Inc.
Publishers and Booksellers
Military and Naval Books Exclusively
One Broadway -:- -:- New York

Printed September 12, 1918

Printed on 12 September 1918, the start of the St. Mihiel Offensive.

After visiting the monument, walk back to the parking and continue to the first bench on your right. From here, you have a magnificent view over Lac de Madine and surroundings. See the 'then' photograph.

2. Montsec: then and now (N48°53.418′ E005°42.839′)

Unfortunately, today the village of Montsec is largely obscured by trees and foliage. However, the outlines of the woods and fields behind it remain largely the same. Looking at the 'then' photo, you can clearly see the massive belts of German barbed wire criss-crossing the fields. This is also a good vantage point to look at the Lac de Madine, which did not exist during the First World War. This man-made lake was excavated in 1965 to drain the area. Because of bad drainage and the continuous shelling during the last months of 1914 and well into 1915 the whole area

View over the village of Montsec. Note the wire entanglements that run through the fields.

had been turned into a swamp. In 1918, American Renault FT17 tanks were seriously hampered by the muddy ground conditions.

Return to your car and descend the hill. Turn right at the T-junction in the direction of Apremont-la-Forêt. Stay on the D12 for about seven kilometres; then turn left onto the D908. When you come at the roundabout, turn right. The Massachusetts Monument is on the right side of the road, just before you reach the crossroads at the church. Park at the side of the road.

3. Apremont-la-Forêt, Massachusetts Monument (N48°51.302′ E005°38.426′)
This monument, a washing or laundry house and water tap, was inaugurated on 4 September 1922 in the presence of Major Carlyle H. Wash, Ambassador of the United States and Toucas Massilon, Sous-Préfet of Commercy. The memorial fountain is dedicated to the American soldiers who lost their lives in Apremont-la-Forêt, which is a bit odd as Apremont lies well within the French sector and no information could be found regarding any American unit fighting in this village or its surroundings. However, financed by the city of Holyoke, Massachuchetts, the building and monument were among the first products of the American Committee of Villages Libérés founded by Miss Isabelle Skinner.

Apremont-la-Forêt, Massachusetts Monument.

Shortly after the war ended, Ruth Isabelle Skinner (1866-1928), a Francophile and businesswoman, decided to visit France. After seeing the French countryside and villages destroyed by the war, she allegedly cabled home: 'War is awful, I can make a difference'. Back in Holyoke and making use of her extensive networks, Miss Skinner initiated and led the effort to rally American cities to raise money and to adopt French villages during the postwar reconstruction, establishing the American Committee of Villages Libérés in New York City in March 1919. Miss Skinner personally funded the rebuilding of all the public service buildings of Hattonchâtel, which as a result makes it a village that is architecturally notably harmonious. See Walk 3 for more information about Miss Skinner and Hattonchâtel.

Apremont was largely destroyed during the war and after the St. Mihiel Offensive the village was handed over by the French to the Americans. As the road that connected St. Mihiel with Apremont and the rest of the former Salient was destroyed, the Americans set to work. The rubble of Apremont was used to rebuild the road (the current D907) that was quickly christened the 'Apremont Highway'. Nowadays, two street names remember the benefactresses of Apremont; the *Rue Belle Skinner* and the *Place d'Holyoke*.

Return to your vehicle and drive back to the roundabout; continue straight along the D907. The road on which you are driving runs approximately along the French front line of September 1918. Pass through Bouconville-sur-Madt (after this village the road becomes the D958), Rambucourt (you have just entered the approximate American jump-off line of the 1st Division) and Beaumont. After you have left Beaumont turn left onto the D28e to Seicheprey, sector of the 42nd Division. Stop at the church. In Seicheprey there are three monuments dedicated to the Americans. Surprisingly, they do not have a direct connection with the St. Mihiel Offensive but with a large-scale German attack on 20 April 1918, when the Americans had just moved into the area to get front line experience.

4. 26th Division, 102nd Regiment Memorial Fountain. (N48°52.169′ E005°47.456′)

In the field to the right of the church stands the State of Connecticut Fountain. This fountain, dating from 1923, is dedicated to the 26th Division, 102nd Regiment, for their part in the Battle of Seicheprey on 20 April 1918.

26th Division, 102nd Regiment Memorial Fountain.

After a failed American attack on Apremont-le-Forêt on 10 April 1918, the Germans launched a large-scale attack on Seicheprey to test American strength and to capture prisoners for interrogation. In the early morning of 10 April, around 3,000 German shock troops started the attack on Seicheprey. Under the cover of thick mist and a heavy bombardment, the first 400 Germans took front line trenches occupied by American and French soldiers. Fierce fighting broke out, but the surprise had been complete; quickly, the Germans pushed on to the centre of the village. However, the American-French troops managed to hold the line. The next day, after thirty-six hours of brutal fighting and heavy shelling, the Germans were pushed out of the village and back to their own line in Hauts de Mad Woods. The German casualties amounted to an estimated 1,200 men. The Americans buried 164 of their own men. They also lost 800 wounded (many were gassed) and 150 were taken prisoner. Because the Americans and French repulsed the Germans from Seicheprey, they declared themselves victors. However, the Germans from the 10th Division also looked upon themselves as victors; they were ordered to test the strength of the freshly arrived American Army and to return with prisoners: mission accomplished. In fact, both sides had approximately similar casualties.

Miss Skinner, (see Walk 3) was the initiator and leader of the effort to rally American cities to adopt French villages during the postwar reconstruction. In March 1919, she established the American Committee of Villages Libérés in New York City. Through this committee, the people of Connecticut raised the money for the memorial fountain and the monument was placed to provide drinking water to the people of Seicheprey. It also emphasized the friendship between France and the US.

5. Seicheprey, Memorial plaque on church
(N48°52.179′ E005°47.439′)
Walk to the entrance of the church; to the left of the doors, you can see a bronze memorial plaque dedicated *'to the god of the armies. In recognition and remembrance of the American troops, January-November 1918.'*

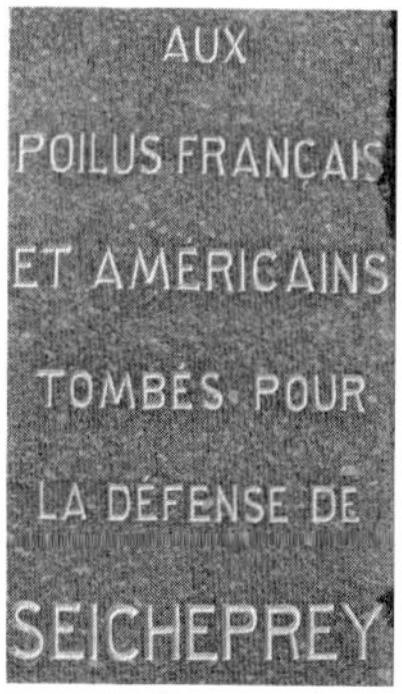

6. Seicheprey, Plaque on French War Memorial
(N48°52.194′ E005°47.441′)
The third monument is a plaque on the French War Memorial that stands to the left of the church buildings. It is dedicated to the people of Seicheprey, but also to the French and American *poilus,* who fell during the liberation of Seicheprey. *Poilu* is a French nickname, meaning the furry, shaggy one, based on the appearance of the bearded French soldiers.

Turn your car around; take a left turn at the T-junction onto the D28a, direction Flirey. Once you have entered

Flirey, go to the church and park there. Opposite the church you will see the Lorraine-USA Monument.

7. Flirey, Lorraine-USA Monument
(N48°52.508′ E005°50.841′)

This monument was erected in the 1930s as a gift from the Department of Lorraine to acknowledge the American divisions and General Pershing that fought during the St. Mihiel Offensive. Forty-eight bronze stars (presumably symbolic of the then forty-eight states in the Union) surround a bronze bas relief showing American soldiers in a heroic pose.

Continue straight along the D958 to Limey. Just before you reach the village, turn left onto a farm track. At the T-junction turn left again. When you reach the highest point, stop. Look at the panoramic photo in the book.

Panorama taken from Flirey in the direction of Ansoncourt Farm.

8. Ansoncourt Farm, Medal of Honor (N48°53.526′ E005°53.371′)
John Hunter Wickersham (3 February 1890-12 September 1918) was born in Brooklyn, New York. He moved to Denver when he was a small boy and was where he received his education. After high school, he went to the First Officers Training Camp at Fort Riley, Kansas in May 1917. He was commissioned a Second Lieutenant and assigned to Company H, 353rd Infantry, 89th Division.

Advancing with his platoon from Limey, Wickersham and his men operated on the far right flank of the 89th

Hunter Wickersham, Medal of Honour.

Division. Their first objective was Ansoncourt Farm, aiming to outflank the heavily fortified Mont Mare Woods from the right. However, Ansoncourt Farm was part of the German first line defences and had been transformed into a stronghold. Between Limey and the farm lay a wide open valley without any form of shelter. Early in the morning of 12 September, at 5.00 am, E and F Companies were leading the attack and soon encircled the stronghold, that comprised three machine guns. The gunners killed, G and H Companies rushed in to support E and F Companies and to continue the attack. On approaching Ansoncourt Farm, Wickersham was severely wounded in four places by an exploding high-explosive shell. Before receiving any aid himself he dressed the wounds of his orderly, who had been wounded by the same shell. Although weakened by the loss of blood, he ordered his platoon to advance and accompanied them on their move forward. Due to the fact that his right hand had been disabled by wounds, he fired his revolver with his left hand until, exhausted by loss of blood, he fell and died from his wounds before first aid could be administered. He was posthumously awarded the Medal of Honor and is buried in St. Mihiel American Cemetery, Plot B/19/12.

Turn your car around and go straight on. When you reach the main road, the D958, turn left. After about one hundred metres, turn left onto the D75, direction Regniéville. After a few hundred metres you will see the Second Division Boulder on the right side of the road.

9. Limey-Regniéville, 2nd Division Monument (N48°53.797′ E005°53.953′)

The recently repainted **US 2nd Division Boulder** (N48°53.797′ E005°53.953′) is situated on the right hand side of the road. Unfortunately, the copper plaque has been removed by vandals. However, this spot marks the German first line, taken at first daylight on 12 September by the soldiers of the 2nd Division.

Second Division Boulder.

Carry on along the D75 until you reach the D3. Park your car in the parking space on the other side of the road. There are several points of interest here and, time permiting, it would be worthwhile to visit these.

10. Regniéville, 5th Division Monument (N48°54.626′ E005°55.676′)

A special monument, although not unique in design, is the US 5th Division Monument that stands at the side of the D3. Like the other 5th Division

Fifth Division Monument at Regniéville.

monuments, the obelisk was erected in the early 1920s. However, this one bears plaques remembering two world wars. The small marble square plaque, a replacement for the original copper information panel, simply reads '5th Infantry Division US Army 12 September 1918'. It commemorates the fact that on the morning of 12 September the 5th Division's jump-off lines started from this point. Europe needed a Second World War to reach political stability and again the Americans came to our rescue. In September 1944, the 5th Division, now part of Patton's Third Army, once more liberated this part of France from the Germans. The plaque reads, *September-October 1944. 5th Infantry Division assigned this sector after 700 mile drive from Normandy beaches. First breach of Moselle River defenses made by 5th Infantry Division, September 1944.*

When you leave the parking space, turn right. Continue along the D3 until you reach Thiaucourt; stop at the church.

War Memorial at Thiaucourt.

11. Thiaucourt, Monument aux Morts
(N48°57.243′ E005°51.934′)

To the left of the church stands the Monument aux Morts. Monuments like this usually depict a French soldier in a heroic pose and commemorates the people that died for France. The monument in Thiaucourt, however, is dedicated to the people of Thiaucourt and to the American 2nd and 89th Divisions who liberated the town. The bronze statue shows a French as well as an American soldier shaking hands symbolizing the friendship between the two nations. The figure of the American soldier was modeled after Captain Cunningham. The shell damage, clearly visible at the bottom of the monument and on the church walls, dates from September 1944, when the Germans were retreating to the Rhine River. The monument was dedicated on 8 November 1925.

12. Thiaucourt, Captain Cunningham Plaque
(N48°57.263′ E005°51.922′)

Walk up the stairs of the church. On the right of the church doors, a bronze plaque is dedicated to Captain Oliver Cunningham. Besides the plaque (note the WW2 shell damage), business colleagues of Oliver's father provided funds for a special set of bells, hung in memory of Captain Cunningham. The original bells had been melted down by the Germans for metal during the war. The new bells were dedicated on 30 May, 1924. The church was rebuilt in 1918 after suffering significant damage. A metal plaque inside the church states the bells' dedication to the memory of Captain Cunningham. Mrs. Cunningham donated money to the town and for 'the reconstruction of the town hall that had been reduced to rubble'.

Oliver B. Cunningham, killed in action 17 September 1918.

Captain Oliver Baty Cunningham, 15th Field Artillery, 2nd Division, was born on 17 September 1894 in Chicago, Illinois. He was the only child of Frank

Church of Thiaucourt and plaque.

Simpson Cunningham and Lucy Eleanor Baty Cunningham. In 1913 he entered Yale University. He also served as a member of the Yale Battery and as an artillery private in the Connecticut National Guard in 1916. Before the first selective service registration took place on 5 June 1917, Cunningham had already enrolled in an officers' training course at Fort Sheridan, Lake County, Illinois and received a commission as a second lieutenant in the Field Artillery. He would later rise to the rank of captain.

On 12 December, 1917, he sailed for France with the 15th Field Artillery, a unit of the 2nd Division. After training in France, the unit took part in several major battles, including Château Thierry, and Belleau Wood, before being deployed in the St. Mihiel Sector. On 17 September 1918, on his 24th birthday, Lieutenant Cunningham was killed by mortar fire near the village of Jaulny. The day after his death his captain's commission arrived, dated 11 September. He was hastily buried in a makeshift grave near the scene of his death. In 1922 his body was exhumed and reburied in Thiaucourt American Cemetery, plot C, row 13, grave 18. Cunningham was posthumously awarded both the Distinguished Service Cross (DSC) and the Silver Star.

Head stone of Captain Cunningham.

Return to your car and proceed along the D3; after about a kilometre, you come to the American Cemetery, on your left. Park here.

13. St. Mihiel American Cemetery and Memorial (N48°57.417′ E005°15.133′)

Built along the D3 not far from Thiaucourt. This cemetery was started in September 1918; immediately after the liberation of Thiaucourt a place was needed to bury the dead. This happened in nearly every village in the Salient, but after the war it was decided that the American cemetery at Thiaucourt was going to become the concentration cemetery for all American dead in the area. This meant that every temporary graveyard or isolated field grave in the Salient was cleared and the bodies reburied in Thiaucourt.

Myth: You are **not** on American soil when you enter the cemetery; the French government has granted free use of land as a permanent burial ground without charge or taxation for as long as the American government chooses to maintain it.

On entering the cemetery, toilets and a small interpretation centre are on the left. On the right side is the office of the superintendent and his staff. The staff speak both French and English and are here to help you and to answer your questions. On the other hand it always helps if you come prepared and have done your homework; if you are looking for a particular grave site this can easily be found on the ABMC website under ABMC burials.

This beautiful maintained cemetery was dedicated on 30 May 1937 and holds 4,153 burials including forty-six Jewish casualties and 117 unknowns. Beyond the burial area to the south is the white stone memorial, consisting of a small chapel, a peristyle with a large rose-granite funeral urn at its center, and a map building. The chapel contains a mosaic portraying an angel sheathing its sword. On two walls of the museum are recorded the names of 284 of the missing. Small bronze rosettes mark the names of six soldiers later found and identified. On the wall facing the door is a large map of inlaid marble depicting the St. Mihiel Offensive. Second Lieutenant Wickersham of the 89th Division is the only Medal of Honor (of three awarded in the area) recipient buried in this cemetery in Plot B row 19 grave 12. For more information see also Car Tour 6, Stop 9.

The cemetery is divided into four plots by paths and trimmed Linden trees. At the centre is an American eagle surmounting a sundial inscribed 'Time will not dim the glory of their deeds'.

Another interesting monument can be found on the right side of the cemetery, between plot B and D. The statue of an officer in front of a cross, the work of sculptor Paul Manship, was initially paid for by the Beale family to honour Walker Blaine Beale. However, as personal memorials were – and are – against ABMC policy, the statue was dedicated to all the soldiers buried in the cemetery and it is now owned by the United States Government. For more information about Walker Blaine Beale, see chapter 3, Car Tour 1, Stop 1.

Visiting Hours

The cemetery is open daily to the public from 9 am to 5 pm, except 25 December and 1 January. It is also open on French holidays. When the cemetery is open to the public, a staff member is on duty in the visitors' building to answer questions and escort relatives to grave and memorial sites. Tel +33 (0)3 83 80 01 01.

Go back to your car and proceed along the D3; note that the road number has now changed to the D67. After ten kilometres you will reach a roundabout. Take the second exit onto the D904. After fifty metres, turn right into the Rue du Château. Right in front of you are the ruins of St. Benoit Château. Although situated on private property, the owners usually do not mind if you make a brief stop to take a look at the ruins.

14. St. Benoit, 42nd Div/MacArthur (N48°59.261′ E005°47.069′)

In 1132, the first Cistercian abbey was built on this spot. Besides accommodation for the monks, eventually six stone barns were built. At the start of the eighteenth century, due to the lack of maintenance, the buildings were in such poor condition that it was decided to demolish the complex altogether. In 1740 the first stone was laid for a new abbey. By

Facade of Château St. Benoit.

using the funds of two other abbeys, there was no lack of resources. The result was a rather sumptuous building that looked more like an eighteenth century château than an abbey. In 1784, as a consequence of heavy debts, a large part of the property was sold; only the two wings behind the facade you see today remained in the monks' hands. During the French Revolution period, in 1790, the wings were destroyed by revolutionaries and only the privately owned Château Benoit was saved.

Occupied in September 1914 by the Germans, the château first served as a hospital before it came in use as a general headquarters building. Typically, the French blame the Germans for the destruction of the

The Château during the German occupation.

château; they claimed the Germans set the place on fire before retreating to the Michel Zone. On the contrary, German officers, knowing the war had been lost, had prevented the burning of St. Benoit Château. Indeed in a number of places they refused to carry out the scorched earth orders. True, eventually the German army was responsible for the destruction of the château, but only after the Americans used the building as an observation post to direct artillery and had positioned machine guns near the château.

General Douglas MacArthur.

On the afternoon of 12 September 1918, the German XIX Corps HQ in the château was evacuated to Metz. On 13 September the château was taken by the 167th Regiment and became the HQ of the American 84th Brigade. General Douglas MacArthur, commander of the Brigade, spent several nights in the Château. He boasted:

> 'The morning of the second day's attack we not only reached but passed the army objective. I am sorry to say we just missed capturing the HQ of the 19th German Army Corps in the St. Benoit Château.

On 24 September 1918, the Germans fired a few salvoes of incendiary shells at the château. MacArthur noted:

> 'From the cuppola of the château which, until the Germans destroyed the château with shellfire, was a favourite observation post for the higher ranking officers of the division, to say nothing of visitors of corps headquarters, I could see the dust of the German trains retreating down the roads towards Metz. Prisoners captured insisted that there was only a small garrison in Metz. I could only come to one conclusion: it was no time to stop! What a wonderful thing it would have been for the division to go ahead even though the outer defences of Metz might have held it up!'

Return to the roundabout and turn right onto the D901 in the direction of Vigneulles. Enter the village. Across the street from the Mairie (the Town Hall) stands the Monument aux Morts, the village war memorial. Park here.

15. Vigneulles, Le jeune Américain (N48°58.846′ E005°42.230′)

The statue at the back of the Monument aux Morts is dedicated to 'A young American who died for France'. At the base of the monument there is a plaque dedicated to Moses Taylor. The plaque reads: Moses Taylor, Jr., 1st Lieutenant, 9th Inf. 2nd Div. USA, born June 8th, 1897, died form (sic) wounds received in action March 24, 1918. This plaque was replaced in 2018 by one with the correct spelling.

Moses Taylor Jr., killed in action on 24 March 1918.

Born in Babylon, Long Island, New York, 1st Lieutenant Moses Taylor Jr. arrived in France in December 1917. On 14 March, after additional training, the Indian Head division was moved to the Verdun/Mihiel area, into the Troyon Sector. Taylor and the 9th Regiment occupied the French trenches between Lacroix-sur-Meuse and Vaux. The story goes that on 23 March 1918 Taylor gathered a group of volunteers for a raid in No Man's Land. The objective was to capture a mill housing several German machine guns. With Taylor in command, at 2.00 am the group went over the top and crept towards the German line. Suddenly, shots rang out and Taylor was hit. Alarmed, flares went up and the Germans started shelling the area in front of their positions. Panic-stricken, the Americans hurried back to their own lines, leaving Taylor behind. The Second Division's History notes:

The War Memorial at Vigneulles, which is also dedicated to Moses Taylor, 2nd Division.

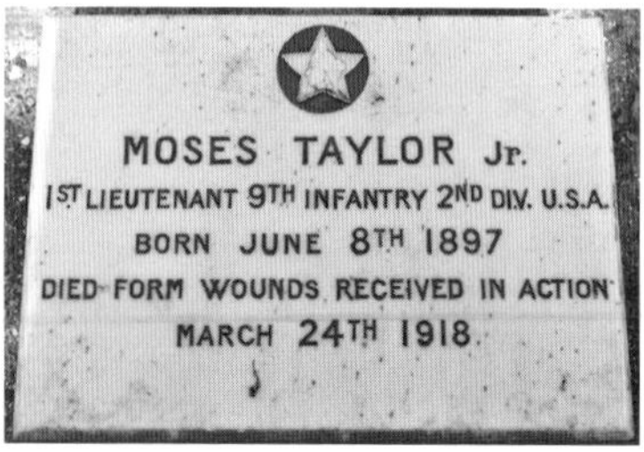

MOSES TAYLOR Jr.
1ST LIEUTENANT 9TH INFANTRY 2ND DIV. U.S.A.
BORN JUNE 8TH 1897
DIED FORM WOUNDS RECEIVED IN ACTION
MARCH 24TH 1918

'The German 82nd Reserve Division lay opposite the Troyon Sector with headquarters in Vigneulles. In spite of rigorous patrolling, the division commander felt his information was incomplete, especially in view of the evidence that Americans were arriving. It had been reported that men wearing brown overcoats (the French overcoat was blue) were seen. On 23 March, 2nd Lieutenant Moses Taylor of the 9th Infantry, mortally wounded while commanding a patrol, had been captured and identified as an American.'

Taylor's head stone in the Meuse Argonne American Cemetery, plot H/44/37.

Taylor's body was buried in Vigneulles by the Germans. After the war his body was exhumed and, rather strangely, re-interred in Romagne-sous-Montfaucon American Cemetery instead of Thiaucourt American Cemetery. The reason for this is unknown. Talyor's grave can be found in Plot H, row 44, grave 37.

Return to your car and drive back along the same road by which you entered the village. Continue onto the D901. At the roundabout, take the first exit on the right and stop at the parking space alongside the road.

16. Vigneulles, First Division Monument (N48°58.703′ E005°42.910′)

The 1st Division Monument here commemorates the significant event on 13 September 1918 when the 1st and 26th Divisions met and cut off the tip of the Salient. The day before, on 12 September, at 5.00 am, the 1st Division had left Seicheprey. In the early hours of 13 September, after a day and a night of fighting, the division arrived in Vigneulles. By closing the gap that morning, thousands of German soldiers were trapped in the pocket and hundreds of guns and tons of supplies were captured. This spot unofficially marks the end of the offensive; officially it continued until 16 September. However, by the night of 13 September most of the fighting was over.

First Division Memorial in Vingneulles.

If you look at the wooded ridge behind the monument, Hattonchâtel can be seen. This village and Vigneulles, among others, were captured by the 26th Division. During this time, the 1st Division lost 98 men killed and 489 men wounded or missing.

Appendix 1

Order of Battle

First (American) Army: General Pershing.
Chief of Staff: Major General Hugh Drum.

Strength:
500,000 US troops of whom 216,000 were in the line.
110,000 French troops of whom 48,000 were in the line.

Army Reserve*:*
80th Division: 317th, 318th, 319th and 320th Regiments.
Major General Adelbert Cronkhite.

I Corps: Major General Hunter Liggett.
2nd Division: 16th, 18th, 26th and 28th Regiments .
Brigadier General John A. Lejeune.

5th Division: 60th, 61st, 6th and 11th Regiments .
Major General John E. McMahon.

82nd Division: 325th, 326th, 327th and 328th Regiments.
Major General William. P. Burnham.

90th Division: 357th, 358th, 359th and 360th Regiments.
Major General Henry T. Allen.

Reserve:
78th Division: 309th, 310th, 311th and 312th Regiments.
Major General James H. McRae.

IV Corps: Major General Joseph T. Dickman.
1st Division: 16th, 18th, 26th and 28th Regiments.
Major General Charles P. Summerall.

42nd Division: 165th, 166th, 167th and 168th Regiments.
Major General Charles T. Menoher.

89th Division: 353rd, 354th, 355th and 356th Regiments.
Major General William M. Wright.

Reserve:
3rd Division: 4rd, 7th, 30th and 38th Regiments.
Major General Beaumont B. Buck.

V Corps: Major General George H. Cameron.
4th Division: 39th, 47th, 58th and 59th Regiments.
Major General John L. Hines.

26th Division: 101st, 102nd, 103rd and 104th Regiments.
Major General Clarence R. Edwards.

15th (French) Colonial Division.

Reserve:
Units of 4th Division

II French Colonial Corps: Blondlat.
2nd French Dismounted Cavalry.
26th French Colonial Division.
39th French Colonial Division.

Appendix 2

Composition of an average American infantry division on arrival in France, comprising some 28,000 officers and men.

Platoon	65 men	Lieutenant
Company	250 men	Captain
Battalion	1,000 men	Major or Lieutenant Colonel
Regiment	4,000 men	Colonel
Brigade	8.000 men	Brigadier General
Division	28,000 men	Major General

Division:
A division's establishment provided for two infantry brigades, each with two regiments, with four battalions per regiment, and four companies per battalion. A company had six officers and 250 men, and the strength of a regiment was 112 officers and 3720 men. All told, a fully established division had 17,666 riflemen, 260 machine guns, and seventy-two guns (forty-eight 75mm and twenty-four 155mm).

In addition there were various units for headquarters, engineering, communications and supply, which brings the total to some 28,000 men.

By the autumn of 1918 and after the enormous casualties of the Spring Offensive, an American division was roughly equivalent to two - three German divisions. The only formations in France roughly comparable in size to the Americans were the divisions of the Canadian Corps; but even these had several thousand men fewer.

The size of the American major formations (ie division, corps and army) was a significant command problem and, taking into account all circumstances, was more a negative than a positive in their performance in the battle. The challenge facing Pershing was that he had too few qualified officers to staff these formations and, inevitably, many of them lacked battle experience and even fewer had experience of command in battle in France and at that level.

Corps:
An American Corps consisted of from two to six divisions – usually three; it had under command a number of artillery, engineering, signal and supply units to support its divisions.

Army:
An American army consisted of from three to five Corps. It had specialist units under command. The American First Army was created in August 1918. In mid October the American Second Army was created and, just as the war was ending, a Third Army.

Appendix 3

Some Facts and Figures

Average American divisional strength in numbers, September 1918

The maximum authorized strength was 991 officers and 27,114 men. The *effective strength in the field* was 16,000 rifles, roughly divided over the four regiments.

Division:	16,000 men = 2 Brigades = 4 Regiments
Brigade:	9,000 men = 2 Regiments
Regiment:	4,400 men = 4 Battalions
Battalion:	1,100 men = 4 Companies
Company:	275 men = 4 squads
Squad:	70 men

Companies A, B, C and D = 1st Battalion
Companies E, F, G and H = 2nd Battalion
Companies I, J, K and L = 3rd Battalion

Also included are three machine-gun battalions, each one attached to an infantry regiment. Each individual machine-gun battalion was made up by four companies.

Losses/casualties

Estimated American losses were: 8,600 killed, wounded and missing; 4,153 are buried in St. Mihiel American Cemetery, although not all were necessarily killed during the St. Mihiel Offensive.

However, these statistics do not convey the entire picture of what the Medical Department faced in terms of the numbers of men they had to treat. For example, the St. Mihiel Operation, from 12-16 September 1918, resulted in 8,600 casualties; however, in addition to those 8,600 there were 18,695 casualties in the sector in the periods 8 January to 11 September and 17 September to 11 November 1918, thus making a grand total of 27,295 casualties; this number included many victims of the second, more lethal, wave of the influenza pandemic.

Approximate American losses during the First World War

There is no exact number of First World War casualties; at best, most numbers are good approximations. The numbers in books and on internet sites usually vary, but most sources that I have checked agree on the numbers below, taken from 'American Armies and Battlefields in Europe', published in 1938.

American losses in the First World War:

116,516 dead and 202,628 wounded, a total of 319,144 of the 4.7 million men who served, a 'modest' total when compared to those of other belligerent nations. An interesting fact is that more American military personnel were killed by disease, usually Spanish Flu (63,114) than by acts of war (53,402). By applying the lessons that had been learnt by European physicians earlier in the war, American doctors were able to reduce the number of deaths caused by shrapnel, infected gunshot wounds and gas. On the other hand, in a shorter period than American involvement in the war, it has been estimated some five to six times as many Americans at home died as a result of the influenza pandemic.

German losses at St. Mihiel remain unknown, but an estimated 16,000 were taken prisoner. Pressured on all fronts, the German administrative system buckled under the strain of the scale of operations from March 1918, particularly from August onwards.

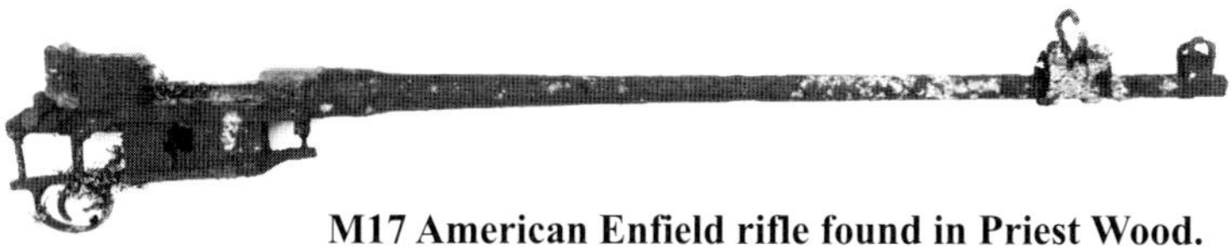

M17 American Enfield rifle found in Priest Wood.

Appendix 4

German Order of Battle

Lieutenant General Georg Fuchs.

Army Group Gallwitz, commanded by General Max von Gallwitz.
Army Detachment C was part of Army Group Gallwitz; the headquarters was based in Conflans.

Army Detachment C, commanded by Lieutenant General Georg Fuchs.
Chief of Staff: Major General Baron Otto von Ledebur.

The seven divisions of Army Detachment C were organized into three army groups:

Combres Group: General Otto von Below
8th Landwehr Division – Lieutenant General O.H.E. Shumann.
13th Landwehr Division – General G. von Gayl.
35th KüK Division - Major General E. von Podhoránszky.

Mihiel Group : Lieutenant General Max Leuthold
192nd Division – Lieutenant General M. Leuthold.
5th Landwehr Division – Lieutenant General Auler.

Gorz Group: General von Harz
10th Division – Lieutenant General Adams.
77th Reserve Division – Major General Gresster.

NB: The information below is taken from *'Histories of 251 Divisions of the German Army which participated in the War (1914-1918)'*, first published in 1920 but which was prepared by the American intelligence staff, based on a variety of sources, including allied, in mid 1918.

Combres Group:
The 8th Landwehr Division
The 8th Landwehr Division, formed in February 1915, was composed of Baden troops who were stationed in Alsace. From its formation until January 1917, the 8th Landwehr held the same front between Altkirch and

the Swiss border. The Landwehr was the third category of the German army, after the Regular Army and the reserves. Landwehr divisions were made up of older soldiers who had come from the reserves; their primary function was security rather than heavy combat. However, they carried out many raids on enemy trenches during their stay in the Alsace.

On 23 January 1917, the division was withdrawn from the Alsace front and sent to the Meuse, where it took over the front west of Fresnes-en-Woëvre, not far from Verdun. The division stayed in the Woëvre sector until the end of the war. In 1918, according to Ludendorff's new doctrine, one shock troop squad was added to each platoon. At St. Mihiel, in spite of being regarded as a fourth-class division, the 8th Landwehr did fairly well.

13th Landwehr Division

The 13th Landwehr Division, a reserve division, was formed in Lorraine in the middle of May 1915. It was made up of regiments from other division that had already been stationed in the Alsace region. Although it briefly occupied other sectors, the division mainly stayed on the Lorraine Front. During the war many different regiments were briefly attached to the Division; the German High Command considered the formation fit to occupy a quiet sector. Still, shock troops had been trained and added to the companies, but mostly the men appear to have been trained for patrol activities rather than for making major assaults.

In June 1918, after a few months' duty in Picardy and Laon, the division entered the line in the Woëvre (Les Éparges area) and remained on the front until the Armistice. In the American attack on the Salient the division lost about 800 men, mainly prisoners. On 12 September it withdrew from Les Éparges to Champlon and Marchéville, some four kilometres to the east, where it stayed until the end of the war. According to the German High Command, it was rated a fourth-class division and was an inferior formation of mediocre morale.

35th (Austro-Hungarian) [KüK] Division

At the start of 1918, under pressure from the German High Command, the Austrian Kaiser Karl agreed that four Austro-Hungarian Divisions would be transferred to the Western Front. In July 1918, 234 boxcars were needed to tranfer the 1st, 35th and 37th Divisions, along with the 106th Reserve Division and heavy artillery units, to the Verdun Front. The 1st and 35th Divisions as well as some heavy artillery, were assigned to Army Group Gallwitz; the 1st Division to the German Fifth Army, east of the Meuse, while the 35th Division joined Army Detachment C, on the Meuse Heights between Dompierre-aux-Bois and St. Maurice-sous-les-Côtes.

The 35th Division was commanded by Major General Eugen von Podhoránszky. Since 1914 the division had been fighting on the Russian and Italian fronts. At the end of July 1918 it occupied a quiet part of the front line in the Salient. On 12 September, early in the morning, the Austrians were caught completely by surprise; they suffered 3,300 casualties, the remaining troops withdrawing to the Michel Zone. The 35th Austrian was regarded as a weak division; by 1918, it had lost a lot of its fighting spirit.

Mihiel Group:
Saxon 192nd Division

In 1915, this division actually started out as 192nd Brigade and only became the 192nd Division in June 1916. It was a composite division made up of troops originating from Saxony, Bavaria and Westphalia. The division spent a lot of time in the Champagne region until it was deployed to the Verdun Front in March 1916, where it suffered heavy losses in the fighting around Avocourt. In September it was engaged in the fierce fighting at Fleury and Douaumont. About the end of October replacements were drafted into the 192nd to bring the division up to something like full strength; now the members of the division were all Saxon. Due to the mediocre quality of the troops, the 192nd spent 1917 in a calm sector of the Verdun Front. After 'resting', the division entered the line at the tip of the Salient on 26 August 1918. Considering the quality of the division, it did respectably well at St. Mihiel. Despite being assaulted by the French on three sides, it managed to extract itself from the front line and retreated to the Michel Zone. On 22 September, when the line had been stabilized, the 192nd was taken out of the line; for the remainder of the war it was stationed close to Etrayes, east of Verdun.

5th Landwehr Division

The 5th Landwehr Division, a second-rate reserve division, was formed in August 1914; it was supposed to have been the garrison of the fortified town of Metz. In December 1914, however, it was engaged in the fierce fighting in Les Éparges, south of Verdun, in an all-out German attempt to force the French from the Meuse Heights and thus to encircle Verdun. As a result of suffering such appalling losses in 1914, the 5th spent 1915 in reserve in the Woëvre Plain in the St. Mihiel sector. In 1916 and 1917 the 5th Landwehr fought the French, just south of Verdun, and was involved in several trench raids. The formation was later further weakened when its best troops were sent to Russia in the summer of 1917.

From 1917 to 12 September 1918, the 5th Landwehr Division occupied a quiet sector running roughly between St. Mihiel and Apremont-la-Forêt. On the morning of 12 September it suffered heavy losses as a result of the bombardment and French trench raids. While on their way to the Michel Zone, hundreds of Germans were taken prisoner; among them was the entire staff of the 3rd Battalion, 65th Landwehr Regiment. The 5th Landwehr was generally regarded as a fourth-class division, a division that did not show any initiative and had no capacity for offensive operations.

Gorz Group:
10th Division

The 10th Division was mobilized at the start of August 1914 and was involved in the battle of the frontiers in Luxembourg and France. Soon thereafter it moved to Les Éparges, on the Woëvre/Meuse front, where it participated in heavy fighting during the first six months of 1915. It stayed in the sector until the beginning of October, after which it became heavily engaged in the fighting around Verdun. The French attacks were so severe that the 10th Division had to be withdrawn from the battlefield. By March 1917, the division was back at full strength and returned to the trenches in Les Éparges. A few months later the 10th Division went by train to the Chemin des Dames where it suffered terrible losses. By the end of March 1918, the division had been badly mauled during the German Spring Offensive, however, in spite of this, it was sent back to the Chemin des Dames.

The losses in men and materiel that the 10th Division had sustained were made up for by the absorption of the 255th Division into their ranks. The newly organized 10th arrived in the Salient on 19 August and occupied the front at Richecourt, Lahayville and St. Baussant. On 12 September, the men of the 10th, who had just returned from a 'quiet' front where they had rested and reorganized, were driven back in a north-easterly direction to Thiaucourt, Jaulny and finally to Rembercourt-sur-Mad, safely behind the Michel Zone defences. Again, the division lost heavily in casualties and prisoners; the Americans had captured entire battalions. Practically destroyed, the 10th Division was taken out of the line; it was refitted in Metz with regiments from other severely damaged divisions. Incredibly, the remnants of the 10th fought in the Meuse-Argonne, where it defended the front line at Stenay, from 3 to 11 November.

The division was regarded a first-class division; however, after severe losses in the German Spring Offensive of 1918, it never recovered its former glory. The inferior qualitity of draftees lowered the status of the division. According to the division's history, the high percentage of Poles worked to its disadvantage; there were numerous Polish deserters.

77th Reserve Division

The 77th Division was formed in January 1915 and four weeks later it went to the Eastern Front, where it was immediately deployed against the Russians in East Prussia. For almost the entire war it stayed in the Courland Region on the Baltic Coast, present-day Northern Latvia, until it was finally sent to France in April 1918. After a short period of rest it returned to the line east of Villers-Bretonneux, in the Somme. In July, the 77th moved to the St. Mihiel Front, where it manned the front line between Flirey and Limey; it held that sector until the American assault on 12 September.

The division suffered very heavy losses, mainly in prisoners; German prisoners told of being completely cut off by the American barrage. The 77th was withdrawn on 16 September and did not return to the front line thereafter; the 77th Division as a formation had been destroyed. What remained of the division occupied the Michel Zone between Prény and Pagny.

255th Division

NB: This division was not part of Army Detachment C, but of the Metz Group which engaged the American 90th and 82nd Divisions.

The core of the 255th Division was formed in 1915 as a garrison unit in the Metz area. Composed of Landwehr regiments, second-class reserve regiments made up of older men, it was part of the Metz detachment, the regiments that defended the Metz sector, the composition of which was remodelled and changed into a division in May 1917. From its establishment as a garrison unit until October 1917, it occupied the same sector between the River Moselle and Abaucourt, a little north of Pont-à-Mousson. On 13 October 1917, after yet another reorganization, it was transferred to the left bank of the River Moselle, where it occupied the front line in Prêtre Wood, which is situated on a ridge to the immediate left of Pont-à-Mousson. The 255th Division continued to hold its sector in Prêtre Wood until the American attack of 12 September. By that point, the number of men in a German company had dwindled to 180, in comparison to an American company composed of 250 men. The majority of the men in the 255th were aged between 37 and 45 years of age; on average, the Americans were 20 years old. Not surprisingly, after the preliminary bombardment the Americans smashed through their lines. However, the 255th was one of the few German divisions to undertake serious counterattacks. After the battle, the division retreated behind the Michel Zone, where it occupied the front line between Prény and Vandières until the Armistice.

IN RESERVE
88th Division
31st Division
123th Division
195th Division

NB: These divisions played no significant part in the fighting in the Salient and so are not described.

Appendix 5

German reports and battle notes, 1 to 16 September.

The translated German reports included in this appendix are taken from Volume 8 of the Military Operations of the American Expeditionary Forces: St. Mihiel.

1 September. From Ludendorff to Group of Armies Gallwitz:
'There are increasing reports to the effect that the Americans intend to attack Metz on both sides of the Moselle. I request that the Saxon 123rd Inf. Div. be moved forward without delay to the boundary between Composite Army C and the Nineteenth Army and that it be held in readiness to support the Nineteenth Army.'

3 September
'By authority of the Supreme Command contained in No. 6729, 24 April, 1918, Composite Army C will fall back to the Michel Position in case of a large-scale enemy attack. Indications are the enemy forces assumed to be opposite the south front of the army have not thus far pointed to enemy intentions to make a full-scale attack against the entire front of the army. Consequently the question arises whether in case of an attack of smaller proportions, possibly in conjunction with an attack against the Nineteenth Army and against the east portion of the south front of Composite Army C, the Michel Movement should also be executed.'

'The army inclines to the view that in case of an attack against the major portion of the south front, the present battle position should be held in order not to concede an early success, particularly since we are dealing with Americans. On the other hand, the Army Group has not been fully persuaded of the success of the defence in an attack against the major portion of the south front unless the requisite considerable reinforcements and their timely intervention can be assured. In view of the present general situation such prospects appear doubtful to the Army Group. The group therefore requires a decision whether in event of a hostile attack against the major portion of the south front, battle be accepted in the present forward battle position or whether, as in case of a full-scale attack against the entire salient, a withdrawal should be made to the Michel Position.'

5 September
'Because of the configuration of the terrain on the south front (Le Mont and Montsec) any enemy attack extending to the west beyond Flirey or Seicheprey must take in the Apremont region and is therefore always to be handled by Composite Army C as a large-scale attack. The preparations necessary in that sense have already been made, in conformity with the directions for the Michel defence contained in No. 1700, 21 June, 1918, Operations Section. Therefore no changes in the present measures will be necessary after receipt of the order of the Supreme Command.'

9 September
'From recent observations, it can be assumed with certainty that the Americans are accumulating ammunition and materiel, perhaps also heavy guns, on the south front of Composite Army C for an attack to be launched there at a not too distant future date. [...] Increasing signs in the last few days that similar preparations are in progress west and south-west of Verdun are an indication that the enemy will not be content with the tactical result of the capture of the St. Mihiel Salient, but have set themselves a higher, strategic goal. They intend to launch a French attack on both sides of the Verdun-Etain Road as well as an American attack on both sides of the Moselle in the direction of Metz, thereby eliminating the Michel Position, which is known to him.'

This proves that the American plan, to make the Germans believe that the attack was to be aimed at Metz, had actually worked. The report continues with plans for a German counterattack against the Americans in the south. Such an attack would have the advantages of capturing large amounts of materiel, facilitating the Michel Movement by forcing the Americans further out, thereby enlarging the Salient. By driving the Americans further away from the fortress of Metz and the iron ore basin at Briey, the morale of the German troops would get a much-needed boost.

Army Group C commander, Lieutenant General Georg Fuchs, suggested in the same report that 'the attack is intended to be carried out as a surprise attack with a short fire preparation, and the line gained will be held. [...] Preparations will have to be accelerated as much as possible; the attack itself will be launched only when the enemy's attack preparations have definitely been completed, thereby giving an absolute guarantee that the blow will really strike him hard.'

Fortunately, the Germans did not know that the American assault was due to take place just three days later, so they were taken completely by surprise. Gallwitz, however, saw things quiet differently and in a more realistic way. He returned the following message that a 'careful study of the plan of attack of Composite Army C disclosed that in the few days available it would be impossible for the artillery to complete its preliminary preparations or for the troops to prepare to overcome the difficulties of crossing the very deep outpost zone. In addition, ever since 8 September, there have been numerous indications which point to the probable cooperation of the French by attacking from the west, while the American attack is directed against the south front of Composite Army C. […] This being the case, we no longer have the means for the proposed offensive to solve the situation which is developing on the southern front of Composite Army C, since there is a serious danger of being attacked from the west face of the salient in the very midst of the south front. The Group of Armies, therefore, believes that the proposed attack should not be undertaken. On the basis of the latest reports, a decision is needed from Supreme Headquarters as to whether it is of the same opinion regarding the whole situation and, if so, the Group of Armies must request an order for the occupation of the Michel Position.'

10 September
To Group of Armies Gallwitz: 'I request that you abandon the proposed attack and again begin to execute the measures for the occupation of the Michel Position according to plan. The withdrawal of the troops from their present positions and the resultant abandonment of the position itself is, if possible, to be postponed as long as the tactical situation will permit, even after the evacuation of the Michel foreground, in order that time may be gained to improve the general situation. LUDENDORFF.'

Late in the afternoon, Gallwitz sent the following message to the HQ of Composite Army C: 'The projected attack will not be carried out. The measures for the systematic occupation of the Michel Position will be started at once. […] If […] there should be an easing of the situation, it appears that the General Headquarters will postpone the Loki Movement [withdrawal to the Michel Zone].'

Early in the evening orders were issued that: 'Subject to the approval of G.H.Q. the proposed attack will not be executed. Since during the past few days there have been increasing indications that the enemy will also attack the west front of Composite Army C, the Army will withdraw to the Michel Position according to plan. The French-American attack against the St. Mihiel Salient is imminent.'

German battle notes 12-16 September

12 September
'Since 2 am there has been heavy fire on the Combres Group and the Gorz Group, particularly in the rear areas; […] on Mihiel Group [the French sector] not so heavy. 12 Noon: Order to the Mihiel Group: Loki Movement is to begin at once. 12:05 pm: The Combres Group [in the American V

Corps sector] has been informed of the order for the Loki Movement. Addition: Position on Combres Heights must be held with all forces.'

The Combres Group was to keep open the route of withdrawal to the Michel Zone. The Michel Group was first ordered to retreat to the Schroeter Position, but at 2.45 pm the situation was such that they were commanded to continue on to the Michel Zone. At nightfall, it was decided that the time had come to evacuate the Schroeter Zone, or what was left of it, altogether. In actual fact, most sectors had already been abandoned, but large bodies of German soldiers had been cut off by the swift advance of the Americans and been taken prisoner.

13 September

'We must expect an enemy attack against the left wing of the Fifth Army and the right of Composite Army C. By daybreak on 14 September, the armies will be ready for action. […] The Michel Position has been systematically occupied by the Gorz Group on the left flank. The majority of the 13th Landwehr Div., the Austro-Hongarian 35th Inf. Div., the 192nd Inf Div., and the 5th Landwehr Div., have arrived at the centre of the Michel Position. The last regiments of these divisions are now passing through it. The movement to occupy the Michel Position is taking place free of pressure from the enemy. During the night only rather weak enemy harassing fire on villages.'

14 September

On this day, the German HQ issued orders to prepare for an American attack on the Michel Zone; regiments were reorganized and reserve divisions were placed at the disposal of Composite Army C. Furthermore, the Germans resolutely declared that the armies 'will hold the main line of resistance with all their forces'. The last point of Gallwitz's orders was a warning not to panic whilst under attack by American tanks: 'The enemy can be expected to employ many tanks. The troops will be reminded again that attacking tanks and even those which have broken through is not dangerous if calmness and presence of mind are preserved.'

'Estimation of the situation [8 to 12 September]: Owing to our movement into the Michel Position, the continuation of the enemy attack has been delayed. On 13 and 14 September: the enemy worked his way forward with advanced guards thus coming into contact with most of the outpost of the Michel Position.'

15 September

'Outpost fighting on the entire army front still going on. Repulsed counter attacks against the new outpost at Soleuvre Farm and near Pagny, inflicting severe losses on the enemy. [...] Combat planes participated successfully in the outpost engagements.'

16 September
'The attack, which we have been expecting to be delivered against the centre of the Group of Armies since 14 September, did not take place today either. This gives us a chance to move up our reserves and dispose of them suitably.

An interesting telegram, dated 17 September 1918, from Hindenburg to Group of Armies von Gallwitz clearly shows how annoyed Hindenburg was over the actions (or rather inaction) of the German commanders during the St Mihiel Offensive. The Salient should not have been lost, on the contrary, if the commanders in the area had kept their wits about them and had launched an attack before the Americans did, the outcome could have been very different - victory for the Germans in St. Mihiel rather than victory for the Doughboys.

'The severe defeat of Composite Army C on 12 September has rendered the situation of the Group of Armies critical. I have, insofar as the situation permits, adjusted the expenditure of forces caused for the most part by faulty leadership and will also give further aid although it is very difficult for me to do so. After the opportunity of striking a blow to the enemy, east of Thiaucourt on 12 September, had been missed, there is now nothing left to do but offer stubborn defence. I can only hope that the Group of Armies will hold the position by using the forces I am allotting to it. The Group of Armies will bear complete responsibility for this. I am not willing to admit that one American division is worth two German. Wherever commanders and troops have been determined to hold their positions and the artillery has been well-organized, even weak German divisions have repulsed the mass attacks of American divisions and inflicted especially heavy losses on the enemy.'

The King of Württemberg on the Western Front; in the centre, Lieutenant General Fuchs. April 1917.

Advice to Travellers and Useful Addresses

The Meuse/Woëvre region is not very densely populated; it is an area dotted with small villages. Most people make their living from agriculture. To do the weekly shop, people normally go to one of the larger towns e.g. Verdun, St. Mihiel or Pont-à-Mousson. On the former battlefield, an area of sixty square kilometres, there are only a few places where you can fill up your petrol tank, buy snacks to take with you on your battlefield tour and have a cup of coffee. However, the area can easily be reached from Verdun; from there, it is only a forty-five minutes drive to the heart of the battlefield.

The car tours are all accessible – at least as of the date of publication – in a standard saloon car and in many cases in a small minibus. However, if planning a tour in a vehicle bigger than a car/camper van, it is advisable to check out the route beforehand. Naturally, the car tour stops are all accessible to those touring by mountain bike or electric bike.

Gas/Petrol stations:
Pont-à-Mousson, St. Mihiel, Verdun, Vigneulles, Thiaucourt

Supermarkets:
Pont-à-Mousson, St. Mihiel, Verdun, Vigneulles, Thiaucourt

Cafés and/or lunch facilities:
Pont-à-Mousson, St. Mihiel, Verdun, Vigneulles, Thiaucourt, Hattonchâtel

Countryside Code
When you are walking in the countryside, and especially when you are crossing over farmland, please follow the Countryside Code – leave gates and property as you find them and please take your litter home with you. Do not obstruct farm tracks with your vehicle (or, if you do, stay close by so that you can move it quickly if necessary). It might sound obvious, but do not walk through fields where there are crops growing – there are plenty of other places e.g the sides of roads and tracks, from which there are excellent panoramic views. The roads in the area are generally well maintained – however, they can be narrow, so please walk along them taking due care.

Where to stay

There are numerous B&Bs in the Meuse/Wöevre area; search on Google on 'Chambres d'hotes' or 'Gites de France'or on Booking.com. Many B&Bs have a restaurant licence and offer good quality three course dinners at a reasonable price. This saves you considerable time on arrival, as you do not have to go out searching for a restaurant; whilst it is also very handy during the rest of your stay.

Ordnance and relics of the war

The bomb disposal unit in the Meuse (Lorraine) consists of ten men who, day in and day out, put their lives on the line to clear the former battlefields of the deadly heritage of (mainly) the First World War. Every year these men collect some hundred tons of shells of all types – gas, shrapnel or high explosive – as well as hand grenades. Gas shells have the potential to be particularly hazardous and one out of three shells fired during the 1918 campaigns contained gas. However, they only collect shells when there is immediate danger; this means that the forests etc have not been cleared. Advice to travellers - do NOT pick anything up off the ground that looks dodgy. Use your common sense and leave well alone. Munitions are designed to kill and sometimes they still do. In summer 2018, a tourist was killed by an unexploded shell. Rusty metal is also an ideal breeding ground for tetanus.

Metal detectors

The use of metal detectors is prohibited, even with permission from the owner of the land. Fines can be as high as 7000 euros and the impounding of the offender's car is a standard procedure.

Maps

A useful, general map of the Meuse-Argonne region is the Michelin 'Sites de la Guerre 1914-1918 en Meuse' map, which can be purchased locally or ordered at www.michelin-boutique.com. If you want to study the area in more detail, the maps in the IGN Série Bleue are highly recommended. Maps 3213 SB, 3214 SB, 3313 SB and 3314 SB cover the whole area as described in this book. (https://ignrando.fr/boutique/cartes/randonnee-france.html)

Driving in France

In France, motorists drive on the right hand side of the road; all car passengers must wear seat belts. The roads in the St. Mihiel area are mostly well maintained. The maximum speed in villages, towns and cities is 50 km/h, on national roads (N and D roads, i.e. N209, D15) it is 80 km/h and on motorways 130 km/h unless indicated otherwise (for example, 110 km/h in rain).

Priorité à droite. Give way to traffic coming from your right. If you are driving along a road, anyone joining that road from your right hand side has right of way – usually, but not always, also indicated by a sign with an 'X'. If you happen to be on a road that has a yellow diamond sign, then anyone on that road has priority. There are variations, but the wisest course is to assume priority from the right. Most intersections are marked by bollards with a red stripe towards the top on the intersecting road(s).

Give Way (Yield) road sign.

Drivers must also carry a luminous yellow vest in the car, in an easily accessible place; should you have a breakdown in France, you have to wear the highly visible jacket when you are getting out of your car. A warning triangle is also essential and this must be readily accessible in your boot. You should also have a first aid kit and breathalyser – the law on the latter is hazy, but better to be safe than sorry. Nowadays, you are required to have a sticker on your windscreen that indicates the emissions category of your vehicle. Failure to comply can result in on the spot fines, usually between €45 and €90.

The weather

In summer, it can be very hot in this area. As regards the rest of the year, the weather is usually quite good but from time to time you may need wellington (rubber) boots – though good quality walking boots should suffice, even in winter, and should be a minimum footwear requirement year round, protective wet weather gear against rain and possibly an umbrella. Tips for a pleasant trip into the forest: apply a good brand of insect repellent. Since ticks, the possible carriers of Lyme's Disease, are particularly common in forest areas, it is advisable to cover up by wearing long trousers whenever you visit the forest.

Water

It is quite safe to drink tap water in this area. The French continually monitor the quality of drinking water. Some of the walks can be lengthy, so be sure to bring a supply of bottled water with you.

Hospital

Should you require medical aid, there is a hospital in Verdun as well as in St. Mihiel. Most doctors and specialists speak English or at least the basics. There are numerous pharmacies and one can usually be found in the bigger towns in the area.

Hôpital Saint Nicolas,
2 Rue d'Anthouard
55100 VERDUN
03 29 83 84 85

Centre Hospitalier Verdun St. Mihiel Saint Anne,
2 Place Jean Bérain
55300 St. Mihiel
03 29 91 81 81

Guided Tours

For guided tours in English (and also Dutch and French), contact museum19141918@gmail.com.

Acknowledgements

My sincere thanks go to Orla Kuiper-Ryan for correcting and proof-reading the manuscript; Bart Metselaar, who once again delivered some superb maps for the tour section; my wife, Didi, for test-driving and walking all the tours with me; Nigel Cave, the series editor, who has joined me many times on trips to visit and explore the Salient; Tom Gudmestad, for photographs, general advice and for sending me a heavy box packed with original divisional histories; Superintendant J. R. Hays and Marie-Lou Meyer-Vinot of the St. Mihiel American Cemetery in Thiaucourt; the American Battlefield and Monuments Commission (ABMC); the National Archives and Records Administration (NARA), Washington, DC, who supplied me with great quantities of much yet unpublished photographic material; Frances Kerber and Paula Gilbert for generously sharing Warren Jackson's original journal. Thanks also go to: Ken McElroy, Suzanne van Baarsen and Harmen Kramer; Pinie Marinus.

The contemporary American photos are from the National Archives, Washington, D.C.; all other photographic material is from my personal collection, unless otherwise indicated.

The short histories of First Lieutenant William McFee and Sergeant Fred Smith were researched and written by Peter Wever, see also the selective bibliography. The story of Mess Sergeant First Class Jay E. Shetler was researched and written by James Shetler. A special thanks goes to the people who put the book together: Matt Jones, Sylvia Menzies, Jon Wilkinson and Dom Allen.

Doubtless there are others: you know who you are and I am very grateful. All errors in this book are solely my responsibility.

Nantillois, August 2019

Selective Bibliography

33rd Division A.E.F., Frederic L Huydekooper, Gustave Soupert, Luxembourg, 1919

92nd Division Summary of Operations in the World War, ABMC, United States Government Printing Office, Washington, D.C.,1944

A History of the 90th Division, Major George White, The 90th Division Association, 1920

American Armies and Battlefields in Europe, American Battle Monuments Commission, Government Printing Office, Washington D.C., 1938

Americans all, the Rainbow at War, 42d U.S. Infantry Division, Henry J. Reilly, F.J. Heer Printing Co. Publishers, Columbus, Ohio, Second Edition, 1936

A U.S. Army Medical Base in World War I France: Life and Care at Bazoilles Hospital Center, 1918-1919, Peter Wever, Jefferson, NC: McFarland; 2019.

Defending the Ypres Front, Jan Vancoillie & Kristof Blieck, Pen & Sword, Great Britain, 2018

Histories of 251 Divisions of the German Army which participated in the War (1914-1918), War Department, Government Printing Office, Washington, DC, 1920

History of the 89th Division, George H. English Jr., The War Society of the 89th Division, Smith-Brooks Printing Company, Denver, Colorado, 1920

History of the 90th Division, Major George Wythe, The 90th Division Association, The De Vinne Press, New York City, New York, 1920

History of the First Division during the World War 1917-1919, Society of the First Division, John Winston Company, Philadelphia, PA, 1922

History of the Seventh Division, Captain Edgar Tremlett Fell, George H. Buchanan Company, Philadelphia, Pennsylvania, 1927

History of the Yankee Division, Harry H. Benwell, The Cornhill Company, Boston, Massachusetts, 1919

Illinois in the World War Volume Two, unknown, State Publications Society, Chicago, Illinois, 1920

Les États-Unis dans la Grande Guerre, Léon Abily, Marines Éditions, Rennes, France, 2010

MacArthur, held van de Filippijnen, Sydney L. Mayer, Standaard Uitgeverij, |Antwerpen, België, 1995

Medals of Honor of the Meuse-Argonne, Maarten Otte, Exposure, Rosmalen, The Netherlands, 2016
My Experiences in the World War, Volume II, John J. Pershing, Frederick A. Stokes Company, New York, 1931
Official History of 82nd Division American Expeditionary Forces, Divisional Officers, The Battery Press, Nashville, TN, 1919
Squandered Victory, James H. Hallas, Praeger Publishers, Westport, USA, 1995
Storm of Steel, Ernst Jünger, Penguin Books, London, England, 2004
The 4th Division in the War, Bach and Hall, issued by the Division, 1920
The Fifth U.S. Division in the World War 1917-1919, Society of the Fifth Division, Wykoop Hallenbeck Crawford Co, New York, NY, 1919
The Iron Division in the World War, H.G. Proctor, The John C. Winston Co, Philadelphia, 1919
The Second Division American Expeditionary Force in France 1917-1919, Colonel Oliver Lyman Spaulding and Colonel John Womack Wright, The Hillman Press Inc, New York, NY, 1937
Unjustly Dishonored, An African American Division in World War I, Robert H. Ferrell, University of Missouri Press, Columbia, Missouri, 2011
US Army in the World War 1917-1919 Volume 8, Military Operations St. Mihiel, Historical Division Department of the Army, Washington, 1948

Index